P9-CZV-072

7601 9100 577 559 4

IN GOOD HANDS

REMARKABLE FEMALE POLITICIANS
FROM AROUND THE WORLD
WHO SHOWED UP, SPOKE OUT
AND MADE CHANGE

STEPHANIE MACKENDRICK

To Mandy Goetze, a founder of The International Alliance of Women, a change agent extraordinaire and dear friend; my hero

KCP Loft is an imprint of Kids Can Press

Kids Can Press gratefully acknowledges the financial support of the Government of Ontario, through Ontario Creates; the Ontario Arts Council; the Canada Council for the Arts; and the Government of Canada for our publishing activity.

Published in Canada and the U.S. by Kids Can Press Ltd.
25 Dockside Drive, Toronto, ON M5A 0B5

Kids Can Press is a Corus Entertainment Inc. company

www.kidscanpress.com

The text is set in Baskerville.

Scout Books & Media Inc.
Edited by Susan Knopf and Kate Egan
Design concept by Annemarie Redmond
Set by Emma Dolan

Printed and bound in Canada in 2/20 by Friesens

CM 20 0 9 8 7 6 5 4 3 2 1

Library and Archives Canada Cataloguing in Publication

Title: In good hands : remarkable female politicians from around the world who showed up, spoke out and made change / Stephanie MacKendrick
Names: MacKendrick, Stephanie, author.
Description: Includes bibliographical references.
Identifiers: Canadiana 20190114576 | ISBN 9781525300356 (hardcover)
Subjects: LCSH: Women politicians — Biography — Juvenile literature. | LCSH: Women — Political activity — Juvenile literature.
Classification: LCC HQ1236 .M33 2020 | DDC j320.082 — dc23

CONTENTS

PART 2: THE PLAYBOOK

PART 3: THE DEEP DIVE

FOREWORD

AS THE FOUNDER of IGNITE, the largest and most diverse young women's political leadership organization in the United States, I am relentless in my desire to make sure that young women are ready and eager to become the next generation of political leaders. So imagine my delight when I read *In Good Hands* — a book that shares so much of IGNITE's vision for empowerment.

At IGNITE we train young women to define their personal call to service by asking them several critically important questions: What is the most pressing issue you see in your community? What is your personal connection to that issue? How would you solve it?

Our goal is to help young women see that their personal experiences — no matter how painful or shameful or hard — are exactly what qualify them to lead. Case in point: one of our alumni spent some time as a teenager in and out of the criminal justice system, like so many young people in her community. That is why her platform for city council was so powerful: She could authentically say to the sitting council member, "What have you done for our community over the last 20 years? Let me tell you how your policies have failed, and let me tell you what I would do." Couple that powerful call to service with real tools, like how to raise money or contact voters or garner endorsements, and you have a real plan for success.

In Good Hands is a must-read for any young woman who is curious about running for office but doesn't know how to make it happen. Providing equal parts inspiration and information, *In Good Hands* tells stories of powerful female role models from around the world who conquered their doubts, ran successful campaigns for public office and then implemented their vision. Young female activists will hear what these leaders accomplished as public servants. More important, they'll get the real story on dos and don'ts for their first time running as a candidate, as well as a handy 12-step roadmap to prepare them for the journey ahead. It can be scary to run for office that first time, but knowing that you have a plan can mitigate some of the fear.

There has never been a more important time to invest in young women who are passionate about bettering their communities and teach them that political leadership is the most direct way to make change.

The 2016 election in the United States sparked an extraordinary level of political activism among young women across the country. In the face of policies that limit their potential, young women are finally emboldened to own political power. They are fed up with the status quo, and they see political leadership as both desirable and tenable. We need to ensure that we take this moment and turn it into a movement to build the next generation of political leaders. That's where *In Good Hands* comes in. Make sure that it gets into the hands of any budding activist or political leader or frankly any young woman who cares about making her community — and our world — a better place.

Anne Moses, PhD
President & Founder
IGNITE
www.ignitenational.org

WHAT'S INSIDE?

DO YOU WANT to solve problems, address issues, bring people together and change the world? Maybe you have thought about running for election in your school, your community or at some level of government. Maybe someone you know has suggested that you should think about running for something. Or maybe you are just curious about what it takes to run in the first place.

Either way, wouldn't it be great if there was one place to go to find out everything you need to know about running for elected office, no matter where and no matter how much — or how little — experience you have? One place for all the inside stuff, the unwritten rules, the things most people don't learn until they are in the middle of running — or worse, after a campaign is all over?

Wouldn't it be even better if you could find out about the stuff that *you* find daunting? Maybe it's speaking in public or asking people for money, or maybe you are uncertain how to get people to listen to you and believe in you. You are holding a book that answers these questions right now!

INSIDER'S GUIDE

In Good Hands is an insider's guide that tells the stories of inspiring women who have put their names on the ballot and how they faced the challenges — big and small — of running for office. It tells you what to expect, how to deal with the tough stuff and why it's worth it to run. And it's not just one woman's view, or from one country or one segment of society. *In Good Hands* is for everyone — it is nonpartisan and inclusive.

I talked to women from all parts of the world, across the political spectrum, about the experience of running for office. What I want to share with you is encouraging and also frank. *In Good Hands* identifies the challenges but, more importantly, shows you how you can meet those challenges and overcome obstacles, even when trying to reach your goals seems overwhelming.

The stories in this book open a window to the thoughts, aspirations and campaigns of other women. You'll see how some of the toughest battles were fought and how you can learn from those battles. Throughout, you'll find guidelines on what's important and what you need to simply ignore. You'll learn about the pitfalls that are specific to women, the ones that systems and institutions create for us and the ones we unwittingly create for ourselves. And you'll get practical strategies that will help you transform "I'll think about it" into "I'll do it!"

WHY *IN GOOD HANDS*? WHY NOW?

The reason I wrote *In Good Hands* is simple: because it's 2020. The time for women to lead is now. As women, our voices must be heard and our perspectives on peace, conflict, power, economics, community, education and family have never been more needed than they are today. Yet we are underrepresented in almost every nation and across local communities, national governments and international bodies.

Elected office is not for everyone, but everyone should feel equally entitled to consider it as an option. As women, we don't — or at least not as routinely, or as often, as men do.

The world needs the full participation of just over half its population. It needs the different approaches that women often bring to public office. And governing bodies need more than one or two token women to provide "the woman's view," as if all women had only one way of thinking.

I came to this project with 20 years' experience fighting in the trenches to help women advance in their careers, in Canada and internationally. I've had a chance to see at close range the cultural, institutional and individual barriers to women's advancement. Sometimes, it's the system that holds us back. But sometimes, it's our own perceptions of ourselves as women. We are often intimidated by the double standard, the one that makes us feel that we have to be twice as good to go half as far. It makes us overly nervous about making a mistake that crosses the narrow space between being nice (read: "too weak to lead") and outspoken (read: "difficult," "unreasonable" or "aggressive"). But sometimes, we just don't believe in ourselves enough. That's one of the things we can change if more women become public leaders.

HOW TO USE THIS BOOK

In Good Hands answers the questions that many of you have about whether to run for office, how to run for office and when to run for office.

You can read *In Good Hands* cover to cover, or you can start with a topic you want to learn more about, a story that sounds intriguing or resources that address a specific issue you are facing.

Whatever approach you take, be sure to read the stories of women who have run in Part 1: The Journey. Find out what they learned and how they made an impact — in the process, you may find a role model.

Part 2: The Playbook includes a step-by-step guide to building a campaign and developing the personal qualities you will need for your run.

In Part 3: The Deep Dive, you'll find articles, books and organizations to consult when you want to find out more — because there is always more to learn.

INTRODUCTION

A MATTER OF CONFIDENCE

SEVERAL YEARS AGO, I had an amazing opportunity to pose a crucial question to a major public figure. The answer to the question I asked was a revelation.

We were in an elegant meeting room in a stylish Washington, D.C., hotel. The speaker was one of the world's most accomplished women, someone who was distinguished and greatly admired — Madeleine Albright, the first woman to be U.S. secretary of state, serving from 1997 to 2001. The room was full of awesome and talented young women, likely top leaders of the future. They had served in the military, advising generals and being groomed for leadership roles; they were fast-rising business executives, entrepreneurs, lawyers and not-for-profit leaders. I looked around the room and thought to myself, *I could be looking at a future president of the United States!* I fought an involuntary moment of panic that made me feel like a party crasher and pushed aside the inner voice asking its own question: *What are* you *doing here?*

I was facilitating a discussion on the role of mentoring in career development and leadership. My own qualifications were strong, but looking around the room, I felt self-doubt. I wondered what I could possibly contribute to a crowd like this. But I was really curious about how such accomplished women had attained their positions, what they enjoyed, what they worried about and what they had faced — and faced down — to achieve their goals. One of the young women I spoke to was the communications director for a five-star American general, and I was surprised when she seemed eager to ask *me* questions about career development and what I had learned both personally and professionally. I had the same questions for *her*.

> MADELEINE ALBRIGHT HAD FACED DOWN TYRANTS AND DECIDED ON MATTERS OF GLOBAL WAR AND PEACE. SHE HAD BROKEN THE GLASS CEILING AND NOT BEEN CUT BY THE FALLING SHARDS. BUT UNDERNEATH THE MANTLE OF POISE AND SELF-ASSURANCE, SHE WAS JUST LIKE SO MANY WOMEN – DOUBTING HERSELF AND WONDERING WHETHER SHE WAS GOOD ENOUGH FOR THE JOB AT HAND.

The guest of honor, Madeleine Albright, was a legendary supporter of women in politics and public life. During the Clinton administration, in the late 1990s, she spearheaded international relations for the Western world's most powerful nation. She oozed confidence and a steely resolve. Time after time, she took a stand, held a strong position and demonstrated a deep understanding of the political intricacies that made her role so challenging. She was tough and seemed absolutely fearless in making the life-and-death decisions that come with the job. She sat at the front of the room, stylish and calm, taking it all in with sharp eyes that missed nothing. She was genial as she chatted before the event, but she also projected an air of authority.

I realized that this was an opportunity I couldn't miss. I had a question to ask the guest of honor. It was a simple one: "What was the single greatest challenge you faced in your career?"

How would she answer? Would she talk about her background? She was born in the Czech Republic and had immigrated to the United States as a child. Perhaps it was being perceived as a foreigner and feeling like an outsider? Or maybe she would say it was continually being one of the only women in a boys'

PINNED

Remaining confident in the face of real challenges is one of the most important ways to unlock true potential. Even Madeleine Albright was dogged by self-doubt. How did she deal with it? One of the ways she bolstered her self-confidence involved a sizable collection of pins and brooches that she used to give herself a boost when she was facing difficult meetings or intimidating foes. Each brooch was a symbol of how she wanted to feel. One of the most famous is a pin fashioned into a snake and an apple, which she wore after the Iraqi press called her "an unparalleled serpent."

What does that mean for you? Should you wear a giant pin on your shoulder to run for class president? Or should you wear a certain color to mark your party affiliation? Choose any strategy that is meaningful to you to offset the discomforts that come with taking risks.

club of international diplomats and country leaders. Could it be balancing family and personal time with a series of overwhelmingly demanding roles? Was it making decisions on military action? Looking at her and knowing her story, I found it hard to believe that she could be daunted by any challenge.

She gave her answer without a moment's hesitation: "Self-doubt."

There was an audible gasp from the audience. *Self-doubt?* How was it possible that this woman who radiated competence and confidence struggled with self-doubt? Madeleine Albright had faced down tyrants and decided on matters of global war and peace. She had broken the glass ceiling and not been cut by the falling shards. But underneath the mantle of poise and self-assurance, she was just like so many women — doubting herself and wondering whether she was good enough for the job at hand.

She often had to make important decisions with significant consequences, and this was daunting. She knew that she was being judged as a trailblazer, her every move considered an indication of whether a woman could handle the job.

She worried whether she had made the right decisions and whether she was doing a good job. It felt relentless. A right or wrong choice could literally change the world.

Wouldn't anyone with those responsibilities doubt themselves? Yes, at least a little. The point of Madeleine Albright's story was that *she didn't let her doubts stop her.*

And that got me thinking about the fundamental importance of self-confidence and how it affects anyone who is trying to decide where to set her sights, how high to aim and how to achieve her goals.

It also got me thinking about the particular relationship between women and self-confidence. There are confident women, just as there are confident men. And there are people of all genders who lack confidence. But research, anecdotes and my own observations all point to the significant gaps in confidence levels between women and men. And because confidence is such an integral part of one's thinking and worldview, people may not even realize how confidence — or a lack of it — is affecting the way they make decisions about their lives.

Just as Madeleine Albright carried out one of the most demanding leadership roles possible, despite the constant challenge of self-doubt, you shouldn't let your doubts stop you either. They are just signals telling you there are factors to consider in a decision you are making or a path you are following. Having self-confidence doesn't mean you ignore doubts, but you keep them in perspective and give them their proper weight.

Because you, as much as anyone else, were born to run.

PART 1

THE JOURNEY

CHAPTER 1

MICHELLE STILWELL

WHEN THE IMPOSSIBLE BECOMES "NO OBSTACLE"

Member of the British Columbia Legislative Assembly, Canada

I HEARD MICHELLE TELL HER story several years ago in Winnipeg, Manitoba, her hometown. She was the guest speaker at a career-development event my organization was running. As she spoke, there were times she was emotional and other moments when you could hear a touch of sadness, but there was never a single note of self-pity. She didn't talk about how wrong things had gone for her, but about how she decided to play the cards life dealt her.

RESILIENCE VS. GOOD LUCK

It would be hard to find someone who better embodies the notion of resilience than Michelle Stilwell. Today Michelle is a member of the British Columbia provincial legislature. But her journey to get to this point wasn't based on good luck. Rather, it required an extraordinary commitment to keep on going in the face of bad luck.

Michelle started out with a lot. She was born smart and athletic. She is a natural organizer and planner. And from an early age, she felt it was important to use her voice to change things she thought needed changing. She has a deeply ingrained drive to make the world a better place.

At school, Michelle was a top athlete in basketball, baseball, ringette (a form of hockey played with a ring instead of a puck) and track. She was class president and headed up the local youth group. Michelle looked like the student most likely to succeed.

COMING BACK FROM CATASTROPHE

But that all changed in an instant. When she was 17, Michelle was taking a piggyback from a friend when she fell. Michelle broke her neck and became quadriplegic. A whole chapter in her life closed and an entire range of interests and activities was suddenly out of reach. Michelle was in shock. As she absorbed the implications of her injury and adjusted to the "new normal," she assessed her options.

While still in the rehabilitation hospital, Michelle was introduced to wheelchair basketball. The sports options for quadriplegics are limited, but Michelle had enough use of her hands and arms to play wheelchair basketball. She credits the sport with making her stronger and more independent, and

MICHELLE STILWELL: PROFILE OF A CHAMPION

2006	World Championships (Assen, Netherlands): Gold in 200 meters. Silver in 100 meters.
2008	Beijing Paralympic Games: Gold in 100 and 200 meters.
2011	World Championships (Christchurch, New Zealand): Gold in 100, 200 and 400 meters. Silver in 800 meters.
2012	London Paralympic Games: Gold with Paralympic Games record in 200 meters. Silver in 100 meters.
2013	World Championships (Lyon, France): Gold in 100, 200 and 800 meters.
2016	Rio de Janeiro Paralympic Games: Gold in 100 and 400 meters.

her teammates with teaching her about living with a disability. Perhaps most importantly, she found a new outlet for her drive and passion to excel. A talented athlete before her injury, Michelle became an even more accomplished athlete afterward. She took the wheelchair basketball skills she learned in rehab, started playing locally and discovered her competitive spirit was very much intact. With her innate athleticism, she developed enough strength in her upper body to propel the wheelchair and shoot the ball.

Soon she was playing for the Manitoba wheelchair basketball team, and within two years, Michelle was on the national team, competing at the world championships in Sydney, Australia, and winning a gold medal. Michelle was the first-ever female with quadriplegia to compete in wheelchair basketball at the international level. Shortly after the 2000 Paralympic Games, though, Michelle suffered complications from her spinal cord injuries and ultimately would have multiple surgeries to deal with issues as they arose. The complications forced her to give up competitive wheelchair basketball. It was yet another loss.

Michelle then focused most of her energy on coaching others. It was at a coaching clinic that wheelchair racing coach Peter Lawless spotted her and noticed that she had very quick hands for someone with her functional ability. Peter was determined to recruit Michelle for wheelchair racing.

Michelle has quadriplegia, which means all four limbs are affected. Her upper arms and back are strong, but her wrists and hands have limited function. She is able to make the movements needed to propel the chair forward — a quick downward motion, flicking back on the wheels — but the lack of function in her hands was challenging for basketball.

Michelle was initially reluctant to switch to racing, as she had been a track athlete before her accident and was afraid that she would be frustrated to go back to something she had excelled at before. But Peter was persistent. When she finally agreed to take it on, she started training and competed in her first race. She was not happy to be beaten by a 12-year-old boy, but the loss only made her more determined. Wheelchair racing turned out to be an excellent fit for Michelle. She ramped up her training and began racing in earnest, starting with local events and building up to bigger, more competitive races. By 2005, Michelle was competing in the European Championships. Just two years after taking up the sport, she competed in the T52 quadriplegic class at the World Championships in Assen,

> I'M A PLANNER AND AN ORGANIZER. THAT'S MY PERSONALITY. WITH MY INJURY, I TOOK THOSE TRAITS AND TRANSLATED THEM INTO BOARDS AND COMMITTEES IN SPORT. I WAS INVOLVED IN THE WHEELCHAIR SPORTS ORGANIZATION. LIVING LIFE USING A WHEELCHAIR, THERE ARE MANY BARRIERS, AND I STARTED TO USE MY VOICE TO MAKE THE CHANGE THAT NEEDED TO BE MADE.

Netherlands, where she won a silver medal and another gold.

Impressive as these athletic achievements were, Michelle was busy in other areas at the same time. She was a successful motivational speaker. She became a community advocate for people with disabilities and children with special needs. She got married and became a mother. During her competitive years, Michelle continued to be active as a leader.

As she was preparing for her record-breaking London Games, politics suddenly and unexpectedly came into Michelle's life. "I never dreamed in high school that I would ever run — or want to run — as a member of the legislature," she recalled. It just wasn't on her radar.

A RELUCTANT POLITICIAN

A local broadcaster who had become a good friend after interviewing her told Michelle she should consider running for office in the 2011 federal election. He had seen her determination, drive, toughness and leadership skills, all qualities that he thought would make her a good politician. The first thing she said was, "Why me? I don't know anything about politics." But she didn't say no. She thought about it, and she realized that she knew a lot about politics. She had been on numerous boards for sports organizations and knew what was involved in leadership from those experiences. "I spent 20 years in Para sports, and I can tell you there is a lot of politics in sports."

She was reluctant, but he persisted. "It can sometimes take a long time to understand what you actually *do* know," Michelle said.

Michelle didn't run then, but she got involved. She worked on another candidate's campaign. "I'm an organizer, so I became the volunteer coordinator, overseeing phone calling, events and the scrutineers [volunteer observers for each party at polling stations]."

When she returned from London, a member of the BC provincial legislature called to ask whether Michelle would speak at a conference. "I was running my own business as a speaker, and I thought it was just another gig, so I said okay," Michelle remembered. But the conference turned out to be the BC Liberal Party Convention. "Again, I asked, 'Why me?'" Michelle said. "And he said, 'Because you tick all the boxes. You are a successful business owner, a wife, a mother, an athlete and you have a disability.'"

"I have trouble saying no," she confided with a laugh, "so I said yes. Once I agreed to co-chair, that's when they put on the full-court press. People at the convention kept coming up to me and saying I should run. There were lots of phone calls, lots of encouragement. Christy Clark, who was then premier of British Columbia, called me and that sealed the deal. I'll tell you she is a great salesperson!"

In January of 2013, Michelle ran unopposed to become the Liberal Party candidate for the riding (electoral district) of Parksville-Qualicum. The election was four months off — not much lead time to learn all she needed to know about politics.

RUNNING ON HER OWN TERMS

Although she was a rookie, Michelle entered into the fray on her own terms. "I was still competing. That was one of the main conditions I insisted on if I was going to run. I was just not prepared to give up sport because I still had goals I wanted to achieve." So after she was named the Liberal candidate for her district, she left for Australia to train and ultimately to compete in the 2013 World Championships in Lyon, France. Her strength of will and amazing organizational skills were key to her ability to be an athlete and a candidate at the same time. She said, "I campaigned over the internet. I did a lot of Facebook and video. We sent out mailers. Then I came home during the writ [campaign period] and campaigned in person." Michelle won her seat by a strong margin.

CHALLENGING BUT REWARDING

Michelle spoke openly of the challenges of her role as representative in the Legislative Assembly. "No one can ever prepare you for it. It's not 8-hour days — it's 12- to 14-hour days. You spend weeks away from home. I spend Sunday to Thursday in Victoria. It's not that far, but too far to commute daily. I have a teenaged son. He is 16 now, but he was just 11 when I was elected. You miss out on a lot and that is something that you struggle with — particularly if you are a woman. I was not at the soccer practices or at the tae kwon do belt trials."

But that is only part of the story. She went on to add, "Having said that, the biggest surprise in all of it was how rewarding it is. You look around the community and see the changes you have had a part in making. Being in cabinet, you make changes that affect the whole province."

As a politician, Michelle was empowered to make the kinds of changes that she used to push for as a community advocate. "I am probably proudest of the single-parent employment initiative that we undertook to help single parents live better lives and get off the welfare cycle. We expected around 400 people to apply to participate in the program, and so far, we've had 4000. We've reached 10 times more people than what we thought. But even something simple like helping a constituent get their electricity turned back on or helping someone get emergency financial assistance so they don't end up homeless, it's just so rewarding."

But with politics, as with life, you can't please everyone. Michelle discovered that even when you make good public policy, there may be people who will react with hostility.

One situation Michelle found especially difficult was connected to improved transportation options for people with disabilities. She was pleased to have made changes to BC's disability bus pass program but was shocked when misunderstanding unleashed torrents of anger on social media.

Michelle remembered, "We weren't taking anything away from anyone, and we were giving more people access to benefits." But the announcement and rollout didn't go smoothly. There was confusion about who would qualify for benefits under the new program, and people jumped to conclusions, assuming that the changes meant benefits would be taken away from some recipients. "Twitter and Facebook just exploded with hostility. I couldn't believe the abuse ... but it's part of what you have to deal with."

Michelle's logical thinking and common sense helped her put it all into perspective. "You can't take it personally but sometimes you do," she said, acknowledging that if you are in charge of social assistance and people are in difficult situations, emotions can run high. "You have to acknowledge what others may be going through. What I have to remember is that while my job is to help, I don't have control over everything and I can't fix everything. There is no magic wand."

Michelle summed it up simply. "I believe that every change I make is making things better, so I just have to go with that."

CHAPTER 2

KYRSTEN SINEMA

FROM HOMELESSNESS TO CAPITOL HILL

Senator representing Arizona, United States

THE PATH TO POWER is rarely straight or easy. Just ask Kyrsten Sinema, who conquered her family's reversals of fortune, poverty and temporary homelessness in childhood before setting out on a journey that would lead her to become the first woman senator to represent Arizona in Washington, D.C.

At the time of writing, Kyrsten had just triumphed in a seesaw battle to win the vacated seat of retiring Republican senator Jeff Flake in the November 2018 election. It had been a no-holds-barred, closely watched race between two congresswomen: Kyrsten for the Democrats and former Air Force pilot Martha McSally for the Republicans. As the election night returns came in, the two candidates were neck and neck, trading the lead back and forth several times. Well into the evening, the race was too close to call, but as the night ended, it appeared that McSally had won the seat by a razor-thin margin, maintaining the grip Republicans had held on the state for decades.

But not all the ballots had been counted, and Kyrsten's run for Senate was not finished. About three-quarters of Arizona's votes are placed by mail, and the process to count them is exacting, requiring the signature on each ballot to be matched to the signature on a voter registration document.

Adding to the lengthy process were the early ballots dropped off at polling stations on Election Day. As the election officials waded through the avalanche of early ballots, the tide began to turn in Kyrsten's favor. It took another six days of counting before Kyrsten was declared the victor, winning 50 percent of the votes against her opponent's share of 47.6 percent. In doing so, she became the state's first woman senator. It was an astonishing feat, all the more impressive given the long road Kyrsten traveled to get there.

FROM SUBURBAN HOME TO HOMELESS

There was nothing in her early life to suggest that Kyrsten would gain four university degrees and become a multi-term legislator known for her independent thinking and passion for protecting the vulnerable.

Kyrsten started life in a middle-class area of Tucson, Arizona. Her father was a lawyer and the family lived in a large suburban home, but that all changed when he lost his job in the early 1980s. The first inkling of what lay ahead came when Kyrsten was five years old. The family car was repossessed, then their home was briefly in foreclosure. Soon, the family was on the brink of poverty.

By the time she was seven, Kyrsten's parents had divorced. Her mother, Marilyn, was struggling to care for her children, relying on food stamps to keep them fed. When Kyrsten was eight, Marilyn married Andy Howard, a teacher at Kyrsten's elementary school in Tucson, and they moved to DeFuniak Springs, a small town on the Florida panhandle, to be closer to Andy's family.

Andy and Marilyn had trouble finding work in their new town. It took Andy a year to find even a part-time job at the local junior college; Marilyn found occasional work as an aerobics instructor. Relying on food stamps and assistance from the Mormon Church, the family ended up living almost three years in an abandoned gas station/convenience store owned by Andy's family.

It was a defining experience that Kyrsten has spoken publicly about, describing the conditions as primitive, with no electricity or plumbing. Although she was young, she was old enough to know that it wasn't normal.

But even then, there were glimmers of hope and possibility. Andy's parents lived nearby and the children spent time there after school and on weekends. They attended school regularly. It took time, but her parents eventually found full-time work, and the family's fortunes improved. By the time Kyrsten was 12, they no longer lived in the abandoned building.

When former neighbors and schoolmates are asked about Kyrsten, they say that there was something special about her even back then. She was known for her big smile and her fierce drive to succeed. The precarious circumstances of her upbringing did not erode her ambitions; the struggles of her family only accelerated her drive to succeed and to find ways to address the issues underpinning the poverty they'd experienced.

DRIVING WITH THE FORCE OF A FREIGHT TRAIN

Kyrsten was unstoppable. When she was 14, in her second year of high school, she decided she needed to take both high school and junior college courses to put herself on the fast track. A college degree meant independence to her. She convinced school authorities to allow the dual-stream studies and graduated at 16. She was tied for top marks in her high school and went on to attend Brigham Young University on a full scholarship. She continued her accelerated approach and earned her first college diploma in two years, graduating with a social work degree.

Kyrsten's battle with poverty continued — but this time, she worked from the other side. She became a social worker focused on families struggling to meet the basic needs of life. This was something she could relate to, based on her own experiences, and she wanted to make things better for others.

At the same time, Kyrsten kept learning. She earned a master's degree in social work in 1999. Then, as she began to think more broadly about poverty and other social issues, she attained a law degree, became a criminal defense lawyer and later earned a PhD in justice studies.

As she progressed through her studies, she set her sights on effecting change on a more systemic level, through political office. She said she was motivated by the belief that "everyone should get the same shot and that the system should not favor those at the very top."

AN EARLY SETBACK

Kyrsten's political career began with a run for the Arizona House of Representatives in 2002. She was an independent candidate affiliated with the Green Party. Like many first-time candidates, she was unsuccessful, gaining only 8 percent of the vote. This rare misstep taught Kyrsten that, even as an independent thinker, she needed to be part of a major political party to gain office.

Learning from experience, she registered as a Democrat and moved quickly through the ranks. In 2004, she successfully ran to represent the 15th District in the Arizona House of Representatives and was reelected to that position three times. In 2010, she ran and won a seat in the Arizona Senate. In 2012, she won a seat in the U.S. House of Representatives for Arizona's Ninth Congressional District, making history as the first openly bisexual politician in Congress.

DOING IT HER WAY

Kyrsten does things on her own terms, in her own style.

In the sometimes-drab political world, she is a burst of color in a sea of navy-blue suits and subdued dresses. She has appeared in Congress and at political events in a magenta blazer, a bold black-and-white print dress, and bright teal and orange tops. Her eyeglass frames are distinctive. But the clothing itself is not important. What matters is that it reflects who Kyrsten is: a woman determined not to fit into any mold.

Kyrsten is forthright in her speech and she doesn't compromise anything about her identity to satisfy her goals. In a state that epitomizes social conservatism, Kyrsten has been completely open about her bisexuality, and she is the only person in U.S. Congress who claims to have no religious belief, having broken from the Mormon Church (also called the Church of Jesus Christ of Latter-Day Saints, or LDS) at 18. She believes that religion should be separate from politics.

IT'S NOT A SPRINT, IT'S A MARATHON — LITERALLY

Kyrsten also makes time for running of a different sort — competing in marathons and triathlons, even the notoriously demanding IRONMAN triathlon.

She has a regular group of running mates who accompany her and also act as sounding boards, people she can talk to when she wants to try out ideas, argue about policy and get honest feedback on how she's doing.

A BIPARTISAN PROBLEM SOLVER

Kyrsten characterizes herself as bipartisan. She is driven by problem-solving and not limited by party lines. She is part of the conservative Blue Dog Coalition and is a member of the bipartisan Problem Solvers Caucus. Being a Democrat from a Republican stronghold state, Kyrsten knows how to work both sides of the aisle to get things done.

She remains firm when it comes to the issues that affect families undergoing the same struggles hers did. Kyrsten's principles regarding welfare were first outlined in the 2006 Arizona Congressional National Political Awareness Test: she supports increasing access to public transportation for welfare recipients who are employed and using the federal Temporary Assistance for Needy Families funds to extend health and childcare subsidies to the working poor. She also disagrees vehemently with the idea of promoting marriage for welfare recipients, commenting in her forthright way, "This is offensive."

Kyrsten is a practical, savvy strategist who has figured out how to be effective in the intersection of right and left in Arizona.

FINDING THE PATH TO SUCCESS

When she took strategic aim to fight a same-sex marriage ban, she had a well-thought-out game plan. Rather than debating the merits of same-sex marriage, she focused on how the ban would affect all unmarried couples. She warned that the initiative to ban same-sex marriage also contained an amendment that would prohibit legal recognition of domestic partnerships, whether same sex or not. That in turn would mean the unmarried partners of employees working in organizations with health care benefits would no longer be eligible for such benefits under their partner's program. It would also prohibit unmarried seniors from visiting each other in the hospital.

The game plan worked. Arizona was the first state to defeat such a proposal at the state level.

Being outspoken also includes not being afraid to disagree with her own party. She criticized national Democrats for moving too far to the left, asserting that the drive for free college tuition and single-payer health care are unrealistic promises to make in a campaign platform.

Even so, Kyrsten favors a wide range of progressive legislation. She supports the DREAM Act to grant legal status to undocumented immigrants who were brought to the United States as children and went to school there. On responsible investing, she aligned lawmakers from both sides of the aisle to force state pension funds to drop investments in some companies doing business in Sudan because of the genocide in Darfur.

And she is staunchly in support of women's health and advancement, including women's reproductive rights, winning the backing of Planned Parenthood and EMILY's List, whose mission is to get progressive women candidates elected. In 2013, she cosponsored the Women's Health Protection Act, which bans many limitations on access to abortion. Kyrsten is a supporter of *Roe v. Wade*, a supreme court decision that protects a woman's right to have an abortion, and she has voted against bills in Congress that would have allowed employers to deny coverage for birth control for their employees. She believes that women and their families should be allowed to make their own personal health care decisions without the interference of politicians.

While she was in the Arizona State Legislature, she supported a bill to prevent nursing mothers from being charged with indecent exposure. In 2017, she cosponsored a bipartisan bill, Working Parents Flexibility Act, to enable families to contribute pretax dollars to a parental leave savings plan, and in 2018, she sponsored amendments to the Congressional Accountability Act to make members of Congress personally accountable for their sexual conduct and to stop them from using tax dollars to settle sexual harassment claims.

KEEPING HER EYE ON THE NEXT PRIZE

Going into 2017, Kyrsten had the next prize in plain sight. In September of that year, Kyrsten announced her candidacy for the Arizona seat in the U.S. Senate, vacated by Republican Jeff Flake.

In a tweet announcing her intention to run, she referred to her sense of obligation to help those who follow behind her: "I owe a large debt to my country.

> **I NEVER BELIEVED THAT BEING HOMELESS WAS GOING TO STOP ME FROM BEING WHO I WANTED TO BE.**
>
> **– 2017 CAMPAIGN ANNOUNCEMENT FOR U.S. SENATE**

I got my shot and now it's my duty to help others get theirs." For Kyrsten, this was a logical next step in making right what went wrong in her own family. Clearly, the drive that has carried her forward since her school days was in full swing. She amassed a sizable war chest, raising $8.2 million by May 2018, more than all three of her Republican rivals combined.

It took all of her iron-man stamina and superhuman drive to battle her way to victory and wrestle the Senate seat from a Republican stronghold.

She remains a fierce champion of society's most vulnerable because she knows what it is like and fights unapologetically for issues that affect those in the margins, no matter how the party lines fall.

CHAPTER 3

JULIANA LUNGUZI

DARE TO MAKE CHANGE

Former Member of Parliament representing Dedza East, Malawi

IT TAKES COURAGE TO PUT yourself out there, to take a stand, to go forward, especially when the odds are stacked against you. But it takes a very special kind of courage to step up when the political system you are dealing with is corrupt and taking a stand can be dangerous. This is the story of how Juliana Lunguzi dared to make change and became a member of Parliament representing Dedza East in Malawi.

Juliana did not set out to be a politician, especially after what happened to her father, controversial former chief police inspector (CPI) McWilliam Lunguzi. In 1983, he and three others were accused in the killing of four politicians who died in a suspicious car accident. By 1995, CPI Lunguzi had been cleared. He had just launched his campaign to run for Parliament the year before, when he himself was killed in a car accident that was considered suspicious by many. Juliana believes her father was killed by his political enemies to prevent him from running for office.

She had a successful career as a registered nurse and advocate for safe childbirth and women's reproductive health. She was well educated, with degrees from universities in Malawi and the United States. After working in the U.S., she returned to Malawi to take on a series of administrative and advocacy roles, championing women and their reproductive health. By 2012, she was working as an international midwifery advisor for the United Nations Population Fund in Khartoum, Sudan. She had steady, meaningful work and financial security. Things were going well, but she was itching to find a new challenge.

THOUGHTS FROM JULIANA

ON BEING A FEMALE POLITICIAN

"I am often asked how it feels to be a female politician. I look at it this way: I am not a politician because I am female, but because I am Juliana." She says it's important for women not to put limits on themselves or let the challenges of being female in a system that is predominantly male stop them from engaging in politics. She says that if you are in politics, those who oppose you "will call you names, whether you are a man or a woman." It just comes with the territory, so she doesn't take it personally and urges other women considering politics not to let that stop them, either. As a woman, Juliana says, "If you have a contribution to make, you go for it!"

ON CHOOSING YOUR BATTLES

"Public life has taught me which battles to fight because you can't do them all. Stick to an issue, focus on it. Health was one of my issues." There were many issues of concern to her and her constituents, like having the electricity out for months at a time, but as she points out, "That was not my issue. You have to let a lot [of other issues] go."

ON DECIDING TO RUN

"Run for the right reason, not to be famous or for money. If you run for the right reasons, you won't be frustrated with the political process. I knew before I ran that the system was broken, so I am not discouraged. It is demanding and expectations are huge. You need patience and you need to understand."

IMPOSSIBLE TO STAY ON THE SIDELINES

She remembers, "I was working in Khartoum. I was lonely and spending a lot of time on social media. At night, I was talking to my friends in Malawi about what was happening at home. The president, Bingu wa Mutharika, was seen as a dictator. There was no electricity and no food [for the people of Malawi]. Then the president died and the vice president, Joyce Banda, became president. We were hoping she would turn things around."

But that was not the case. Juliana kept getting alarming reports from friends back home. Politicians from the government were thought to be siphoning money from the public coffers, offering cash gifts in return for votes. On social media, criticism of politicians and their corrupt electioneering and lack of impact was intense. "I was following politics closely. One day it dawned on me: if all the blame is on the politicians, and if we think we are good, better than them, why not run for office?" Juliana dared to make change.

ARE YOU CRAZY?

But Juliana's friends did not agree. She had a good job with the United Nations (UN) and everyone thought she was crazy. The woman who was her boss at the UN was blunt: "You can't just quit and do African politics." But something inside of Juliana told her to try politics, to help her country. Nobody — family or friends — supported the idea at the beginning, when she quit her job.

WE ALL NEED CHAMPIONS

Juliana had one champion, a friend she had met in the U.S. who believed in her. He issued a challenge to her: "If you win the primaries [for election to Parliament]," he said, "I will help your campaign." And by help, he meant both strategic advice and support in fundraising.

She made the decision in October 2013 to run in the May 2014 election to become the member of Parliament in the Dedza East constituency for the Malawi Congress Party (MCP). She returned to Malawi and won the primaries by a landslide, winning four times as many votes as her opponent. She had strong name recognition, as her father had been widely known, and she used social media to get her message out and engage the voters. It worked.

Next step: the general election, and the fight to defeat the incumbent president, Joyce Banda, a controversial politician who headed the ruling People's Party after being expelled from another of Malawi's major parties, the Democratic Progressive Party.

FACING CORRUPTION

In February, Juliana started raising funds for her campaign, and that's when she had to summon all her courage to take the risks that come with engaging in Malawi's politics.

She was up against a culture of corruption, where it was common for candidates to give money in exchange for votes, and common for voters to ask for specific favors or services. Juliana said, "They ask, 'How many coffins are you buying us? Can you transport this sick person?' There are so many challenges [in each community], and it's all about money and handouts."

But Juliana wasn't prepared to do favors in exchange for votes. Instead, her approach was to ask for money and tell donors to her campaign that the best she could do in exchange for their contributions was to thank them. It wasn't always a welcome message.

She used a Facebook page to reach out and enable people to give small amounts, since that approach had worked in other situations. "We used it to fundraise for school books and raised 1200 dollars. A dollar or 50 cents makes a difference," she said. Other candidates were more visible, but she garnered support using social media. And she went door-to-door and spoke directly to voters.

It also helped that she was running in the home village of her father, which made her name familiar.

THERE ARE RISKS

Juliana faced down a lot of criticism. "I was not married; I was too vocal. The *Nyasa Times* made [negative] personal comments about me." On the internet, there were slurs about her personal life, especially by news organizations that were aligned with other parties. But she is philosophical and practical. "As I see it, if the intentions of the commentators are not good, I ignore it. If they identify a problem, I will lose sleep for a day or two. As a public figure, I have to deal with it, so I do.

"You can't win fighting on social media. If you abuse it, it will abuse you. So, I am not commenting on the president, but on his policies. I don't personalize things. It's about systems and rational choice of words. Getting ideas out is the important part."

AND THERE IS COURAGE

"Politics in Africa is dangerous. My dad was killed. I am a threat because I oppose the president and vice president in what they do. I take precautions — I am cautious and sensible — but I don't want to stop believing in trying to make a difference through politics. I have had threats and blackmail. You can't let even that stop you. I say, 'Okay. You threaten me and you can choose someone else, but I will not stop doing what I think is right.' It is tough. Threats are always there, but I pray about it and then I just put it in the back of my mind."

In a cliff-hanging primary battle in November 25, 2018, when the votes came in, Juliana trailed her rival Patrick Bandawe by six votes — 821 to 815. That's when a seesaw battle began. Juliana appeared to have lost but on November 26, the MCP declared her the winner and their candidate for the 2019 election, citing apparent irregularities at the polls. Just when it looked like Juliana was on her way to defend her seat, on January 8, 2019, Bandawe launched and won a legal appeal to prevent MCP from declaring Juliana the winner of the primary and it looked like Juliana was out of the race. Then on January 24, the courts vacated that earlier judgment, so Juliana was back in. Ultimately, her opponent won the seat running as an independent. But that hasn't stopped Juliana who remains active and outspoken in her advocacy.

CHAPTER 4

CATHERINE MCKENNA

SHE'S NO "CLIMATE BARBIE"

Member of Parliament representing Ottawa Centre, Canada

IMAGINE YOU HAVE A MASTER'S degree in economics from the London School of Economics, a law degree from McGill University and an undergraduate degree in international relations from the University of Toronto. You've trained in human rights and international justice and worked as a lawyer in Indonesia, and you have become part of a critically important review of the military justice system in Canada. You've founded a charity bringing together the power of people, education and law to create a more equitable and just society. You have a passion to make the world a better place and you've accomplished a lot in a short period of time. That might be a lifetime of success for many people, but Catherine McKenna aspired to more.

Catherine decided to run for office because she cares passionately about Canada and its role in the world. No one thought she could do it — and even her mother advised against it — but she worked hard, got elected in the Ottawa riding where Canada's Parliament sits, and within weeks, she was sworn in to cabinet as minister of the environment. It was a proud moment.

But just days after her cabinet appointment in November 2015, a media organization known for its skepticism about human-caused climate change, was calling Catherine "Climate Barbie." This was a shorthand way to undermine all Catherine had done. It was an assault on her and her accomplishments and amounted to an accusation that she didn't belong in a position of responsibility.

At first, Catherine tried to ignore the demeaning comments. But when she faced the media at a climate conference she was running, bringing together environment ministers from each of Canada's provinces and territories, Catherine had an important decision to make — would she continue to ignore the attack or would she confront the opposition?

TOO MUCH TO IGNORE

When a reporter for the media organization that had called her "Climate Barbie" asked a question about an electricity project, Catherine decided in an instant that enough was enough and confronted him about it: "I certainly hope that you will no longer use that hashtag. Can I get a commitment from you that you will not use that hashtag and not use that name in your articles?"

The reporter said he did not use the epithet himself but couldn't speak for everyone in the organization, and he pushed for an answer to his question. Catherine said she would provide an answer but first pressed her own point. "I want a commitment that you will not call me names, that you will not comment on the color of my hair and you won't make fun of me."

Then she came to the heart of the matter. "The reason I am asking you not to do this is because I have two daughters," Catherine said. "There are lots of girls that want to get into politics and it is completely unacceptable that you do this."

Catherine explained why she felt it was so important to take a stand. "I tried to take the high road and to not be seen as a victim. I was ticked off for a long time but I didn't do anything." Then at the climate talk press conference, the first question was from them. "It was a split-second decision," she said.

"So often, people make insulting comments, even friends, and you kind of want to say something, but you don't," she elaborated. "But it's okay to call people out in the moment. It shames them, it keeps them on their heels. If you wait until later or write them a letter, it doesn't have the same impact."

TAKING CONTROL OF THE CONVERSATION, TAKING CONTROL OF DECISIONS

Catherine believes the incident also underlines the need to take control of your own decisions. "As women, we sometimes feel we need permission about what we do. What will people think? We are judged all the time and you think, should I be this way? If I had asked someone [whether to call out a media organization], I would have been advised not to. But it was the right thing to do."

It did not stop the gender-based attacks on her credibility right away. Despite the measured tones Catherine used to challenge her harassers, the founder of the media organization answered with a tweet that characterized Catherine as being unable to control her emotions, unqualified and only chosen for cabinet because of a gender quota.

THE RIGHT THING TO DO

Catherine's stand was widely applauded. "The reaction was overwhelming. I had a lot of comments supporting me, a lot of dads with daughters … it showed me that there are a lot of people out there who don't want to see this kind of behavior." Not only did the reaction support her efforts to differentiate sexist insults from legitimate debate and criticism, but it also vindicated her decision to run for office in the first place.

Back in 2012, Catherine had been disturbed by the changes in Canada's approach to international affairs under the Conservative government. Things were moving from peacekeeping to military operations and from aid-focused policy to a trade-first orientation. There was a rejection of participation in multilateral initiatives in favor of inititives that directly favored Canada. The government also began targeting charitable organizations, undermining those whose work did not align with Conservative policies. The complex demands of auditors coupled with legal bills were crippling many foreign aid, human rights and poverty organizations.

For Catherine McKenna, this had been the last straw. "I care about Indigenous rights, about human rights, and I was running a charity that was being targeted by Revenue Canada." She had also been thinking about running for office for several years. The first time was in 2008, when the then-leader of the Liberal Party and leader of the Opposition Stéphane Dion asked her to run in Hamilton, where she grew up but had not lived for almost 20 years. Catherine was six months pregnant, and the timing wasn't right.

JOINING A NEW GENERATION OF POLITICIANS

But when Justin Trudeau was elected leader of the Liberal Party in 2013, she was ready. "Once [Trudeau] was nominated, I decided I would run, that he would need good candidates. It's a new generation of politics and I knew others would step up and run, too."

As she weighed the decision, Catherine asked a lot of people whether they thought she should run. "There were people who said, you can't win so don't run," she said. But she wanted to be part of a new political conversation, win or lose. "My mom didn't want me to run. She worried about how I was going to manage with three kids, how I was going to be a good mom, then. She worried that I would be hurt — though she has totally come around and supports what I am doing."

Catherine was not approached by the Liberal team to run this time and realized that it was a decision that she had to take into her own hands. "Women sometimes wait to be asked. I wasn't asked this time and I did not wait to be asked. I decided really early to go in."

ELECTED! TWO YEARS AND 100 000 DOORS LATER

Since she lived in the riding of Ottawa Centre, Catherine set her sights on that seat, a New Democratic Party (NDP) stronghold through the last two elections. She gave it her all.

"My campaign lasted almost two years when you include the nomination race," she said. "I knocked on 100 000 doors. I remember when I got to the last door. It was 8:00 p.m. [on Election Day] and we had been getting out the vote. I was so happy! I didn't know if I would win, but I felt great. We had introduced new ideas, we had stood for something." The tide was with her as the Liberals won a majority and her hard work paid off. At the end of her marathon campaign, Catherine was elected with 43 percent of the votes compared to her NDP opponent's 38 percent, a convincing victory. Goal achieved!

There's a lot to juggle with a major cabinet post and a young family. Catherine makes a point of bringing her children with her to events and on travels, though she admits that living in and representing an Ottawa riding makes the balancing act much easier for her than for someone who might represent a riding across the country. On October 21, 2019, Catherine was reelected, winning by a convincing 20% margin — 63 612 votes to her nearest competitor's 22 049.

A CHANGE IN CONTROL

When asked what she knows now that she wishes she knew when she started down the road to politics, she said, "I wish I'd known that I would have so little control over my life. I used to make decisions about which meetings I would take, what my day would look like. But because of the volume of what I do, my life, my scheduling, is not my own. Where I do push back hard is around incursions into my personal life, my time with my children and family."

Her upbringing in a family who encouraged her to pursue her goals — and who support her now — helps Catherine juggle all the aspects of her busy life. In fact, in many ways, Catherine's early life and career were ideal preparation for her high-profile role in government.

The eldest of four children, Catherine was raised in Hamilton, Ontario, known as a gritty steel town. She attended French schools at the insistence of her father, who believed that all the children should be fluently bilingual. This turned out to be a huge asset when Catherine began considering national politics in Canada.

She excelled in academics and sports; she's smart and she's tough and competitive. At the University of Toronto, she was captain of the national varsity swim team and still swims competitively in the masters' category of the local YMCA team.

After graduation, Catherine focused on human rights and social justice, practicing law in Canada and Indonesia. She served as a senior negotiator with the United Nations Timor Sea Treaty peacekeeping mission and cofounded two charities: Level Justice, supporting access to justice for marginalized communities, and Canadian Lawyers Abroad, helping law students and law firms do pro bono legal work in developing countries. She led a public policy organization for young leaders at the Banff Forum, and taught at the Munk School of Global Affairs.

CATHERINE'S MESSAGE TO YOUNG WOMEN

Beyond her own ambitions, Catherine is passionate about encouraging young women to consider running for office. She has started an initiative called Running Like a Girl and finds opportunities within her busy schedule to speak on the subject. She has an important message about the positive aspects of running for office: "Running is awesome whether you win or lose. I was able to get a whole bunch of people together — friends, people I didn't know — who all believed in something bigger. Politics can be very positive when you run it your own way. It creates a community. People like that you are running for your own reasons. It's such a positive experience. It's important that women get out there and run — lots of women. It's a great experience and politics matters." And along with encouragement, she also sounds a warning. "We can't be apathetic and we can't be scared. If good people don't run, who will?"

CHAPTER 5

MICHELLE WU

THE UNEXPECTED PATH TO POLITICS

Member-at-large and past president, city council of Boston, United States

IN 2007, MICHELLE WU was hurtling toward success like a high-speed bullet train. She had graduated from Harvard University with a degree in economics and was working at a prestigious consulting firm in Boston. She loved the city that she now called home, and she was attaining success by her own standards and also by the measure of her family's hopes and dreams for her. Michelle's parents had emigrated from Taiwan and settled on the south side of Chicago, where Michelle grew up. As first-generation immigrants, they pursued the dream of creating a better life for their children. With a good education, a stable job and financial security, Michelle was fulfilling that dream and then some.

A LIFE-CHANGING CALL

Then, out of the blue, came a call that sent Michelle's life and career tumbling off the track. The caller was her sister, then only 16 years old, and the news was not good. "Something's wrong with Mom," she told Michelle. Her mother had stopped eating and sleeping and appeared headed for a serious mental health crisis. As the eldest of four children, Michelle was the one her sister turned to. At the time, Michelle's youngest sister was only 10 years old. Her brother was away at college. Her parents had recently separated and her father was working overseas. There was no one to take care of her sisters — except Michelle.

Michelle took a temporary leave of absence and flew home, determined to take care of her family and then resume her fast-track career. Her mother had been well and happy up until this crisis, and she hoped her recovery would be as swift as the onset of her illness had been. Michelle was optimistic about turning the situation around.

But even with her sisters pitching in, it soon became clear that her mother wasn't going to snap out of the crisis and that she would not be capable of taking care of the younger children. "I was going to have to make a permanent plan for taking care of Mom and the family," Michelle remembers.

A MAJOR TEST OF CHARACTER

There was no possibility of staying with her company and transferring to Chicago, so Michelle resigned from her job. She was only 22 years old, yet overnight she became full-time caretaker of her mother and two younger sisters.

This was a major test of character for Michelle. She immediately went to work fighting for the support services her mother needed and ensuring that her sisters could focus on school. Michelle persevered, even when the tasks were arduous. She also put another plan into place. Her mother had always dreamed of running a tea shop, and Michelle thought there was some promise in that idea. "When I assessed the situation, I said to myself, I'm going to start this business," she said. "I thought, as she gets better, [my mother] could take it over. It would be a lovely extension of her warm personality and an extension of her culture."

Michelle found a location, applied for permits and untangled miles of red tape that went along with setting up shop. She chose a selection of loose-leaf teas herself, and named each one after a literary character. She supported the family and took concrete steps toward fulfilling her mother's long-held dream. After a year, though, it became apparent that her mother would never be able to run the business, and Michelle had to take yet another serious look at her life plan.

ANOTHER CHANGE OF COURSE

That's when necessity forged an inspired path and she made a gutsy decision. Michelle recalled, "I ended up applying for law school. I sold the business, came to Harvard Law School and brought the entire family." Their life in Boston was vastly different from their life in Chicago. "I was able to get my mom treatment in Chinatown where they spoke Mandarin, her native language. There are world-class hospitals in Boston. My middle sister started school again after she had floated around for a while, and I became the official guardian for my youngest sister."

It was a big decision and the right move. "If I was going to truly take care of my family," Michelle said, "I needed to be in a city that I wanted to be in, where I wanted to raise [my own] family."

A MOTIVATING EXPERIENCE

The experience of trying to settle her sisters into school and get treatment for her mother in Chicago had left its mark. "There was this injustice around how our family had had to struggle, as small business owners and caretakers," Michelle said. "The government just wasn't acknowledging that it was a burden to have to come to city hall and wait all day for an appointment. It's a hardship when you need an inspector, and it's all on the city's schedule." To get one permit, Michelle had to take a bus across town to pick up a paper copy of a form that was not available online, a simple task that should have taken minutes but instead took several hours. This was an example of the challenges Michelle saw for hardworking, everyday people.

USING THE LAW TO ADVOCATE FOR FAMILIES

Michelle chose law school to equip herself to fight for other families, with the goal of representing families and small businesses who didn't have the resources and skills she had to fight through all the red tape.

"I wanted to see how the laws were written, how I could help and implement change. I was thinking, I'll be in city hall and work behind the counter."

Though she wanted to be an advocate, politics was not on her mind. "I had no thought of running for office when I was growing up," Michelle said. "I just didn't think about it. It wasn't even so much that I thought I couldn't do it, it was that I didn't even know it was something someone like me could [aspire to] do."

"POLITICIANS DON'T LOOK LIKE ME"

For one thing, Michelle was a very shy girl growing up. "Every report card I got said I needed to speak up more." For another, her perception of what a leader and politician was did not in any way match Michelle's own qualities. "Growing up, I always assumed that a leader — a politician — was someone who was tall, loud, able to command a crowd," she said, "someone who was often angry and would be shaking his fist at a room, things I was not and couldn't change."

Politics also seemed a remote possibility because it was never part of her daily life. "The immigrant ethos of working hard, keeping your head down and not causing trouble so that you could one day be financially successful did not allow much room for politics," Michelle said. Growing up, she never encountered politicians, never went to a city council meeting and didn't discuss politics at the dinner table. Her first political discussion did not occur until she was a freshman at Harvard.

When people advised Michelle about her future, they sometimes advised her to become an athlete. "[Figure skater] Michelle Kwan was the only well-known Asian-American female at that time," Michelle said. "There were so few examples for young Asian girls to look up to." But she didn't have money for figure skating lessons and she never took up that challenge.

FOLLOWING A TRADITIONAL PATH

What Michelle intended to do was follow the same path as her mother. "I remember saying that I planned to go to school, work, have kids and then become a stay-at-home mom," she recalled. "That's what my mom did, and she took the whole force of her being and poured it into raising her family."

But when she enrolled as an undergraduate at Harvard, she had a lot of negotiating to do with her parents, who defined success quite narrowly. "They wanted me to be a doctor, an engineer, or get a business degree," Michelle said. "I just wanted to help people and to learn what makes groups come together. I wanted to take history or social studies, but that would doom me to a lifetime of my parents thinking that I was not successful." The compromise was a degree in economics, and Michelle graduated with a clear plan. She would do a two-year stint in consulting and then apply to business school.

When her mother's crisis changed things, Michelle chose law instead of business and excelled. She was named a Rappaport Fellow in law and public policy, interning in 2010 for Michael Weiss, chief of staff for then-mayor Thomas Menino. She was asked to pick a project to work on during the internship, and

Michelle knew exactly what she wanted to do. She told them, "I'm going to streamline permitting for opening a small business."

UNTANGLING RED TAPE

While her boss didn't exactly roll his eyes, his reaction was not what she expected. The chief of staff showed her evidence that this project had already been tried. "He unfurled a four-foot poster showing arrows going off in all different directions." Michelle said. "The previous interns had mapped out the system and it was a mess."

But she had the advantage of direct experience with the system. "I made my own guide to the process, recognizing a lot of small things that are a problem, like none of the applications being available online," she said. Michelle knew from experience that to open a restaurant, she'd had to go to three different locations to get the forms.

By the end of the summer, she had created a roadmap guide to opening a restaurant in Boston and led a business competition that saw the launch of the first three food trucks in Boston.

And 2010 was also the year Michelle took her first steps toward becoming a politician. The internship in the mayor's office had given her a firsthand look at how city politics worked and how change could be accomplished. She applied for and was accepted into Emerge America's six-month training program to prepare women to run for office. The 70 hours of instruction covered all the key aspects of becoming a politician, from public speaking, fundraising, media and messaging to ethical leadership and cultural competency.

A ROLE MODEL TO FOLLOW

With politics now firmly in her sights, Michelle had another watershed moment, when she studied contract law at Harvard with Professor Elizabeth Warren. Elizabeth was more than a professor to her — she was a role model and mentor as well.

At the time, Elizabeth had been appointed and was serving as chair of the national Troubled Asset Relief Program (TARP), which followed in the wake of the 2008 world economic collapse. "Having Elizabeth Warren as a professor was amazing. When she was not in class, she was overseeing TARP in

Washington," Michelle said. "Mondays and Tuesdays were terrifying because she would call us out if we were not prepared. Then Tuesday evening she would fly to Washington and we would watch her grill the regulators."

That admiration turned into action when Elizabeth ran for the U.S. Senate in 2012, and Michelle signed up to help with the campaign. She started as a field organizer, inviting people to events. But she soon took on more responsibility, working her way up the chain of command to become the constituency director in charge of outreach to marginalized communities of various religious, ethnic and language groups, as well as the LGBTQ community. Her job was to find networks of citizens who had not been engaged, who weren't being heard. "I remember at the end, doing all sorts of things, showing up at mosques and temples, finding social networks, all so we could figure out how to shape [Elizabeth Warren's] platform," said Michelle.

She was very proud of the end result. "We came up with 11 different versions of the palm card [an information piece with basic details, the size of a business card] in different languages and for different groups," she said. "I was proud not only because the content was different in each one, but also because we had taken the time to listen to people."

GIVING PEOPLE A VOICE

Michelle had a major "aha" moment when she saw the turnout on Election Day, especially the influx of first-time voters who had never been part of the political process before. She had always been focused on the importance of good municipal policy, but all that changed in an instant: "It made me realize how important politics is, bringing people into the tent and having a voice for those who didn't have a voice." It was a welcome transition from setting the framework through policy-making to taking direct action as a politician.

AN UPHILL BATTLE

The next year, Michelle saw an opportunity to leverage all the lessons she had learned from Elizabeth Warren's Senate campaign and from the Emerge America training program. Michelle decided to run for Boston city council, vying for one of the four at-large spots on the thirteen-member council.

Not only was Michelle ready, but 2013 marked a particularly good opportunity. Four of the thirteen seats on the council had been vacated by councillors who were running for mayor, and two of those were at-large seats. Michelle built her campaign platform on increasing access to municipal services and connecting families to opportunities for business and education. She was committed to helping other families avoid the challenges she and her family had had to struggle through.

Michelle was in many respects fighting an uphill battle. She was young, not from Boston, an Asian American, female and not wealthy. But she was well prepared. She had a clear vision of what she wanted to accomplish at city hall and a track record from her time as an intern.

And compared to many first-time candidates, she had developed strong political skills. She was ready to hit the ground running.

A SERIES OF FIRSTS

The hard work paid off. Michelle won an at-large seat, coming within a fraction of a percent of winning the most at-large votes in the election. She came in just a hair behind Ayanna Pressley, who would go on to win election to the U.S. House of Representatives in 2018, becoming the first African-American member of Congress from Massachusetts.

Michelle earned her own firsts in that 2013 campaign. She became the youngest-ever Boston councillor and the first Asian-American woman on the council. She focused on several important issues in her first term: improving employment conditions for domestic workers, outlawing LGBTQ conversion therapy and extending late-night transit services.

Michelle quickly gained the respect of her fellow councillors. She was the lead sponsor of Boston's paid parental leave ordinance, a measure she championed after she became a mother and discovered that city employees had no parental leave provisions. She also sponsored the health care equity ordinance that banned discrimination based on gender identity. Both ordinances were unanimously passed by council.

Then, two years into her tenure, shortly after being reelected in 2015, Michelle was voted president of the council by her peers. She was just 30 years old at the time. In 2017, she was convincingly reelected, winning the most votes for an at-large position. In 2018, she decided to step down as president and

MICHELLE'S ADVICE TO YOUNG WOMEN

"Don't be afraid to define leadership differently. And make a decision not based on whether you yourself think you're as ready as you should be; make it based on whether you're going to be the best candidate out of everyone else who will step up if you don't."

concentrate on her own policy agenda: economic mobility, racial equality and climate justice. In October of that year, she proposed the first car-free day for Boston and she remained staunchly supportive of Boston's status as a sanctuary city — a municipality that limits cooperation with federal authorities to enforce immigration law.

Michelle's leadership has been widely recognized, and she has received several awards for her work, from being named to *Marie Claire*'s New Guard list of the 50 Most Influential Women in America to winning the 2017 Eleanor Roosevelt Award from the Massachusetts Democratic Party.

Her life has taken unpredictable turns, but she makes a point of tackling challenges one by one and taking advantage of the surprises her career has allowed.

CHAPTER 6

HALA LATTOUF

THERE ARE NO CAMEL TAXIS

Minister of social development, Jordan

TO FIND OUT WHAT you're really made of, it's often advised to step outside your comfort zone, to challenge yourself, to push the limits. Whether you succeed or fail, the greatest risks often bring the most rewarding personal growth and sense of self-confidence. This is the kind of advice that is much easier to say than to actually do. But not for Her Excellency Hala Bsaisu Lattouf, Jordan's minister of social development. Early in life, she set herself on an unconventional path and has since answered the call not once, but twice, to serve in key public office appointments.

GOING AGAINST EXPECTATIONS

As a teenager, Hala Lattouf left the carefully prescribed route set out for girls in the socially conservative country of Jordan and put herself forward for a student exchange program that would transport her more than 6200 miles to the heart of the American Midwest. She went from a largely cloistered, small school in Amman, Jordan — where there were only 16 girls in her year who all attended class together and where everyone knew everyone else — to wandering the halls of a typical American high school in Madison, Wisconsin, where there were thousands of students and more than 800 in her graduating class. She was just 16 years old when she chose this challenging path.

She was way far out of her comfort zone in the wildly different world she found herself in. To start with, the parties. "Going to school [in Jordan], I had never seen anyone drunk or on drugs." (Jordan is a largely Muslim country where observant Muslims don't drink alcohol.) And the scale of the school was equally jolting. "I was not used to so many people. At home, we all knew each other, so we all said hi to everyone. I didn't realize when I came to America that you didn't do that. They didn't know how to react at first to this girl who went down the hall saying hello to every person, but after a while, they would say hi back to me and they became used to it."

Once they got to know her, the American students got a good taste of Hala's sense of humor. "I had a blast talking about home," she said. "They used to think it was amazing because I spoke English and didn't look different. I told everyone that I got around town by camel taxi," she said, laughing at the memory. This was in the 1980s, and all that her classmates knew about Jordan were stereotypes. They expected that the whole country was full of camels, even in the city.

FROM A TRADITIONAL BEGINNING TO A LIFE-CHANGING EXPERIENCE

About her early life, Hala told me she wasn't someone who started out knowing she wanted to serve in public office. "I came from a Palestinian middle-class family. We cared about education, but as girls, we had no aspirations. I didn't think it was possible to even think of being in public life. It was just accepted that my path would never include that." She was expected to follow a traditional route through adolescence, from education to marriage and motherhood. Husbands and families came first; careers were something women fit in before they married or after their children were grown.

Although she did go on to marry and have children, Hala had a different path in mind. She wanted to travel and she wanted to meet people from different countries. With her parents' support, she applied to the exchange program. She said spending her graduating year at an American high school was a defining experience. "It changed my life, in a positive way." It gave Hala a wider perspective and a less homogeneous experience. "You learn to accept all humans and all families. It taught me not to have stereotypes myself and to love and accept everybody."

Hala also learned how to persevere when things don't go exactly as planned. The first family she stayed with in the United States wasn't a good fit, and Hala did not feel comfortable or accepted there. But she didn't let that stop her on her grand adventure. "I had to change families. Sometimes you work hard, but it doesn't work. It's important not to take failure as a personal issue, to be able to step back. It didn't work, I tried my best, I moved on."

Hala's persistence paid off. "I went to another family and had the time of my life. I called them Mom and Dad … I'm still in touch with them. It was a great family and they made me feel so welcome."

Did broadening her horizons through travel teach Hala to think independently? Or did she want to travel and do something different because she was already an independent thinker? It's hard to say, but either way, Hala believes that the ability to think independently is an essential quality for all, but especially for women.

This independence of thought applies to choices about what kind of education you want, who you socialize with, where you live, who you marry. It also applies to how you relate to your beliefs and religion. Hala explained her perspective. "I am a Muslim, I pray five times a day," she said. "But I have done my homework. I don't let anyone tell me what my religion says to me. I studied and I know Islam is a strong religion for supporting women. It's very, very important not to let other people define you, to tell you what to do. Especially, you cannot empower others to use religion as a tool to tell you what to do."

DEFINING HER GOALS

Returning home from the U.S. after graduating high school, she obtained a bachelor of science degree with distinction at Jordan University. But Hala continued her exploration of other cultures, winning a scholarship to the London School of Economics. There, she earned a master's degree in international accounting and finance.

Hala began her career in banking at the Jordan Investment Bank and then at the Arab Bank, where she had a chance to use her finance and accounting skills. She enjoyed the work but discovered that banking couldn't hold her attention. She felt there was something missing. "I wanted to do more development," she confided, "something more closely related to who I am." So, out of her comfort zone Hala went once again and took a job at the United Nations

HALA'S MESSAGE: IDENTITY + POSITIVITY

Hala has a message for young women that goes beyond communication skills and involves identity and positivity. It's important, she said, to be comfortable and proud of who you are, of being from your country, and to be comfortable in your own skin. "Don't change who you are," she said. "Don't let people decide your state of mind for you. You control the outcome of the conversation."

Equally important, even when the conversation is difficult, is avoiding negativity and anger. "No matter how challenging, you raise the bar. You never go lower. You take the time to drive negative into positive, to move ignorance into knowledge." In a divisive world, she advises young women to "explain rather than defend or go on the attack." She acknowledges that this takes a lot of discipline, but it's worth the effort.

Effective communication brings people together, and this is a fundamental part of leadership. "Young women have to believe in themselves, that they can be part of the leadership. If women are not part of leadership, we can't have the society we are capable of reaching in developing dignity and human rights," she said. "Hope is the only thing stronger than hate."

Development Programme, a global development network that works in around 170 countries to eradicate poverty while protecting the planet. "I started at the UN in 2001, my first contract. I created new IT projects, including a national network, which His Majesty [King Abdullah] opened. We were able to turn ideas into reality." In that role, she was also put in charge of the poverty and gender team. She then worked as project director at the World Bank.

MORE EFFECTIVE FROM INSIDE?

Hala then turned her attention to public leadership, seeing the possibilities to effect change through government. She advanced through a number of senior posts in the ministry of tourism and antiquities, followed by a position as secretary general of planning and international cooperation.

At first, this seemed to be an ideal way to make a positive impact on development. "It was the culmination of everything I learned in my career in public office," she said. "I thought, there is so much more I can do, I had so many ideas, so much I wanted to do. Working in the public office, I felt that I could help more *and* be who I am and who I want to be."

But it didn't turn out the way Hala had hoped. As she got into the role, she realized she was not having the impact she wanted. "I was not doing reform," she said, "and that's what I came to do. So, I resigned from government. When you resign from government, you have to give up your pension. I gave up my pension." This was a steep price, but one she was willing to pay to be true to herself.

Was it a courageous thing to do? Hala doesn't speak of it in those terms. She said it was not easy, but simply necessary. "It is very tempting just to stay in office, but I don't like to compromise who I am, because then I stop being who I am. That's very important. I tried to be true to my principles."

And it speaks to something fundamental: the need to really understand what you are striving for when you enter public office. "You have to decide," she said, "are you in it for the politics and political power, or are you in it for impact and change?"

Hala is committed to change and reform. "For me, it's a passion, my whole self."

FINDING A NEW PATH

Hala returned to the private sector and found other ways to pursue her development work outside of government. She worked in a consultancy that focused on the areas she felt passionately about: poverty reduction, youth empowerment and the protection of vulnerable groups.

Then another life-changing moment connected her back to government. She was recruited by Queen Rania of Jordan. She wanted Hala to work with her team as office director. The queen is known for her activism and her initiatives to address social issues such as poverty alleviation, women's advancement, education and child welfare. These issues were important to Hala, too.

"I worked with Her Majesty and it was a great learning experience." She describes Queen Rania as very smart and passionate about the work she does. But what struck Hala the most was the queen's empathy. "She is always thinking

> IT ALL BOILS DOWN TO THIS: IF YOU DECIDE TO GO INTO POLITICS, YOU MAY RUN FOR OFFICE, BUT IN FACT, YOU ARE RUNNING FOR YOUR LIFE, THE ONE YOU WANT TO CREATE FOR YOURSELF AND FOR OTHERS.

not only of being queen, but also how everything she does affects the people. That aspect is in every decision. It was humbling because she always found the time to do the work, yet ask you about your children, to make you feel part of a special team and appreciated for the work you do. It makes you work harder because you feel you are not just part of a team but part of the family."

And to Hala, that's not just a nicety, it's essential to the future and the key to bridging gaps between people, ideologies and nations. "It is critical that we connect as humans first," she said.

COMING FULL CIRCLE

"When we stay connected at a human level, there are no differences. We don't choose how we are born, how we look or what nationality we are. Everybody is simply human. And it allows relationships to form where you care for other people like you care for yourself."

Hala has kept this foremost in mind as she has taken on a series of important roles. After working with Queen Rania, she was appointed minister of social development, a post she held from 2007 to 2011 when she returned again to the private sector to consult. Then, in 2016, she was appointed to the Senate of Jordan, where she headed the labor and development committee. In June of 2017, she resigned from the Senate to become minister of social development for a second time. (In Jordan, the cabinet is appointed by the prime minister and is responsible to the elected lower house. While ministers can also be appointed from the lower house of the Parliament, called the Chamber of Deputies or

House of Representatives, that is a relatively recent development, put into place in 2011.)

Now, Hala is back in government, focusing on the issues she is passionate about, working to create change and have a positive impact on the people of Jordan.

IF ONLY SHE HAD KNOWN ...

Social pressure can have an adverse impact on how you live your life, Hala observed. "When I hit 40," she said, "something really changed in me and I stopped caring what people thought of me. I wish I was like that before! I would look for smiles of approval. I cared about getting recognition, that my ideas were accepted. Something made me change and it was like being liberated."

HALA'S THOUGHTS FOR YOUNG WOMEN

Independence of thought needs to be applied when choosing an educational path. "It's a very big step in one's life to decide," she said. "You have to go for your passion because then you go wholeheartedly. You don't just do it to pass the exam — you want to take in all the knowledge, to read more and know more. It's how you keep on gaining knowledge to stay ahead in the field you are working in."

Knowledge also fosters independence of thought. "If you lead in knowledge, you will find creative ways to solve problems and you will be part of the small group who looks at things differently."

And a related quality comes into play, one Hala thinks is essential for young women. "How we communicate dictates the path we pursue," she said. "Coming from a conservative culture for women, it's very important to give this weight. We should teach young women about conflict resolution and negotiation."

CHAPTER 7

KIM CAMPBELL

BREAKING BARRIERS WITH NO REGRETS

Former prime minister of Canada

THE AMBITION TO LEAD came early in life for Canada's first — and so far only — woman prime minister, Kim Campbell.

"When I was very young, I wanted to become secretary general of the UN. In high school, when I became student council president, I ran because there had never been a girl as president. But I didn't think of it as politics then, more as organization. I didn't come from a political family," she said. "Girls were not necessarily encouraged to get involved in leadership and politics. People then didn't see us as future legislators, so I made my own way."

EDUCATION FIRST

Kim was born Avril Phaedra Campbell in Port Alberni, British Columbia, but as a young teenager, she decided that she would be called Kim. She studied political science at the University of British Columbia, becoming the first woman president of the freshman class. After graduation, she went on to pursue a doctorate and lectured in political science at two universities in Vancouver.

The idea to pursue politics came when she was teaching. "I started to think politics might be a way to make a difference. One of the students I knew was the president of the Young Conservatives. He gave me some of [former Conservative

Party leader Robert] Stanfield's speeches to read. He said, 'Pick politics, not a party. Become a star and the party will come to you.'"

ENTERING THE FRAY

In 1980, Kim launched her political career at the municipal level. "My husband at the time had served three terms on the Vancouver school board and was running for city council. People suggested I should run for the Vancouver school board." She agreed, but she raised eyebrows when she went against all advice on a small but telling decision. "I ran under my own name — Kim Campbell — instead of my husband's name. A lot of people seemed disappointed because they thought if I ran under my married name, there would be greater recognition and a better chance of getting elected. But that's not the name I used, so I ran as Kim Campbell. We both got elected, but I got more votes."

At the time, she wasn't sure how she would feel about being in the public eye. "I didn't know whether I had the temperament for it, whether I would be able to stand the public scrutiny, the demands, whether I had the personality for door knocking. But I found I enjoyed it."

Kim served two terms at the school board while also attending law school. She said it was "a voyage of self-discovery. The municipal level is great training for developing political instincts. There is great variety in what you deal with at that level and a direct link between what you are doing and the people. I was involved in everything from strategic planning to finance. It really was very interesting and enjoyable."

But it wasn't perfect. "School board politics are fractious. I got used to being in situations where people were yelling at me and I found it didn't bother me. I knew that people were giving their opinions and it was part of the game."

Kim brought a broader perspective to these boisterous occasions, having specialized in Soviet studies as a student. "I thought to myself, you can't do this in Soviet countries. It really is a privilege. So, I welcomed the debate and disagreements."

MOVING UP

Kim moved on to provincial politics. After an unsuccessful campaign in 1983, she served as a member of the British Columbia Legislative Assembly and

> I DIDN'T KNOW WHETHER I HAD THE TEMPERAMENT FOR IT, WHETHER I WOULD BE ABLE TO STAND THE PUBLIC SCRUTINY, THE DEMANDS, WHETHER I HAD THE PERSONALITY FOR DOOR KNOCKING. BUT I FOUND I ENJOYED IT.

cabinet minister with the Social Credit Party in 1986. "Though our party was in government, I did not get on with the premier [Bill Vander Zalm]. But I got to do interesting things and I really enjoyed it. Going into politics gives you a chance to get to know the community in a way you never would otherwise." She was involved in everything from heritage conservation to construction and forestry.

"I got to know the province very well. I was *interested* and it reinforced a practice that I had learned at the school board; I learned to listen to people, to consider how they will be affected by the legislation and actions we were taking. This saves you from making some stupid mistakes down the road."

Kim turned her sights to federal politics when another trailblazer, Pat Carney, left politics. Pat had been the first woman member of Parliament elected as a Progressive Conservative from BC. Kim ran for the nomination in Pat's riding of Vancouver Centre. She won the nomination and in 1988 Kim was elected when Prime Minister Brian Mulroney swept to power with a majority government. In 1989, she became minister of what was then called Indian Affairs and Northern Development. Then came more firsts: first woman justice minister and first woman minister at the departments of National Defense and Veterans' Affairs.

A FOREGONE CONCLUSION?

"People would say to me, 'When [Prime Minister] Mulroney steps down, you will be our next leader.' I remember asking a colleague, 'What's happening?' He said, 'I think you are going to lead this party one day, and I think it's going to happen naturally.' They saw me as a leader, not just as junior leader."

Kim credits her success to her care and attention to being a team player. She believed in a model of inclusive politics, bringing different interest groups together for discussion and working toward compromise. She was also a staunch supporter of ensuring that women and Indigenous peoples were included in the process. During her tenure as justice minister, she convened the first-ever national symposium on Women, Law and the Administration of Justice. She co-chaired with the Yukon minister of justice a symposium on Aboriginal justice. She introduced major amendments to gun control legislation and oversaw a bill on abortion that was a compromise between the polarized views within the governing party. She also oversaw the 1992 rape shield legislation also known as the "no means no" law.

Then came a huge opportunity when Prime Minister Mulroney announced in February 1993 that he would leave politics in June. Although his successor would become prime minister as leader of the ruling party, it left little time for the new leader to make an impression and build support for the election looming in November.

With the opportunity to run for the leadership of the Progressive Conservative Party of Canada came a dilemma. While her personal political capital was strong and rising, the popularity of the incumbent prime minister was low and falling. The public was not happy with the government. Chances for a hollow victory — winning the leadership but losing the election — were high.

"I was of two minds. I had all this support; everyone was saying I should be the next leader. We were governing at the time and that was good, we were in power. But I was also worried because Mulroney was unpopular in polling — the most unpopular prime minister ever. That's not criticism, it just is. I did not run for the Progressive Conservative Party leadership just to be the first female prime minister, but when it came down to it, I couldn't not run."

So, she ran for the party leadership. Given Kim's popularity, many prominent potential leaders did not enter the race, but it was far from a given that she would win. Mulroney backed Kim's main rival, Jean Charest, an MP and cabinet minister from Quebec with almost 10 years' experience. The race turned into a tight one, but eventually Kim won the leadership with 52.7 percent support compared to Charest's 47.3 percent. With that vote, history was made. As leader of the party in power, Kim automatically became prime minister and was officially appointed by the governor general on June 25, 1993, becoming the first, and so far only, woman to attain that position. It was a huge moment and an emotional one for many of the delegates. Kim recalled, "I remember the final night of the leadership convention, a man came up to me with tears in his eyes and said, 'This is for my daughter.'"

Kim's political momentum was strong and her personal popularity was the highest of any prime minister for 30 years. She was more popular than her main opponent, Liberal Party leader Jean Chrétien, and her party was drawing close to the Liberals in popularity. Everything seemed set for success.

Immediately, she streamlined the cabinet structure, reducing its members from 35 to 23 by consolidating a number of ministries. In July 1993, she attended the G7 Summit in Tokyo, bringing together the leaders of the United States, Canada, Britain, Germany, France, Italy and Japan. "People liked that I reduced cabinet and that I had a successful G7 Summit. They liked me governing." However, the underlying political currents had turned against her.

Kim's candor and directness were admired while she was vying for the party leadership and in her early days as prime minister. However, they did not play as well once the election campaign began in September.

A DIFFICULT TIME

It was an unusual election. Canada has more than a dozen political parties, but for decades it had been a three-way race between the Liberals, Conservatives and New Democrats. With the creation and growing strength of the right-wing Reform Party from Western Canada and the surging separatist Bloc Québécois, the vote was newly fragmented. Nonetheless, the Liberals remained her main opponent, led by Jean Chrétien, a seasoned politician who had served in key roles under previous prime ministers. He had more than 20 years' experience, including a major role in creating and bringing into force a new Canadian Constitution.

In the media, the election race was characterized as the Tortoise and the Hare, with Kim as the overconfident, unreliable sprinting bunny who had only been in federal politics for five years compared to her older, slower, more

ADVICE FROM KIM'S POLITICAL PLAYBOOK

EXERCISING POLITICAL POWER

"Going into politics is about political power and the ability to exercise it. There is something very energizing about having to deal with real decisions, to get the information you need and the processes to make the best decisions.

"If you are happy with the way things are, fine. But if you're not happy with the way things are, think about how to get someone else in there — and maybe that person is you.

"Power exists. Someone's going to have it. To young women I would say, if you have it, exercise it ethically."

MEETING THE CHALLENGES OF POLITICS TODAY

"You need to find ways to connect and communicate directly (with the electorate) and not have your message distorted and not be subject to campaigns of disinformation. Door-knocking continues to be important because it is the one way you can be face-to-face with people."

THINKING ABOUT DEMOCRACY

"More than ever, we have to be conscious that democracy matters. It's a blunt instrument, but it's incredibly important because if we lose it, there are devastating consequences. It also means that those who understand the importance of democracy need to present themselves for public office."

DEALING WITH DIFFERENCES

"Understand not everyone is going to like and support you, either because they disagree or they are partisan and against you. There are partisan disagreements and substantive disagreements. Don't fall into the trap of meanness when you disagree."

A CALL TO ACTION

"One doesn't really have the choice of *whether* to get involved. The question is *how* we do it. It is our choice. You can be an active voter, a volunteer, check writer, door-knocker, campaigner or be a candidate. To think it doesn't matter is very dangerous."

experienced rival. Her candor was seen as a liability in the election campaign, especially when she said bluntly that unemployment "would not be much reduced by the end of the century," while Chrétien was promising more jobs. In addition, Kim had to battle party infighting and the sexism of a country that had never had a woman prime minister.

Perhaps the most difficult obstacle she faced was the rise of the far-right Reform Party that was taking significant support from the right wing of her own party. Adding to the challenges, negative ads mocking Chrétien severely backfired and eroded public support for the Conservatives.

When the general election came, the results were disastrous. The Progressive Conservatives were decimated, winning only two seats and losing their status as Official Opposition. The new Reform Party went from 1 seat in the 1988 election to 52 seats in 1993. The Bloc Québécois went from 10 to 54 seats.

It was a momentous turn of events. More than half the voters had changed political parties from the previous election. Kim was ousted as prime minister, lost her own seat in Vancouver Centre and resigned as party leader on December 13, 1993. All in all, she held the top post for 132 days.

RESILIENCY WITHOUT REGRET

How does Canada's only female prime minister feel about her place in history? She said, "I don't really have regrets. You do what you can. In the short term, it often seems disappointing and devastating when you lose or things don't work out. I liked politics the most of all the things I've done and I did the best in politics, but there are no guarantees. There is life after politics, that's an important lesson to learn. I went on and reinvented myself. I've had a very interesting and happy life since then."

She has been active as a teacher and research fellow, and in organizations of world leaders working to promote and strengthen democracy.

"One of the reasons I came back to Canada recently (after an extended time in the U.S. as Consul General and at Harvard) is because I think it's important to remind people I'm around. People say, 'She was only in office for 10 minutes so we don't have to count her.' But actually, I am the third shortest-serving prime minister. Are they going to go down the corridor of the Parliament buildings and take down the portraits of [the two shortest-serving prime ministers] Sir Charles Tupper and John Turner? Somehow, as a woman, I'm the one who doesn't belong."

Kim added, "I was out of Canada for a long time. When I came back I heard from so many women about what it meant to them that I had been prime minister. They would say, 'I was in grade 8 when you became prime minister, I still remember.' All sorts of people come up to me and tell me that it was really important. I was concerned about whether losing the election would dampen enthusiasm for women in leadership. But I don't think it did. We lost the election but it was a breakthrough."

CHAPTER 8

JACINDA ARDERN

PUTTING THE BLAZE IN TRAILBLAZING

Prime minister, New Zealand

NEW ZEALAND HAS A long history of trailblazing when it comes to equality for women. It was the first country in the world to give women the vote, in 1893, and so far, three women have held the top post of prime minister.

But none have demolished barriers or expectations quite like Jacinda Ardern. She was elected prime minister in September 2017, at the age of 37, becoming the youngest female leader of a country in the world and the youngest New Zealand prime minister since Edward Stafford took office in 1856, also at age 37. She leads the Labour Party in a rare government coalition that embraces both the right wing New Zealand First Party and the left wing Green Party.

She's young and outspoken, and she fearlessly tackles tough issues on the home front, including mental health, conditions for workers and paid parental leave. She's also taking on her country's international role, reviving discussions on the mothballed Trans-Pacific Partnership. She is accessible, hugs people with abandon and flies economy on commercial flights.

TESTED BY TRAGEDY

The world's eyes were on Jacinda in March 2019, when a gunman from Australia opened fire on two mosques in the New Zealand city of Christchurch, killing 50 and wounding dozens more.

Jacinda didn't hesitate. She came out immediately with a passionate denunciation of the gunman's actions and Islamophobia in a speech to the nation from New Zealand's Parliament.

Referring to the fact that the gunman came to New Zealand to perpetrate an act of terrorism, she said, "You may have chosen us, but we utterly reject and condemn you."

She called out Facebook for the role its platform played in the rise of extremism, as a live video of the shooting taken by the gunman went viral. She called on social media to take more systemic action to curb its use in spreading hate.

In condemning the attack, Jacinda backed up her words with action. In a decisive and lightning-fast move, she introduced legislation to reform New Zealand's gun laws by banning assault rifles and military style semiautomatic guns — just 10 days after the shootings.

In the immediate aftermath of the attack, Jacinda was crystal clear on the values of New Zealand: "We represent diversity, kindness, compassion," she said. "A home for those who share our values. Refuge for those who need it. And those values will not and cannot be shaken by this attack."

She further emphasized the point, saying, "Many of those who will have been directly affected by this shooting may be migrants to New Zealand; they may even be refugees here," she said. "They have chosen to make New Zealand their home, and it is their home. They are us. The person who has perpetuated this violence against us is not. They have no place in New Zealand."

EARLY CHALLENGES LEAD TO LIFELONG INSPIRATION

Jacinda was born in Hamilton, New Zealand, the second of two daughters of Ross and Laurell Ardern. Her father was a police officer who went on to become New Zealand's high commissioner to the island of Niue, and her mother worked as a catering assistant at a school. The family was part of the sizable Mormon community in New Zealand, where missionaries had been active since the mid-1800s. Jacinda's family were devout followers and her uncle Ian was a senior official in the Mormon Church. As is customary in the Mormon faith, Jacinda canvassed door-to-door to promote her religion, and her family remains with the church. However, in her 20s, Jacinda left the church when she could no longer reconcile its opposition to gay marriage with her own beliefs.

Jacinda spent the early part of her childhood in Murupara, a community known for its gang violence and poverty, an experience that left a lasting impression on Jacinda. Seeing these desperate conditions was one of the things that inspired her later interest in politics.

After Jacinda's older sister was beaten up at school, the family packed up and moved to Morrinsville, just south of Auckland, when Jacinda was eight years old. Morrinsville sits in a largely rural farming area, a quiet, idyllic community that in many ways was the opposite of Murupara. Jacinda attended primary and secondary school in Morrinsville before going to the nearby University of Waikato, to study politics and communications.

HIGH SCHOOL YEARBOOK: STUDENT MOST LIKELY TO BE PRIME MINISTER

Jacinda showed early signs of political potential. One of her former teachers, Gregor Fountain, recalled Jacinda in the *NZ Herald* "staying behind in class to talk about issues, because she really wanted to grapple with them." And in her high school yearbook, Jacinda was named "most likely to be prime minister."

Jacinda has achieved a lot in a short period of time, partly because her interest in politics developed early. When she was 14 years old, she tracked down then-MP Marilyn Waring for a school project, peppered her with questions about a nuclear-free New Zealand and asked for her views on the most pressing issues facing the younger generation. By age 17, Jacinda had joined the New Zealand Labour Party and was handing out leaflets for the political campaign of Harry Duynhoven, the Labour member of Parliament (MP) for New Plymouth.

Apart from a part-time job in a fish and chip shop and some volunteer roles, Jacinda's career has been entirely within the world of politics and policy.

Jacinda was a straight A student, and after graduating from university, she became a researcher on the staff of Labour MP Phil Goff, which in turn led to a role as researcher for then–prime minister Helen Clark. In 2005, she traveled, but when she ran low on money, she applied to be a policy advisor in the London cabinet office of U.K. prime minister Tony Blair. Although she disagreed with Blair's decision to enter the Iraq war, when an offer came, she took the job. In 2007, she was elected president of the International Union of Socialist Youth (IUSY), traveling to many countries in that capacity, including Algeria, China, India, Israel, Jordan and Lebanon.

EXPLAINING NEW ZEALAND'S ELECTORAL SYSTEM

New Zealand national elections are held under the mixed-member proportional representation model (MMP). Citizens have two votes: they vote to select a candidate in their local district and they vote for a party they would like to win a majority in the national elections. If there is a disparity between the proportion of seats won by a party and the overall proportion of votes it won, it is equalized by selecting members of Parliament (MPs) from a list that each party creates for this purpose.

In 2008, she returned to New Zealand and campaigned as a Labour Party candidate in the Waikato district, an area where Labour was historically out of the running. She was trounced, losing by 13 000 votes. However, under New Zealand's mixed proportional-representation system, there are two streams to enter Parliament: one by winning a district seat and a second by becoming a "list" MP, which is how Jacinda became a member in 2008. At 28, she was the youngest member in the House of Representatives.

After joining Parliament, Jacinda spent nine years in Opposition, becoming Labour Party spokesperson for a broad range of portfolios, including justice, youth justice, arts, culture, heritage, youth affairs, small business, social development and children, honing her political skills. She has championed adoption reform to include adoption by gay couples and introduced the Child Poverty Reduction and Eradication Bill. Then, in February 2017, she won a by-election, becoming the MP representing Mount Albert.

Although later it seemed as if Ardern was an instant success, she was already a seasoned veteran by the time she led the Labour Party to power.

FROM THE WORST JOB IN POLITICS TO "JACINDAMANIA"

When Labour Party leader Andrew Little stepped down abruptly on July 31, 2017, Jacinda was unanimously selected to be the new party leader. She stepped in to the role of party leader less than two months before the general election, when the campaign process was already well underway.

Expectations were low. The Labour Party had been languishing in Opposition for almost a decade, losing three times in a row. With just over six weeks to go, the polls — and the odds — were definitely against them. Would the Labour Party suffer a fourth consecutive defeat?

Then something extraordinary happened. Ardern inspired what is sometimes called "Jacindamania," an outpouring of enthusiasm and admiration unprecedented for a politician in New Zealand.

That tide of popularity swept her into office in September 2017. It was a dream come true by almost any standard. Having risen to head of state at a young age, Jacinda believes her sensitivity is an asset. She recognizes that resilience is a key to success in politics.

"I'M JUST PREGNANT, NOT INCAPACITATED"

In January 2018, she announced that she was expecting a baby in June 2018 and planned to take six weeks' maternity leave. Deputy Prime Minister Winston Peters would be in charge while she was away. When she announced her pregnancy, just four months after taking office, she dismissed any questions about how she would cope with the dual role of prime minister and expectant mother. With a laugh, she told reporters, "I'm just pregnant, not incapacitated." Her partner, TV presenter Clarke Gayford, planned to be a stay-at-home dad. And when Jacinda gave birth to a baby girl in June 2018, they proceeded with this plan.

Jacinda pushed forward on other fronts, too. While she was happy to talk publicly about her plans for motherhood and how she would combine them with the country's top job, she fiercely defended the right of women to keep their own child-bearing plans private from their employers.

She has a strong record of support on many issues that affect women. She vowed during the 2017 election campaign to liberalize abortion laws and remove abortion from the New Zealand Crimes Act. She stated that she intended to have a gender-balanced caucus and would use her administration to push for stronger pay equity measures for women. Women now represent 46 percent of her caucus.

While she is openly and proudly feminist, Jacinda makes it quite clear she is only human. She is clear that she does not want to be thought of as some kind

AN INTERVIEW WITH JACINDA

Q: What initially sparked your interest in politics?

A: I was one of those kids who wanted to change the world. As I got older, I worked out that politics was a great place to start.

Q: What has politics taught you about yourself? About the world?

A: That everything takes longer than you think, but it's worth the effort. And about myself? Probably something that applies to everyone — we're all tougher than we think.

Q: What do you wish you had known then (before entering public life) that you know now — in other words, what advice would you give to your younger self?

A: You don't have to have 100 percent confidence in your ability to take on something new before you start. Everyone has doubts. The trick is knowing how to feel the fear and do it anyway.

Q: You have been open about your struggle with anxiety, something that a lot of young women relate to. You said before you became party leader that you didn't want the top job because of the pressure and time demands that you saw up close working for Helen Clark. What have you learned about coping with anxiety that you would like to share with young women?

A: There is nothing wrong with self-preservation. If you're not feeling on top of your game, then turn off social media, cut yourself some slack and always try to sleep!

Q: Was it as difficult as you thought it was going to be?

A: Yes. But it's also just as rewarding as I thought it would be.

Q: What advice would you give to young women considering running for an elected office?

A: Do it. And when you do, be yourself.

of superwoman, because she believes it is important that no one expect women to be superwomen. She has said publicly that her ability to combine motherhood and being prime minister is only possible because her partner Clarke has the ability to be a full-time caregiver.

THE FIGHT FOR WOMEN'S EQUALITY IS FAR FROM DONE

Jacinda believes that most of us can name a woman who has been a role model and has blazed the trail for those behind, but she is adamant that the fight must not flag and that progress cannot be taken for granted. After all, when Jacinda was elected, she was one of only a handful of women heads of government around the world.

While she is pleased to have become prime minister, she would be just as happy if there were less attention paid to her rise to power; she looks forward to the day when a country having a female leader becomes commonplace and not worth remarking on.

CHAPTER 9

KIRSTEN GILLIBRAND

WANTED: FULL-TIME DRAGON SLAYER

Senator representing New York, United States

WHEN YOUR POLITICAL OPPONENTS are breathing fire at you and your eyebrows are getting singed by the flames, you could be forgiven for stepping back in retreat. But if you are Senator Kirsten Gillibrand of New York, chances are you will brandish your sword and step forward into the fray. Where others might falter, Kirsten stands resolved. And while the dragon can take on many forms, Kirsten's response is consistent: stand your ground!

Whether it's bullying tweets from the commander in chief, sexual assault in the military, campus sexual assault or sexual misconduct in Congress, she is prepared to do battle — often against the odds — when the stakes are high.

TAKING ON A PRESIDENT

And the stakes probably couldn't get much higher than taking on U.S. president Donald Trump, denouncing his alleged sexual misconduct, among other issues. Her criticisms got under his skin, and in December 2017, Trump's Twitter attacks came to a peak. He called Kirsten a "lightweight" and "a total flunky for Charles Schumer," the senior U.S. senator from New York. But those were not the parts of the tweet that set the Twittersphere alight with outrage. That happened when he said she had come to his office "'begging' for campaign contributions not so long ago (and would do anything for them)," implying that she had offered sexual favors in return for campaign money.

Kirsten blasted back, emphasizing that women's voices matter and must be heard: "You cannot silence me or the millions of women who have gotten off the sidelines to speak out about the unfitness and shame you have brought to the Oval Office," she tweeted.

That is just a small taste of how this fearless warrior has shown that she has the political chops to gain power, raise funds, mobilize a movement and occasionally jump in where others fear to tread.

This fearlessness was in full evidence when in March 2019, she announced her intention to run for president. When you look at her background and her track record, this move comes as no surprise.

BORN FIERCE

Kirsten's political savvy and her take-no-prisoners approach to fighting political battles come to her naturally. Her mother and grandmother provided Kirsten with an inspiring blueprint for raising a family while not giving any ground on accomplishing goals on a larger scale outside the home. Her mother, Penny Rutnik, took her criminal law exams two days after giving birth to her first child, Kirsten's brother, Douglas. She stood for the New York bar character exam three days before giving birth to Kirsten. Her grandmother Dorothy, known as Polly, was a five-foot dynamo who skillfully wielded her influence in the Democratic Party as a founder of the Albany Democratic Women's Club and as leader for 40 years in Albany mayor Erastus Corning's political machine. She told dirty jokes, swore a blue streak and was known to whiz down the halls of Albany's legislature in roller skates.

AIMING HIGH, STAYING BALANCED

It's not surprising that Kirsten sets her own sights high. She followed her mother's footsteps and became an attorney in 1991. In 2001, she married a British national, Jonathan Gillibrand, after they met on a blind date while he was studying for his MBA at Columbia University. They have two sons and live near the state capital of Albany. The balancing act is second nature to her. Kirsten picks up her kids between 5:00 pm and 6:00 pm every day. She considers this to be her most important commitment, so she fits everything else in around it.

Kirsten started her career as a corporate lawyer, causing controversy when she represented the interests of tobacco giant Philip Morris, among others. However, she defends her role by pointing out that she also did considerable pro bono work — helping women experiencing domestic abuse get divorces from abusive men and aiding a housing alliance in suing landlords over lead-paint problems.

At the same time, Kirsten was getting deeply involved in political action. She became part of the Women's Leadership Forum of the Democratic National Committee, eventually becoming its leader. During the last year of the Clinton administration in 1999, she served as special counsel to Andrew Cuomo, secretary of Housing and Urban Development (HUD), the federal agency responsible for affordable housing.

A DEFINING MOMENT

Kirsten credits a speech at the Women's Leadership Forum by Hillary Clinton, then first lady, for inspiring her to become a candidate herself. Hillary cautioned the group against leaving all the decision-making to others — otherwise, you only have yourself to blame if you don't like the results. Hillary's challenge hit home and galvanized Kirsten to step up.

She began working on Hillary's 2000 U.S. Senate campaign, recruiting young women to join the effort. She went all-out volunteering for the campaign and also backed her conviction by making significant campaign donations.

In many ways, her involvement in that campaign laid the groundwork for Kirsten's own political career. She proved successful at targeting young, first-time donors, and many of the young women she recruited for Hillary later worked on Kirsten's campaign. Perhaps even more important, a friendship was forged with Hillary, who then became a mentor. When the time came for Kirsten to consider running in 2004, it was Hillary who advised her to wait until 2006 when she believed conditions would be more favorable. (Although, since 2017, when Kirsten said in an interview that she believes Bill Clinton should have resigned the presidency over his affair with White House intern Monica Lewinsky, their friendship has become distanced.)

So it was after almost 15 years as a lawyer — and 6 years after Hillary's successful Senate race — that Kirsten took aim at winning a seat in U.S. Congress.

Enter the dragons.

DEFYING ALL ODDS

This was no cushy, safe seat. Kirsten took up her sword to face the 20th Congressional District in upstate New York, in the heart of a right-leaning, Republican-dominated district. In fact, the challenge she took on seemed almost guaranteed to stop her political career right in its tracks. Who could possibly give good odds when you were up against a well-established incumbent and in a district Democrats had held for only 4 years since 1913, the last time being more than 30 years before? Even worse was the fact that the Republicans had registered more than twice as many voters as the Democrats. At the time, there were 197 473 Republicans registered versus 82 737 Democrats. Most fledgling politicians might run the other way, but not Kirsten. She simply charged.

It was a close race, but Kirsten won by 6.2 percent, winning 53 percent of the vote to her opponent's 47 percent, and she has never looked back.

BIG NAMES VS. THE UNDERDOG

Fast forward to January 2009 when Hillary Clinton vacated her Senate position to become secretary of state. Under New York law, the governor chooses the interim replacement until a special election can be held, which in this case was set for November 2010. A number of prominent people expressed interest in the role, including Caroline Kennedy, who had campaigned for President Obama and addressed the 2008 Democratic National Convention; actress Fran Drescher, who had been a public diplomacy envoy for women's health issues during the George W. Bush administration; and Andrew Cuomo, who was New York State attorney general at the time. But Kirsten had other ideas. She stayed out of the spotlight and worked tirelessly behind the scenes lobbying for the post. She had a lot going for her: the Democrats were looking for a woman candidate; she had experience in Congress as an upstate representative; and she was seen as a centrist with the ability to win against Republicans. She got the nod, becoming, at age 42, the youngest senator in the 111th Congress.

When the special election came in 2010, she then had a huge advantage as the incumbent. Kirsten breezed through the Democratic primary, with help from party officials who didn't want a divisive battle and so discouraged high-profile candidates from standing against her. She went on to win the special

PICK YOUR BATTLES

Kirsten has focused on issues that matter most to her, and she advises aspiring women leaders to do the same. Here is a sample of the issues she champions.

- Kirsten was a leading voice in the effort to repeal the "Don't ask, don't tell" policy that banned gay people from serving openly in the military.
- She has waged a bipartisan battle for more resources to investigate campus rape cases and enforce the laws in place, as well as calling for more transparency and accountability from colleges on reporting.
- She wrote part of the STOCK Act, which made it illegal for members of Congress, their families and their staff to financially benefit from inside information.
- She successfully led a long fight to provide permanent health care and compensation to the 9/11 first responders and community survivors who became sick from the toxins at "ground zero."
- Kirsten has also been pressing for accountability and transparency in government, becoming the first member of Congress ever to post her official daily meetings, earmarks and personal financial disclosures online.

Senate election with a strong team and support from Democratic luminaries, including Hillary and former president Bill Clinton.

In 2012, Kirsten was reelected for a six-year term, and with her seat secure, she began, year by year, to consolidate her stature as a rising star and a legislator who is not afraid to tackle controversial issues or tough opponents, including the president.

A WARRIOR FOR WOMEN PAYING IT FORWARD

As a strategy for advancement and stemming from a deep conviction, she has been a tireless champion for women. Long before Harvey Weinstein and the #metoo campaign, Kirsten was calling out sexual harassment and battling sexual assault against women on campus and in the military.

The idea of paying it forward was inspired by Hillary's early support of Kirsten's entry into politics, and she became determined to give a hand up to women coming behind her. Kirsten strongly encourages more women to join public service, even going so far as to say to women considering politics: "If you want to run, give me a call. I'll help."

STARTING A MOVEMENT

Kirsten set in motion an entire movement, called Off the Sidelines, to encourage women to run for office, which had the side effect of vaulting her into the role of influential rainmaker and high-profile national political figure.

Off the Sidelines started as a simple website in July 2011, its goal to reverse the drop in the number of women elected to Congress in 2010. The Off the Sidelines Political Action Committee, a fundraising group that donates to campaigns, was established in 2012. And in 2014, Kirsten published her political memoir and feminist political manifesto, titling the book after the movement.

The success of Off the Sidelines is evidence of Kirsten's fearless advocacy and remarkable talent for attracting supporters and donations.

PULLING OFF A MINOR MIRACLE

It turns out that Kirsten is an ace at fundraising. In her very first campaign, she raised more than $2 million, more than any other first-time representative in the House. That included the rendering of a small miracle. In March 2006, she found herself $100 000 short of the $500 000 she needed to make the list of the Democrats' preferred candidates — with only one day until the deadline. She decided she would attempt to achieve what anyone else would consider the impossible; she spent 14 straight hours phoning friends, family, college classmates, law firm partners and associates, neighbors — everyone she knew — asking urgently for donations. She raised $125 000 in that one day, surpassing the total she had managed to raise in the six months previous. It proved to be a turning point, and she's still going strong.

FROM BENEFIT EVENTS TO BANKROLLING — MOVING WOMEN FORWARD

As a defender of women's rights, Kirsten's gone far beyond words of encouragement and well-orchestrated cheerleading. She's not just talking about engaging women in politics, she's funding their campaigns. The genesis of the movement was small scale, starting when Kirsten began holding fundraising lunches for women candidates in tight races. From there it has become a well-oiled machine. On opensecrets.org, the Center for Responsive Research reports that her political action committee (PAC) has donated $538 000 to Democratic candidates. And the momentum is growing.

One of the factors fueling her drive to get more women into Congress is her belief that women are more likely to work in a bipartisan way, which she considers essential to pass important social legislation. She encourages women from all parties to step up to run, though her funding efforts are solely focused on Democrats.

Influential, well-funded, fearless. It's no surprise that Kirsten took aim at the highest office in the land, jumping into the race on March 17, 2019, as a presidential primary candidate for the Democratic Party. Kirsten brought all her energy, fundraising skill and campaigning savvy to the battle, but in a crowded field of more than 25 candidates, she was not able to get the traction she needed and dropped out of the race on August 28, 2019. Though this campaign did not put her on the 2020 presidential ballot, she remains a formidable force in the senate. Dragons beware.

CHAPTER 10

STAV SHAFFIR

CORRUPTION STANDS NO CHANCE

Member of the Knesset, Israel

STAV SHAFFIR, THE YOUNGEST-EVER female member of the Knesset, streaks like a fireball across the political horizon in Israel, taking aim at budgetary corruption and fighting for her vision of Israel as a country that takes care of all its people, regardless of which region they live in and what their religious or ethnic roots are. No person or practice is off-limits in her fight for greater financial transparency; she happily upsets the status quo. She is blunt, unapologetic, fearless and super-focused.

Stav was first elected as a member of Knesset (MK) in 2013 at the age of 27 and won a second term in 2015. She was recruited by the Labor Party after playing a leading role in the 2011 social and economic protest movement, mobilizing protests across Israel that involved hundreds of thousands of people. She was fiery and articulate, the kind of charismatic leader that people like to follow.

While the tent cities and massive gatherings that marked the protests had already faded by the time the 2013 election came along, the echo of their energy still sounded on the campaign trail. The protests gave life and attention to many of the issues that Stav's campaign focused on: affordable housing and reform of education, welfare and health systems to narrow the gap between rich and poor — pushing the perennial concerns of security, war and peace further down the list.

Stav was also on a mission to expose corruption and dishonesty in the

Knesset in order to gain the support of youth who showed apathy and distrust toward government. In fact, it was the depth of this cynicism — which she discovered during a cross-country fact-finding tour to determine the next steps for the protest movement — that led Stav to consider a role in politics in the first place.

She observed a divide over the question of whether the movement should turn to politics or not — people over the age of 40 thought the next step should be entering politics, and people under 40 were wary of politics in general. Her mission was to encourage her generation to believe in politics as a way of taking responsibility for communities and lives.

So Stav focused on appealing to a younger demographic in her campaign, holding voter forums in bars and restaurants and engaging in events like a mock election at a high school near Tel Aviv.

The "same old, same old" just wasn't going to cut it in 2013. "We need to make politics sexy again," Shaffir told Reuters during that inaugural campaign, as she sat on a bench on a trendy avenue filled with cyclists and dog walkers.

Her campaign slogan was "It's Our Time." She was right and she was elected.

FIGHTING CORRUPTION

Although she is the youngest member in the legislature, Stav is one of its most influential and definitely among the most outspoken. She took on the titans of the Knesset and won greater transparency in how financial transactions for the government are handled and reported. She has a seat on the powerful finance committee, where budgets and spending for Israel are overseen, and almost immediately following her election, she called for greater budgetary oversight. In her second term, she continued the revolt against backroom budget deals between political parties, accusing her opponents of massive corruption. She created and chaired the transparency committee, taking her battle to the Supreme Court of Israel, which agreed with her complaints.

What drives this fiery political warrior and activist? The key to understanding Stav's goals lies with her early family life.

BATTLES ROOTED IN PERSONAL HISTORY

Stav grew up in a close-knit family that includes a brother eleven years younger than she is, and her sister, Shir, who is four years younger. Shir, who has severe autism as well as developmental and cognitive impairment, was a powerful formative influence on Stav. As with any family with a child with such overwhelming needs, the struggle to meet those needs has an enormous impact; it can rip a family apart or bring it closer together. Stav has seen her mother and father fight tirelessly on Shir's behalf since she was born, and their determination and kindness has informed her whole worldview.

"Who I am today is entirely because of the way we grew up," she said in the Israel Policy Exchange. "You come to understand that it's possible to solve almost everything simply because you have no alternative. When you go out on the street and your sister starts screaming and raving, and people around her stare at her with hostile glances, you are her protecting wall and her shield. You get used to the feeling that you must never fall."

Stav is under no illusion about how Israel's policies affect families like hers. "A middle class family with an autistic kid suddenly finds itself spending all its income in their treatment; an assistant in the kindergarten, a personal tutor, travel expenses, a speech therapist," she said. "They start losing their income and they can lose their jobs. No one will help you cover those expenses, because there's no social welfare. That's the middle class. There are a lot of people that seem OK on the outside, but that are slowly falling apart."

With her sister's well-being on the line, Stav learned early to be fearless and to protect her at any cost. This determined attitude has shaped her style as a politician. "I'm really sensitive and hold things dear to my heart," she said. "But there's no way anyone can stop me or move me out of the way when I believe that something is right. They have no chance, thanks to [Shir]."

Stav credits her parents with creating an atmosphere of harmony and support, and that sense of responsibility for caring for others has informed Stav throughout her life.

Stav was born in 1985 in Netanya, Israel, a city of more than 200 000 that lies between Tel Aviv and Haifa in Israel's north-central region. Her Jewish heritage includes ancestors from Romania, Lithuania, Poland and Iraq. Her father was an accountant and her mother was a teacher who later joined her husband in the family business.

A LIFETIME OF ACTIVISM

Her activism started early. At the age of only eight, Stav was a young journalist for the children's and youth magazine *Kulanu.*

When she was 11, her family moved to Pardesiya, a town of just over 5000 in central Israel, where her parents started an accounting business. Stav was active in organizations promoting social justice, such as HaNoar HaOved VeHaLomed (the Federation of Working and Studying Youth), which is dedicated to democracy, Zionism, peace and social justice. But she also knew firsthand the challenges faced by her sister, and she volunteered to help children with disabilities. After high school, Stav worked for a year with underprivileged children in the town of Tiberias on the Sea of Galilee.

FROM PILOT TO JOURNALIST

She dreamed of becoming a pilot or an astronaut, and in 2004, Stav enlisted as a cadet in the flight academy of the Israeli Air Force. It was highly competitive to be accepted and even more difficult to make it all the way through the program. After five months and 15 flight hours, Stav was transferred to a position as a military journalist. She covered major events, including the Israeli disengagement from Gaza and the 2006 Lebanon war.

After she finished her military service, Stav found new direction as a journalist when she began working freelance for a variety of publications, including *National Geographic.*

LEADING A MOVEMENT

In the summer of 2011, Stav was living with a friend in a dilapidated apartment in Tel Aviv. There were no windows and plenty of vermin. Her roommate saw a Facebook page about a demonstration to protest rising housing costs, reduced public services and low income. Stav and her roommate joined the protest, and Stav quickly became a key spokesperson for the group.

The protesters pitched some tents next to a main road in Tel Aviv, touching off the biggest protest in Israel's history. Stav rose to national prominence after she participated in a July 2011 televised debate on the protest with Miri Regev, a member of the Knesset. She went on to help establish more than 120 tent camps throughout Israel and a strong lobby to members of the Knesset to pursue a social justice agenda. She was a cofounder of one of Israel's largest social protest movements, created to provide cohesive leadership for the fragmented social justice movement. After the post-protest cross-country tour to hear the concerns of citizens, Stav was recruited by the Labor Party, who saw her as a promising leader, and the group disbanded.

She accepted their overtures, though this was a complete turnaround for Stav, who had had disdain for politics and had avoided it until the tour. She thought politics was corrupt and found politicians untrustworthy. Although she voted in elections, she never felt that her vote was meaningful.

But then she had a revelation: to fight corrupt practices within the political power structure, she herself would need to gain political power and work from the inside.

Stav reflected on the disillusionment that she and many other young adults felt about the government of Prime Minister Benjamin Netanyahu. She was raised to believe that if she studied and worked hard, she would be successful. But after she completed her military service, the opportunities that she and many others of her generation had been anticipating just weren't there. Instead they found corrupt politicians who were not looking out for young people's interests.

Stav ran in the party primaries in January 2013 and was placed eighth on the Labor Party list. She was elected to the Knesset in 2013 on the Zionist Union electoral list, which combined candidates from the Labor and Hatnuah Parties. While in Knesset, her relentless battle for greater transparency in the budget process brought her more attention, and in the January 2015 primaries, she rose in the party rankings, placing second in the Labor Party, which put her in fourth position on the Zionist Union list.

After joining the Knesset in 2013, Stav continued her battle for better quality and more affordable housing, culminating in the passage of the Fair Rental Law in June 2018. The law provides guidelines for tenant–landlord relations, including minimum requirements for an apartment to be considered "livable."

ELECTIONS TO ISRAEL'S KNESSET

There are 120 members in Israel's Knesset. Members of Knesset are elected using a proportional-representation system in which parties — or sometimes coalitions of parties — prepare lists of candidates, and voters cast a single vote for the list of their choice. The number of seats won by a party is equal to the proportion of the vote received by that party. The party list presented to voters is determined by primaries in which party members vote for candidates. Candidates are then ranked in order of the number of votes each received, and the higher the candidate's ranking on the list, the better their chances are of making the cut of those being included in the Knesset.

A CRUSADE AGAINST CORRUPTION

But it was on the finance committee, which she joined at the beginning of her first term, that her reputation as an implacable crusader against corruption began.

When she arrived in the Knesset, Stav was taken aback by the practice of transferring billions of shekels (Israel's currency) from one budget item to another in secret deals among political parties and interest groups, all done after the budget had been approved.

Stav began to probe, but her questions weren't welcomed and the information was not forthcoming.

Newcomer though she was, she took action, responding to each proposed budgetary transfer with a filibuster. (A filibuster is the practice of continually speaking or asking questions to extend debate and delay a vote on the matter being discussed.)

LEVELING THE PLAYING FIELD WITH SOCIAL MEDIA

When she was still unable to get the information she needed, she recruited a team of researchers to investigate each transaction to find out exactly where the money came from and where it was going. She then posted the results on Facebook.

This bold step was like poking a hive of angry bees. Her opponents regularly tried to shut her down, compared her to tyrants, attempted to have her physically removed from finance committee meetings and even tried to have her suspended from the Knesset for her fiery accusations of corruption.

When she made no progress in the Knesset to reform what she considered illegal practices, she took the fight to Israel's Supreme Court, which agreed with Stav's position and ruled that the finance ministry must reach a compromise with Stav on a new method for budget transfers.

VICTORY!

The treasury eventually agreed to publish information online about budgetary transfers several days in advance of any vote by the Knesset finance committee. This eliminated the practice of calling for surprise votes without prior circulation of information, which had obscured the details of the transfers.

In 2015, Stav made an impassioned speech to an almost empty Knesset that became known as the "Who Is a Zionist?" speech. She had been angered by verbal attacks on her party and, in the heat of the moment, she rose to the podium to speak. In her speech, she argued that true Zionism (a movement for the development and protection of Israel as an independent country) is not a question of funneling resources toward expanding territories or settlements, but rather it means distributing money equitably to all regions of the country and to all groups, especially looking after society's most vulnerable citizens. It was heartfelt but also shrewd; she effectively joined the concerns of both the left (Zionists) and the right (advocates of proper use of taxpayers' money), making it difficult for either side to argue against her position. A three-minute YouTube video of her address went viral. Within weeks, it had been seen by approximately 300 000 people, according to the *Jewish Journal*, and perhaps up to a million, according to Stav herself.

There's no question that Stav "walks the walk" when it comes to advocating for financial transparency and responsible use of taxpayers' money. She was one of only eight members of the Knesset to forgo their 2015 pay raise, calling it "distasteful" in light of wage stagnation in the Israeli job market. In addition to being the youngest MK, she is also the MK with the lowest net worth, and owns neither an apartment nor a car.

Stav's work on financial transparency has ventured beyond Israel. In 2017, she was appointed chair of a newly established committee on government transparency for the Organisation for Economic Co-operation and Development (OECD). The committee, which shares knowledge, research and methods between different parliaments across the world to expose and end political corruption, is a joint initiative led by Stav, the Israeli foreign affairs ministry and the OECD representative in Israel. The first meeting, which took place in Paris in February 2017, was attended by representatives from more than 90 countries.

CHAPTER 11

JAIME HERRERA BEUTLER

STANDING UP, STANDING OUT

U.S. representative, Washington, United States

EVER SINCE SHE WAS a young girl, Jaime Herrera Beutler has been a fighter. As far back as elementary school, this feisty, outspoken congresswoman was canvassing for local Republican candidates and marching in parades to support conservative causes.

A QUICK START

Jaime wasted no time when it came to deciding her own future; she took aim at a political career while still in her teens, learning the ropes through political internships. In 2007, at age 29, she managed to convince both Republican and Democratic county authorities that she should be appointed to fill a seat made vacant in the Washington House of Representatives when its occupant became embroiled in a sex scandal. Her tenacious efforts at persuasion paid off: she won the appointment and went on to win the seat — with 60 percent of the vote — the following year.

Less than three years after Jaime's political debut, she turned her attention and energy toward national politics. In 2010, she ran for U.S. Congress, not only succeeding in that election, but also in the next four consecutive contests. Jaime became the representative for Washington State's Third Congressional District, known as Battle Ground, an aptly named constituency for the scrappy young politician. In March 2019, she announced that she intended to seek a sixth term in Congress in 2020.

HEARTLAND VALUES

Born in 1978, in Glendale, California, Jaime grew up in rural southwest Washington State. According to a 2011 article in the *Seattle Times*, her dad, Armando, and her mother, Candice Marie, are both evangelical Christians who passed along their belief that the social safety net is best provided by the community, not the government. Her conservative fiscal and social values are bred in the bone.

In many ways, Jaime's childhood was typical of rural America. She participated in community activities like the 4-H Club and spent lots of time enjoying the area's lakes and rivers. Jaime was homeschooled through ninth grade, then attended public school and graduated from Prairie High School in Vancouver, Washington. After high school, she studied at Bellevue Community College and went on to earn a degree from the University of Washington.

Throughout her student years, she sought out experiences in community service, spending countless hours volunteering at "ground zero," the site of the 2001 terrorist attacks in New York.

THE INSIDE EDGE

Jaime set her sights on learning the inner workings of state and federal politics during her time in college. She interned in the Washington State Senate and also in Washington, D.C., at the White House Office of Political Affairs. She won another internship in the Bush administration after she graduated, working with Washington State senator Joe Zarelli during the later stages of the president's reelection campaign.

A turning point came for Jaime in 2005, when she landed a job as senior legislative aide for Congresswoman Cathy McMorris Rodgers (R-Spokane) in Washington, D.C. As lead advisor for McMorris Rodgers on health care policy, education, veterans' and women's issues, Jaime got a firsthand view of how policy is shaped on Capitol Hill. She was able to hone her political skills as she assisted in drafting proposals, including a health information technology bill and an education-based competitiveness bill, both of which passed in the House of Representatives.

All of this early, inside experience gave Jaime the building blocks for her own run for office. When she became a congresswoman herself, Jaime wasted no time, speaking out in clear terms from the very start about the policies and measures she believes are in the best interests of her constituents and the country.

She supported the repeal of the Affordable Care Act but voted against the Republican bill to replace the American Health Care Act because she said it cut too deeply into the social safety net and didn't do enough to lower costs.

She felt that the bill left people vulnerable. She was one of only two Washington State Republicans who voted against the bill, and in doing so, she parted ways on that issue with Congresswoman Cathy McMorris Rodgers, who had been her close mentor. McMorris Rodgers was a strong proponent of the bill.

In 2008, Jaime disagreed with the economic stimulus package put in place by Democrats after the global financial collapse. Instead, she favored tax cuts to boost the economy, due to her conviction that fiscal conservatism extends to both individuals and governments. Jaime believes that governments have to live within their means, even if that involves making hard choices and unpopular cuts to programs.

AN ECONOMIC EYE

Many key issues that others see as social policy, Jaime frames in economic terms. For example, she articulates her stance on abortion in economic terms: she is against any spending on abortion, but believes in supporting full access to family planning.

Jaime has also acted to protect living organ donors from losing their jobs as a result of time off for the procedure, ensuring they are covered under the Family Medical Leave Act. To her, this is a matter of economics as well as compassion. She said in a press release, "Organ donations save lives, save Medicare millions of dollars and cut costs across the health care system, which means it helps meet my goal of delivering better health care to Southwest Washington residents."

In March 2019, Jaime vehemently opposed a Democrat-sponsored bill to provide public funding for private campaign donations, at a ratio of six dollars for every dollar donated. She issued this blistering response in a press release: "Who on earth thinks we don't have enough money in politics? [...] When I ask people about how government should best spend the public's money, some say they want more to go to schools. Some say our military. Some say research for curing diseases. Never once, in my entire life, have I had someone say to me 'I'd like the government to send money to political consultants to pay for more TV campaign ads.'"

ROLE MODELS AND DEEP ROOTS

As a fierce defender of conservative values and strong leaders, it's no surprise that Jaime counts among her role models these two formidable women born centuries apart: former British prime minister Margaret Thatcher and former first lady Abigail Adams.

Margaret Thatcher was known as Britain's "Iron Lady" for her indomitable leadership style. Jaime admired the former prime minister's focus and dedication as well as the strength of her leadership, even in the face of opposition.

Jaime also admires Abigail Adams, the influential wife and political advisor of John Adams, U.S. president (1797–1801), and mother of John Quincy Adams, also a president (1825–1829).

Like her role models, Jaime stands up for what she believes. But that's not the only thing that makes her stand out. Jaime is also the first Hispanic person to represent a Washington State district in the U.S. House of Representatives, and she is currently (in 2019) the only Republican woman of color in the House. She is also the first member of U.S. Congress to have been homeschooled since the early 1900s, when mandatory public education came into practice.

Jaime is proud that she's not typical. "I love being a young Hispanic mother who's a Republican," she told *Marie Claire* magazine in 2015.

A LIFE-ALTERING SITUATION

Jaime met her husband, Dan Beutler, when they were both working for Congresswoman McMorris Rodgers. Dan proposed in 2008, and soon they seemed on the path to becoming one of Washington's power couples. Dan was just finishing his first year of law school when the couple learned that they were expecting their first child.

Their elation at the news abruptly turned to anxiety when a routine ultrasound showed that the baby had Potter's syndrome, an often-fatal condition that results in abnormally low amniotic fluid from poor kidney function. It affects the development of the lungs, and babies with this condition often die within days of being born. Soon doctors discovered that, in fact, the baby had no kidneys at all. The situation looked dire for the unborn girl.

But when the plight of Jaime's baby became public, a man they did not know — who had had a child with the same condition — stepped forward to suggest that they try an experimental procedure that involved injecting saline solution to substitute for the missing amniotic fluid. It took Jaime several tries, but she finally found a doctor at Johns Hopkins University who was prepared to try the procedure. The results were immediate. The baby rallied, so Jaime drove to Baltimore every day for over a month to continue the treatments.

They were not out of the woods yet. No baby on medical record had ever survived being born without kidneys. But having achieved one unexpected miracle, Jaime and Dan hoped for another.

Their daughter, Abigail Rose Beutler, was born prematurely at 28 weeks, and was named in honor of Abigail Adams. She became the first child known to breathe on her own without kidneys, and she went home from the hospital after six months. At age two and a half, Abigail received a kidney from her father in a successful transplant. Later that same year, Jaime gave birth to the couple's second child. On May 21, 2019, Jaime gave birth to her third child, Isana Mae Beutler.

The experience of becoming a mother and managing Abigail's harrowing health scare gave Jaime an entirely new view of her life in politics. It was one she hadn't expected.

She was overwhelmed and touched by the support she received from both her Republican and Democrat colleagues. It was an important reminder that human experience can transcend political difference.

It's no surprise that, since then, Jaime has been a stalwart champion of maternal health and access to health care, especially for children with complex medical conditions. She introduced a bill, known as the Preventing Maternal Deaths Act, which was signed into law in December 2018. It tracks and investigates pregnancy-related deaths and looks for ways to prevent them in future.

The personal support from both sides of the House moved her and bolstered Jaime's belief in the importance of bipartisan relationships to accomplish important goals.

That's why, although she's been a lifelong conservative and Republican,

Jaime is crystal clear that she has no tolerance for ultra-partisan politics or extremism. As she told *Marie Claire*, "I wouldn't call myself a moderate, but I would call myself an adult."

She prides herself on forming relationships that transcend politics. She believes that even if you hold strong positions, you can accomplish a lot in politics by treating people with respect and maintaining good relationships.

In March 2019, Jaime was one of a handful of representatives introducing bipartisan legislation to address the shortage of affordable, high-quality child care, especially in rural areas. She worked with two Minnesota Democrats — Congressman Collin Peterson and Senator Amy Klobuchar — as well as Republican representative Dan Sullivan from Arkansas.

Sometimes, taking a stand puts her at odds with powerful leaders. Jaime is prepared to hold her ground, even when it means disagreeing with the president. Jaime did not support Donald Trump in the 2016 Republican primary process, choosing to write outgoing House Speaker Paul Ryan on her ballot instead.

While Jaime has been vocal in her support of building a physical barrier along the southern U.S. border — in alignment with her views on immigration policy — she drew the line and refused to support President Trump's declaration of an emergency in order to appropriate funding for a wall. To Jaime, it was a vital matter of principle. She condemned the emergency declaration as a breach of the constitutional separation of powers between the legislative and executive branches of the U.S. government. From her vantage point as the top Republican serving on the U.S. House Committee on Appropriations, the emergency declaration by the executive branch of the government (the president) to take funds for a wall usurped the constitutional powers given to the legislative branch (the House) — the body responsible for allocating funding.

"This is a constitutional breach," Jaime told the *Columbian* newspaper. "It [the emergency declaration] is not speaking to the validity of the need for a wall."

And it was a matter she believed was so important that she couldn't stay silent in disagreement. "The constitutional protection and the separation of powers to me are bigger than any one single issue," she said.

It was not the party line, but it was a battle that the firebrand Jaime Herrera Beutler was prepared to fight.

CHAPTER 12

RONA AMBROSE

BE AUTHENTIC, BE BOLD

Former leader of the Opposition and leader of the Conservative Party of Canada

When charting new territory, Rona Ambrose challenges herself and asks, "Why not? What's the worst that can happen?" Behind that simple question lies one of the defining characteristics of the way she approaches both politics and life. It's a focus on possibility, not fear. It's about seizing life's opportunities and taking calculated risks, not waiting until everything is perfect.

START WITH BROAD HORIZONS

Rona had no notion of running for office as she went through school and started her career. But she had a lot going for her. Born in Alberta, her horizons were broadened early as she spent much of her childhood in foreign countries while the family followed her father, an executive for an international company. She lived mostly in Brazil, but also in Singapore, Borneo and Egypt, returning to Canada in her teens. Rona grew up an independent thinker, comfortable speaking her mind.

CHAMPIONING WOMEN — WALKING THE WALK

From an early age, Rona was engaged in supporting the rights and advancement of women. She earned a bachelor's degree in women's and gender studies as well as a master's degree in political science. Before she entered politics, she was a committed volunteer at women's community service organizations, including the Edmonton Women's Shelter and the Victoria Sexual Assault Centre. "I was involved in women's studies, I marched for women's issues, I've protested policies that limited women's opportunities," she said.

I'M A WHAT?

The road to politics started when she was studying for her master's degree in political science. "I got involved because a classmate in our electronic data and privacy class, James Rajotte, had run for election, and he asked some of us if we could help him," she said. "We did some fundraising, which was something I had already done with charitable organizations. Gradually I got more involved." As the course went on, another member of the class, Shannon Stubbs, also ran for provincial government, and she noticed Rona. "She said to me, 'You're a libertarian and a conservative!'" Rona didn't have any affiliation to a political party. Although she had never attached a label to her beliefs before, she began to see that these two labels fit.

BEING A "POLICY WONK" PAYS OFF

Then James, who had become a member of Parliament, asked Rona to do a caucus briefing on the implications of privacy legislation the government was proposing. "I studied the issue and reviewed the legislation," she recalled. "I actually recommended that they vote against it because of concerns it raised around privacy [for individuals]. Eventually the caucus voted for it, though some opposed.

"That led to a call from (then-leader of the Opposition and Conservative Party leader) Stephen Harper. He asked if I would be interested in running. He said he wanted me to consider it because I was smart, young and strong on policy. I really was a bit of a policy wonk. I said, 'I'm into policy but not politics.'"

TURNING DOWN THE PARTY LEADER AND FUTURE PRIME MINISTER

Rona wasn't shying away from the opportunity but was thinking very strategically about it. "I didn't see myself doing this and, equally important, the situation was not ideal. There was a sitting MP [member of Parliament] that I would be running against for the nomination. Trying to beat an incumbent [for the nomination] is difficult, disruptive and messy because it's often a situation where the party no longer supports the incumbent. That was not the way I wanted to start a political career. I said no."

SAYING YES TO A CLEAN SLATE

But that wasn't the end of it. She got a *second* call from the Conservative Party leader after a new riding had been created and there was no incumbent who would need to be ousted in the nomination process. "That totally changed things for me. It was a challenge, but it was a positive one, with a clean slate. I was not taking someone out; I was competing for the nomination with a field of others on a level playing field. So I said to myself, *Yes, I am going to do this.* But I was realistic. Although Stephen Harper had asked me to run, I knew he absolutely could not intervene in the nomination race." But she wasn't entirely on her own.

GET SUPPORT AND DON'T BE AFRAID TO FAIL

Rona had embraced the notion of "don't be afraid to fail." But she also had the other half of the formula: really strong support. "The people around me were great. My parents said, 'Why not?' I never had a sense of being told to be careful about this, or what about that. Rather than that, they encouraged me." And Rona asked herself, *What's the worst that can happen?* I would lose and go back to my job. But I had a great social circle and they were very supportive. My boss was also supportive and I arranged a leave of absence from my job. It was such a long shot. He said, jokingly, 'I'll see you back here in six months.' No one thought I could actually win because the odds were extremely steep."

PREVAILING IN A FIELD OF 13

Rona ran in a field of 13 vying for the nomination. "I felt like it was possible, but there was no external pressure because no one really thought I could win. The pressure was all internal because I *wanted* to win."

She put together a strong team, mostly good friends and family, people from all over. "Many of them couldn't even vote for me because they were out of the riding. It was a diverse group — my campaign manager was openly gay, and I was a woman candidate. But we were all Conservatives."

Rona won the nomination and went on to win a seat in 2004 as a Conservative MP for the newly formed riding of Edmonton–Spruce Grove, even in a year that saw the Liberal Party form a minority government.

"Even if I had run and not won, it would have been *so* worth it. You learn so much about yourself; it builds so much confidence. Running in itself is a fantastic experience."

PROUD ACCOMPLISHMENTS

Then in 2015, the Conservatives lost the general election and Prime Minister Harper resigned. Rona was chosen by the party to serve as interim leader until a leadership convention could be held. "I am most proud of leading the party. That was a huge undertaking. Everything came together for me to be leading a national political party, and there was no doubt, [I did it] successfully. The usual situation is that the party would be left with a 'caretaker' [type of leader] with funding low and all sorts of infighting. It was the opposite with me." Rona seized the opportunity to do more than just hold steady while the next leader was chosen. She set goals and was determined to rebuild, setting the scene for the next leader.

"When I led the party after the election, our fundraising was four times higher than the Liberals. I turned around the communications. I'm a team builder and I worked really hard." Rona didn't accept the status quo — she asked, "Why not?" and succeeded where others had failed.

WHY SHE LEFT POLITICS

As interim leader of the party, Rona was disqualified by party rules from running for party leader. While she had accomplished a great deal, she decided to leave politics when the party chose a permanent successor and her job was done. "It was the right time to step away. After 13 years [in office] and having led the party — and turned it around — it was time to move on. It was a hard decision but the right one for me."

Rona's parting words when she retired on July 4, 2017, expressed her hope that she had been able to "inspire women to consider public service." And she has already started. At least one of her former staffers is considering running, and Rona has been coaching her all the way. It's a mission that she gladly takes on.

A FOOTNOTE: LIFE AFTER POLITICS

Since leaving office, Rona has remained politically active. She became a visiting fellow at the Canada Institute at the Woodrow Wilson International Center for Scholars. And in August 2017, Justin Trudeau's Liberal government appointed her to a 13-member North American Free Trade Agreement (NAFTA) advisory council to provide opinion and feedback on negotiations with the United States and Mexico.

TIPS FROM RONA AMBROSE

BE BOLD

Women want to meet ten out of ten criteria before they will run or apply for a position, compared to men, who will go if they meet six of ten criteria, a phenomenon that Rona saw often in her time in office. She said, "Not only do women want to tick ten out of ten boxes, I find they even want to add extra boxes!" That's a self-imposed limit that Rona would like to see less of. So even when someone like Rona reaches out to encourage women to run for office when she can see what they bring to the table, it still takes a lot of support and encouragement. Her advice: Be bold. Don't try to be perfect. If you are more than halfway there, go for it.

BE TRUE TO YOURSELF

"It is more important to be authentic than to try to be something you think is required for the job," Rona said. In her early days as a member of Parliament, the party leadership assigned Rona to ask a question of the government during Question Period, a daily opportunity for the Opposition to seek information from the government on specific issues. She did not like the way the question was phrased and wasn't comfortable putting it forward. Many rookie MPs would have asked it anyway, but Rona felt it was important to be true to herself. She said, "I'm not asking that" and requested that the question be rewritten or, if not, that someone else be assigned to ask the question. "You don't have to compromise yourself on those issues," she said.

GET INVOLVED LOCALLY BEFORE YOU RUN

Women should engage in their local area. In Canada, there is an electoral district association in each riding for each federal party. Rona advises, "Get involved, join their board."

DON'T LET THE PROSPECT OF A NOMINATION BATTLE DISCOURAGE YOU

"Nominations are difficult because it is one partisan versus another running to see who is the best of a field from the same party. It often gets difficult and nasty because it is about personal abilities. Don't be discouraged if you face challenges at this stage, understand that the hardest part can be this first part."

DEAL WITH THE UNPLEASANT STUFF; DON'T RUN FROM IT

"Don't let the unpleasant aspects stop you from running. Instead, focus on being prepared to handle whatever comes your way, and keep in mind that most criticism is not actually personal. As women, support each other to get through whatever you need to get through. Rely on your strong support system."

All candidates — or public figures of any sort — get threats. "It is just bully tactics and it happens," Rona said. "The majority of it is not real. You may hear things like 'pull out or we'll share something terrible about you,' as I did — even though I couldn't think of what that could possibly be. The underlying message was 'Who do you think you are? You are just some girl getting above yourself. We are going to destroy you.'

"My reaction was, 'Really? We are all adults here and this is what we get?'"

HANDLE SOCIAL MEDIA CAREFULLY

Have a plan: "You need to have strategies for dealing with social media, and I've been advising other women candidates about this. Twitter really is a small component of your total communications strategy. Stay off Twitter. Have someone you trust on the team do that for you. Get a really good social media manager. And don't read online commentary of any kind. It's full of trolls and negativity and it just brings you down. I had someone tweet as the spokesperson for Rona Ambrose."

Know which platforms matter: "I didn't tweet even once as interim leader of the party and it didn't matter. You have to recognize the level of importance and the context. I can guarantee you that Hillary Clinton doesn't read tweets. The back-and-forth nastiness is like an echo chamber; it's not reaching as many as you think in politics."

Don't go down the rabbit hole: "I've seen what happens if you get too far into social media. You implode and melt down. You really have to use social media as a tool and as a benefit to you — and not use it if it doesn't leverage a positive outcome."

Speak out about threats: "I didn't speak up about it [online threats]; I just kept campaigning. I didn't think people would believe me back then, but I think that has changed, and now I would say something. Women are speaking up."

Know when to bring in the authorities: "It is very important to call out the serious threats on Twitter, and I have. I've contacted the police and asked them to investigate. You let them look into it."

SUPPORT EACH OTHER

Looking out for each other is something that can make even mundane challenges easier to deal with. Rona adds, "With the small group of women in the

Conservative cabinet, we created a little book for women who were in office for the first time. There are so few; it was isolating. So we thought at least we could put together a small guidebook to help women take care of the practical everyday things that can add up and get in your way. We gave advice on things that we learned the hard way, from a little tip such as where the closest dry cleaner is, to where to find a good hairdresser and where to get office supplies in Parliament."

TAKE CREDIT FOR YOUR ACCOMPLISHMENTS

"As a woman, don't forget to take credit for things. Men do and women don't," she points out. As an example, she now realizes that when the Conservatives lost the election in 2015 and she became interim leader, she fell into the trap of not fully owning her accomplishments. "I made the transition look effortless, but it wasn't. It was hard work. If I had been a guy, it would have been the turnaround of the century! But I would say, when asked about it, 'I was lucky.'" She would do things differently today.

BEWARE OF OVER-SHARING

"I am a very private person. This is one of the first times I've talked about my life in politics. You have to understand that if you put things out personally, in a way it gives people the opening to talk about you personally, to criticize you personally. You don't have to share everything, and I would be careful about how much personal stuff you put out there."

DEAL WITH THE DOUBLE STANDARD

"The double standard is real. There were so few women in cabinet we didn't have the support we should have had … Parliament is still a boys' club. Women have to work twice as hard and be twice as careful and endure constant public scrutiny.

"One of the ways I dealt with it, and a lot of women do this, is to be over-prepared whenever I went to cabinet. I couldn't get over seeing senior men at cabinet who obviously didn't know the file and had handed it off to someone else. They didn't feel they needed to know policy; they would just be the political person. Women in cabinet are pretty well always well prepared — they know their files, and that, to me, is the right standard. I want the men to be more like us!"

INSPIRING FINAL THOUGHTS

"You can conquer real and imagined obstacles. Just running for elected office is rewarding in itself. You learn so much. And there are now role models for women leaders who show that you don't have to be like a man to succeed. Women can see themselves sitting in Parliament and that should not be underestimated."

CHAPTER 13

JENNY DURKAN

INTREPID CHANGE AGENT

Mayor of Seattle, United States

NO MATTER HOW DAUNTING the situation, when something she believes in is at stake, Seattle's mayor Jenny Durkan is not one to back down from a fight. Whether it is standing toe-to-toe against the National Rifle Association (NRA) to push for safe gun-storage laws, shutting down Russian hackers or fighting on behalf of travelers caught in transit during President Trump's sudden travel ban, Jenny has been fearless in taking on the tough challenges.

And while most would agree that it takes great courage and determination to stand against the tide, to hear her tell it, taking on these foes is simply the only option she could consider.

"Standing up to the NRA wasn't a hard decision at all," she said. "The true heroes in this fight are the teachers, students, survivors and victims of gun violence. They are a constant reminder of shattered and lost lives that could have been saved if only we acted more urgently."

And so she acts. Despite vociferous opposition from the NRA, as Seattle's mayor, Jenny stood firm in her fight, supporting laws crafted to improve safety yet not infringe on the United States' Second Amendment right to bear arms. Nonetheless, the NRA sued Jenny and Seattle — and lost.

"I always believe you must fight for what is right, even if you have to take on special interests like the NRA," she said.

SUED AGAIN

Then again, the NRA was just the first to sue Jenny for taking a stand. In 2012, when she was a U.S. attorney with the department of justice, the Seattle police was put under a consent decree, a mechanism that required measures be introduced to reduce the department's reliance on excessive force. The consent decree ordered that police officers be retrained and that all incidents involving force be reported, among other measures.

"When I pushed for police reforms and the consent decree as U.S. attorney, I was sued by those trying to stop reform," Jenny recalled. But she prevailed. "Most officers embraced the changes, did everything asked of them and led the nation on reducing use of force through de-escalation and crisis intervention." In fact, a 2018 report showed a sea change had taken place with a new emphasis on de-escalation over the use of force.

However, that wasn't the end of the fight. In late 2018, the city was called before a judge tasked with overseeing the consent decree. At issue was the police contract Jenny had just negotiated and whether it met all provisions of the reforms that were being implemented under the decree.

It was Jenny, not the city attorney, who stood before the judge to argue that the new agreement maintained the force's reforms. Jenny won the day, and the contract was approved by city council 8–1.

UNCHARTED WATERS: BEING THE "FIRST"

It may have been a first for a sitting mayor of the city to personally argue a case, but there have been many "firsts" in Jenny's career. She was the first openly gay U.S. attorney, appointed by President Barack Obama in 2009 to represent the Western District of Washington. She ran and won in her first-ever election in 2017 and started at the top, defying the odds, to become Seattle's first-ever openly gay leader and the city's first female mayor in almost 90 years.

As remarkable as she is, in Jenny's family, she is just one of a group of high achievers. She was raised in Issaquah, Washington, the fourth of seven children.

Politics was part of the fabric of everyday life in the Durkan household. Her father, Martin Durkan Sr., had served in the Washington State House of Representatives and later in the Washington State Senate before becoming a lobbyist. He twice ran unsuccessfully for governor of Washington. While some families try never to talk about religion or politics, for the large Catholic Durkan clan, that was definitely not the case. In her family, as Jenny told the *Stranger* newspaper, "that's all we talked about."

Jenny's mother, Lorraine, known as Lolly, was a free spirit who wanted to see the world. After college, she spent two years in Germany with U.S. Special Services before returning to the U.S. to marry Martin. She was active in community volunteer roles and later became the executive editor of the *Ballard News Tribune.*

The example she set made a deep impact on Jenny. "My mom went to college and worked at jobs women could never have gotten if it were not for World War Two," she said. "She was whip smart and a great writer … Once she had kids, she mostly stayed home for many years raising us. But she always taught us to believe in ourselves, in the goodness of people and the ability to make a difference. When she went back to work, she did all those things working as the editor of a local newspaper."

ALASKA: MOOSE, BASKETBALL AND BECOMING A BOTTLE OF BEER

Like her mother, Jenny dreamed of seeing the world. After she graduated from college, she headed to a remote Yupik fishing village in Alaska. For most of her time there, she was a girls' basketball coach and English teacher with the Jesuit Volunteer Corps Northwest. Before returning to Washington, she also landed a memorable but poorly paid gig as a beer bottle in a beer commercial, and for a short time, she was a member of the Teamsters union, as the only woman baggage handler at Wien Air Alaska in the town of St. Mary's.

Later, these adventures served to bolster Jenny's image as an indomitable, larger-than-life person. She was described by the *Seattle Met* newspaper as a "steely-eyed moose skinner," referring to an episode in Alaska when she was conscripted by a local nun to prepare a moose carcass for butchering.

Jenny acknowledges her time in Alaska as a formative experience. She said, "I ended up being the one who learned so much — from my students, from the people of the local villages and particularly from the Native American Elders who opened their homes and families to me. The lessons I learned have stayed with me for a lifetime"

When she returned to Washington, Jenny earned a law degree. "I wanted to be a lawyer since I was five years old," she told the *Seattle Post-Intelligencer* in 1992. When she graduated from law school, her mother quipped, "Finally, someone is going to pay you to argue!"

SIDING WITH THE UNDERDOG

It was during her time in law school that her instincts for tough fights on behalf of the underdog really took shape. Jenny volunteered in a prison counseling project and got her first courtroom experience at a criminal defense clinic, working with the public defender's office to represent clients in Seattle's municipal court.

She learned a lot from these difficult cases. They showed her "the importance of fighting not only for individual justice but also for systemic changes that ensure broader and longer-term impacts," she recalled.

After graduation, Jenny moved on to the other Washington — D.C.— and worked for the prominent Williams & Connolly law firm on a range of civil and criminal cases, taking up yet another fight representing journalists who had been subpoenaed by the government.

FIGHTING THE CITY SHE WOULD LATER RUN

Returning to Seattle in 1991, she established her own practice, which included criminal defense work and representing plaintiffs. Though it would be many years before she ran for office as mayor, she led a number of actions *against* the city, seeking justice for clients whom the city had failed to protect. It was her job to understand how the city had acted in each of those cases and what needed to be done to remedy each situation.

Jenny described the effect of these experiences. "[They] showed the lasting and deep impacts our system of justice can have on individual lives and broader communities. This prepared me to represent victims in the worst of circumstances — like the families of four firefighters who died in a warehouse fire and a woman denied the right to see her partner in the hospital after a flash flood took her life."

When she became U.S. attorney, Jenny specialized in fighting cybercrime, especially the work of Russian hackers. She is particularly proud of those efforts and told the *Seattle Times* that the crackdown on hacking "demonstrated our ability to bring to account people who feel like they can hide behind a keyboard."

In early 2017, she also fought on behalf of travelers who had arrived lawfully in the U.S. on the day that President Trump's travel ban went into effect, targeting people who had come from predominantly Muslim countries.

While working as an attorney in Seattle, Jenny was also raising a family. While she is open about the nature of her same-sex relationship, she is also fiercely protective of her family, keeping details of their lives private. According to the *Seattle Times*, Jenny has been enrolled in a program that allows state criminal justice employees who have received serious threats to shield their home addresses from disclosure in public documents.

Growing up in a politically active home and being engaged through her clients with the city she called home, the idea of running for office had crossed Jenny's mind over the years.

As she explained, though, "I contemplated running for office at different times, but a variety of factors always argued for continuing the work I was doing."

Jenny embraced other ways to engage in democracy and political action. "I also tried to maximize positive change by supporting people running for or elected to office," she said. "I have witnessed how institutional actions can cause widespread injustice or create broad opportunity. So, having the right people in charge of the institutions is critical."

She cited a few examples that stand out for her. "I saw this firsthand many times, particularly when I served in President Barack Obama's administration, and when I watched Governor Christine Gregoire sign the marriage equality law. Elections matter," she said.

EVERYTHING CHANGED

But then came a watershed moment. Jenny described the impact like this: "First, President Trump was sworn into office and it became clear that states and cities were going to have to lead the way on a progressive agenda. Then Seattle, my hometown and favorite city, needed a new mayor. I knew it was time to step up. It was time to act, for my kids, my community and my country. I believed I could lead the city at this difficult time and be a positive influence for broader good.

"We are a city," she continued, "that dreams and then acts on those dreams. Our businesses and aspirations are second to none. On progressive actions we've led the way: combating climate change, raising the minimum wage, advancing criminal justice reform and securing LGBTQ rights. We are strong, resilient, determined, innovative, generous and — in my view — just a great city. I knew we had to continue leading the way to show the country what it looks like when people turn their progressive values into action.

"But to lead this adventure, I had to be mayor. So I ran."

A STEADY HAND, A LONG-TERM VISION

Jenny campaigned on providing stability and a sure hand after the chaos of her predecessor, who left office amid allegations of sexual abuse. With her large local network and unrelenting campaigning, she set a record for fundraising. On Election Day, she won a decisive victory by a considerable margin, garnering 61 percent of the vote against her opponent Cary Moon.

Since she took office, Jenny has stayed true to her passion: to advance a vision of Seattle as a bastion of creative and progressive policies. In fact, she has been nicknamed the "impatient mayor" because of the relentless pace with which she has been moving forward on her agenda.

In her first year, she passed an education levy to bolster the public school system, passed a safe-storage gun law, added shelter beds to address the needs of the city's homeless population, negotiated a new police contract and had marijuana convictions vacated (which means the verdict is set aside as if the trial and conviction never happened). And while she keeps pushing on immediate improvements, much of Jenny's work is focused on fighting for systemic changes that will outlast short-lived trends. Her eye remains on maintaining the role of Seattle as one of the most progressive American cities.

AN INTERVIEW WITH JENNY DURKAN: CARRYING THE TORCH

Q: What has being in politics taught you about yourself? About the world?

A: What it taught me is that we are all called in different ways and you cannot be afraid of forging your own path. At this moment in time, we need more women, especially young women, charting our future. The world is seeing the rise of division and disparity. Women can reach across these divides in new and different ways. This is not just because of the unique perspective women can have but because women have been kept "outside" the political establishment and know what that means for people.

In one of the most progressive cities in the country, generations of kids in Seattle grew up never seeing a woman or a mom as mayor (and definitely not an openly gay woman). There is no question that women are still held to different standards and face barriers in the political arena. But we also have different talents, tools and approaches to bridge the gaps.

Q: What kinds of issues, actions, events or accomplishments contributed to this learning?

A: I've had the great opportunity to know and work with many different people from a broad range of life experiences. Some of the most influential lessons in my life have come from listening to people just trying to live their everyday lives.

Q: What issues drive you?

A: [My] belief in systemic change is the thread that connects much of my work: from helping create the region's first drug court and mental health courts, to creating a civil rights section in the U.S. attorney's office and pushing for police reforms, to building better ways to detect and combat cybercrime, to creating a free college program for Seattle public school students and a bill of rights for domestic workers.

Q: What made your campaign so successful?

A: On the campaign side: don't get pulled off track. Run your campaign on the change you are trying to make. I focused on things like my plans for free college, building more affordable housing and ideas to solve our homelessness crisis. And fortunately, voters wanted to hear more about those plans.

I also did a hundred town halls and forums, so I could share those plans in the community.

Q: Can you describe what it's like to run for office?

A: Remember two things: first, running for office is rewarding and an amazing adventure. You will laugh and cry. You will meet some of the most interesting people and unforgettable characters. You will hear some of the saddest stories and some of the most inspiring. You will learn new things every day.

Second, no one does anything on their own. While your name may be on the ballot and you are on the front lines, running for office is a team sport. Build a strong network of personal and political support. I had the best on both fronts and relied on them every day. And the best news is you do not have to start from scratch. There are many resources across the country for women to progress in leadership. Don't know how to file, raise money or send a press release? Good news: there's a TON of help! Women can join candidate training programs like EMILY's List, EMERGE America and Run for Something.

Q: How did you stay motivated and manage the demands of running for office?

A: Women have been marginalized for a long time and tend to sell themselves short. My best advice: trust yourself and remember why you ran. Campaigning is hard, physically and emotionally. It requires long hours of "being on" and being under the microscope. Your words, your positions and even your clothes and hairstyle all are scrutinized, amplified and distorted. Social media only makes it worse. The only thing you have 100 percent control over is your own actions.

On the personal side: carve out time for yourself, and for your friends and family. You need it not just to maintain relationships, you need it to keep perspective and stay effective. Your experiences and life relationships brought you this far. Nurture them, too.

Q: What advice do you have for young women who are interested in public leadership but are unsure about whether they "fit the mold"? What are the qualities that you think are most important for someone considering running for office?

A: Ignore the stereotypes and break the mold! We are facing serious and significant challenges throughout the world — and we did not get here because too many people in power were different. We got here because the "mold" hemmed in thinking and locked good people out. We need an infusion of new blood and real people, with good ideas and creative thinking. We need people who believe in good and in kindness. The two most important qualifications for running are integrity and wanting to make a positive impact. Trust yourself and ask why you want to run. (The corollary advice for the candidate: trust yourself and remember why you ran). You can chart your own future whether you're a single mom, an attorney, an educator, an activist, a business owner, a veteran or an artist.

Do not listen to anyone who whispers you can't succeed because of your race, sexual preference, economic status or other personal traits. Too many women are proving them wrong. Be one of them!

I wasn't expecting to run for mayor. I had never run for office before. For decades, I took a varied route. I was a mom, social activist, criminal defense attorney, civil litigator and ran my own law office before I became a U.S. attorney under President Obama. I served on various civic and legal committees, but also drove carpools and brought snacks to my kids' games. That is not the usual profile of someone running for public office; fewer still run for the chief executive role on their first run. So never doubt yourself.

Having women in leadership positions leads to a different style of governance but has a society-changing effect. It shows every little girl to think they can be whatever they want — and every little boy to expect and believe that, too.

Q: What do you wish you had known before entering public life that you know now?
A: I do not think anything can really prepare you for the loss of privacy and "self" time. The impacts vary greatly by the office, but if you are thinking of running, you should take an honest inventory to make sure you are prepared for the long days and constant scrutiny. You also need to have frequent conversations with your loved ones, to make sure they are supportive and ready, too. Then, during the campaign and after you win, you need to stay on top of how they are faring.

More than many jobs, you have to make adjustments and reconfigure your life, especially with kids. Calendar discipline is a must. Fence off times for loved ones and for yourself. There will always be more requests than hours in the day, and you will have to say no to some requests — so say no for the best reasons (sanity, sleep and love). You cannot be a good candidate or public official if you don't keep the important people in your life. And you have to take care of yourself, too.

Personally, I am hoping to move the calendar to 30-hour days to work it all in.

Q: Who were your role models in public life?
A: I am lucky there were so many women before me who broke barriers and were part of so many firsts. I admired and learned from women like [former Texas governor] Ann Richards and [Washington State governor] Christine Gregoire, who served as some of the first female governors. They broke many molds and got things done. They cared about and never forgot the people impacted by their decisions. They believed in kindness and joy. Other women like Barbara Jordan, Hillary Clinton and Sandra Day O'Connor all stepped up when it was even harder for women. Each of them chipped away at "the mold" and tried their best to break the glass ceiling.

Q: Jenny Durkan's final piece of advice:
A: Now it's your turn!

CHAPTER 14

JO SWINSON

RUN EARLY, RUN HARD

Former Member of Parliament, East Dunbartonshire, Scotland, and leader of the Liberal Democrat Party, United Kingdom

JOANNE KATE "JO" SWINSON, member of Parliament for East Dunbartonshire in Scotland, has accomplished a lot in her 39 years. She has run in six major elections; she has been voted into office three times and she has lost three times; and she has spent 11 years in office as an MP, serving in a variety of circumstances. And, in July 2019, she attained a position no other woman before her had achieved: becoming the first female leader of Liberal Democrat Party.

DAVID VS. GOLIATH: JO VS. JOHN

Jo's political career started in 2001 with a David-and-Goliath election battle for the U.K. riding (electoral district) of Hull East in northern England, where she was living at the time. Jo was a 21-year-old political neophyte not long out of the London School of Economics. She had been active in the youth branch of the Liberal Democrats (Lib Dems) and was encouraged to take long odds on a run. While she did not challenge the prime minister, Jo took aim at the next most senior politician in the 600-member Parliament, Deputy Prime Minister John Prescott, who was the local candidate.

Unlike David, Jo did not win this uneven contest. But that didn't deter her. She made a strong impression on the electorate and managed to pull 6 percent

> JO STAYED THE COURSE. AT 23 YEARS OLD, SHE HAD PLENTY OF TIME TO WAIT FOR THE RIGHT OPPORTUNITY TO TRY AGAIN.

of the vote away from the deputy PM. She knew it wouldn't be her last election.

After her defeat, she worked in marketing and public relations, remaining active in the Lib Dems and building a reputation as an outspoken advocate. She was vocal in her opposition to Britain's participation in the 2003 Iraq War and the subsequent move by the governing Labour Party to create national identity cards. She supported reducing the voting age to 16 to encourage young people to get more involved in politics and became a strong voice for women's equality.

NOT DEFEATED BY LOSS

Jo ran again in 2003, this time to be a member of Scottish Parliament (MSP), the regional Parliament for Scotland in her home district of Strathkelvin and Bearsden. Again, however, she was not elected, coming third behind the Independent and Labour candidates with just under 5000 votes.

A less determined person might have given up at that point, but Jo again stayed the course. At only 23 years old, she had plenty of time to wait for the right opportunity to try again.

Jo credits her mother, Annette, with sparking the idea to take a third run for public office in 2005. Her mother used to send her wedding announcements from the local paper to encourage her to think about marriage. But when one of these newspaper cuttings mentioned a change to the boundary of Jo's home seat that might benefit the Liberal Democrats, Jo saw it as an opportunity.

SUCCESS ON THE THIRD ROUND

In 2005, Jo ran a third time, defeating Labour Party candidate John Lyons by 4061 votes to become MP in her home district in the U.K. Parliament, East Dunbartonshire, Scotland. She was the first-ever member of Parliament to be born in the 1980s and became the youngest MP at the time, a status she held until 2009.

One of the factors in her success was her adept use of social media, making it an integral part of how she campaigned for election and then communicated as an MP. She used Facebook and YouTube videos to explain her positions on issues and to link her voters to petitions or motions she put forward in Parliament, as well as relevant documents or legislation. Jo also posted video clips of her activities in the House of Commons, asking and answering questions, allowing her constituents to have unfiltered access to what she said on their behalf in Parliament. She was an early adopter of Twitter and still uses it to keep her constituents informed of timely events and thoughts.

Jo attributes her ability to take on tough battles to her upbringing in Milngavie, Scotland, a small town near Glasgow. Jo was always asking questions, and her parents were strong supporters of this trait. They encouraged her and helped her believe that there was no goal too lofty to aspire to.

As a child, Jo loved to argue, foreshadowing a career where debating is an essential skill. She put her verbal skills to good use as she approached her teen years. Even at a young age, Jo was keen to challenge injustice where she saw it. She wrote to her MP and other government ministers about topics such as sex education in schools. She also tried to make change on a smaller scale; when she was on her school council she campaigned for girls to be allowed to wear trousers as part of the school uniform.

CHOOSING "GUTSY" OVER "GOOD"

Jo was involved in the debating society at her comprehensive school, the Douglas Academy. In her final year, Jo won the Senior Dux, an achievement award that came with a trophy and her choice of any book she wanted. The book she picked was telling of the future; she chose Kate White's *Why Good Girls Don't Get Ahead but Gutsy Girls Do.*

TEENAGE ACTIVIST

Jo joined the Lib Dems as a teenager, becoming active in the Lib Dem youth leadership. The Lib Dems appealed to Jo because of their focus on two key issues: reforming education and instituting an election system with proportional representation.

A pivotal moment for Jo was when she attended the Activate Weekend organized by the Lib Dem Youth and Students (now known as Young Liberals). It was an introduction to the party and a chance to meet other young, like-minded people from all parts of the country. This experience gave her the confidence to attend her first party conference when she was just 18 years old because she didn't have to worry about not knowing anyone there.

Jo was elected to the national executive committee of the Lib Dem Youth and Students and made her first speech at the following conference. She found herself gaining huge political momentum.

She encourages others to get an early start, as she did. Through her experience in politics she gained valuable skills at an early age, including event organization, negotiating, developing policy and working in a team.

Jo also took on a lot of responsibility in her 10 straight years as MP.

When she was first elected in 2005, the Lib Dems were not in power and so became what is known in the parliamentary system as the Official Opposition. Where the party in power forms a government and appoints ministers, the Opposition names spokespersons for important areas or issues. Jo immediately became an Opposition party spokesperson for a succession of key portfolios, including culture, media and sport, communities and local government, women and equality, and foreign affairs. When the Lib Dems came to power in 2010 by joining the Conservatives in a coalition, she became the parliamentary secretary to the Lib Dem leader, Nick Clegg. In 2012, she became the junior equalities minister, and in 2017, she became the deputy leader of the Lib Dems.

In July, 2019, Jo convincingly defeated Sir Ed Davey with 47 997 votes to 28 021 to become the leader of the Lib Dem party after Sir Vince Cable stepped down in May 2019. Her rise to leadership came at a time when the two traditionally strongest parties, Labour and Conservatives, were waning, and the Lib Dems along with the new Brexit Party were surging in popularity.

GAINING CONFIDENCE

Early in her career, her role as spokesperson for women and equalities gave her increased confidence as she realized that she was "living the brief" and had the knowledge to go toe-to-toe with anyone in the House of Commons.

Jo had marveled at the way many of her male colleagues spoke with such confidence. One day she had a revelation as she listened to an MP speak with great authority; she suddenly realized he didn't know what he was talking about. The research did not support his position. The experience taught her not to assume that others knew more than her just because they seemed confident.

SWEPT AWAY

Then in 2015, Jo was swept out of office on the tide of Scottish nationalism, losing her seat to John Nicolson, whose Scottish National Party (SNP) won almost all the seats in Scotland, including East Dunbartonshire.

She wasted no time getting on with her life. She founded her own consultancy, Equal Power Consulting, specializing in helping businesses improve results through greater gender diversity, building on much of the work she had done throughout her parliamentary career on women's equality.

Her husband, who had been an MP himself, was also defeated in the election. Their son was two years old at the time, and they decided then that having a two-MP family required too much travel and juggling of schedules. If politics were to be in the future, only one of them would run. Jo's husband, Duncan, took a post as the head of an anti-corruption charity.

Jo was confident going into the 2017 election. In 2015, the SNP won a landslide victory despite the fact that less than half the population of Scotland backed the party's main goal of Scottish independence. Prior to this election, the country had never before been represented by the SNP in so many seats — they won all but three of Scotland's 59 seats. Since the SNP campaigned on a platform of Scottish independence, Jo believed the electoral result was uncomfortable for the 55% of Scots who had voted against independence in Scotland's 2014 referendum.

It had only been two years since Jo had lost her seat, and she was able to campaign on her track record, still relatively fresh in voters' minds. She was elected by a comfortable margin.

In February 2018, Jo published *Equal Power*, a book that explores why gender inequality is so persistent in business, politics and culture and outlines how individuals can create change.

> **IF WE WANT GENDER EQUALITY, WE HAVE TO FIGHT FOR SPACE FOR WOMEN WE VIGOROUSLY DISAGREE WITH, AS WELL AS THOSE WE SUPPORT.**
>
> – JOSWINSON.ORG.UK.

With her reelection in 2017 and the birth of her second child, Jo was able to experience many of the changes that she put forward as an MP, including one of her proudest accomplishments, the passage of a bill for shared parental leave. Jo was able to take advantage of the House of Commons nursery again, a feature she campaigned for long before she had her first child.

But the ups and downs of her career continued as 2019 neared its end. In a December 12, 2019, snap election called by Prime Minister Boris Johnson to give his Conservative party a clear mandate to exit from the European Union (Brexit), Jo campaigned vigorously on an anti-Brexit platform. But a powerful tide was against her. In Scotland, the Scottish National Party captured 48 of 59 seats. Jo lost her own seat by a heartbreaking 149 votes.

But it's unlikely that this latest turn of events will keep Jo down for long. Immediately after the election, there were rumors that she could be appointed to the House of Lords, Britain's upper legislative house, and continue her political career there. And there are future elections to consider.

After all, she's still only 39.

CHAPTER 15

BETH FUKUMOTO

POLITICAL COURAGE IN THE MOMENT OF TRUTH

Member of Hawaii House of Representatives, United States

THE TERM "MOMENT OF truth" comes from the world of bullfighting. *El momento de la verdad* is when matadors must put themselves in the most vulnerable of positions, leaning over the head and horns of the bull to deal the final blow. It is a point of reckoning, when bullfighters discover whether they have the courage to risk being maimed or killed in order to make the final move.

So, imagine you're Beth Fukumoto and you're standing at the podium, about to speak to a room full of people at the Hawaii Republican Caucus in March 2016. You are one of the GOP's rising young stars, elected in 2012 at age 29 as one of only seven Republicans in the 51-seat Hawaii House of Representatives. In 2014, you became the youngest Republican minority floor leader and House leader in the legislature's history. The audience in front of you are all fellow Republicans. It's the meeting where state delegates will cast their votes to decide the party's presidential candidate for 2016. It's also your moment of truth.

Beth may not have been a matador, but she faced a charging bull of a different sort. She knew there would be trouble if she refused to come around and endorse the party's leading candidate for the 2016 presidential nomination,

Donald Trump. But she believed his style and rhetoric betrayed the party's values and encouraged racism and sexism. She was also increasingly disturbed by what she saw as extreme partisanship and intolerance of dissent and debate within the Republican Party.

FINDING HER POLITICAL COURAGE

At that moment, Beth knew exactly what she had to do. She would hold her ground and tell her peers that when it came to supporting the party's presidential nominee, she could not make that commitment. She knew that the minute she opened the floor to questions, she would be met with a barrage of criticism for challenging her party's direction. Some, she knew, would even see her stance as disloyal. Like the matador, she steeled herself and resolved that she would speak out no matter the consequences. She found her political courage and made her move.

The reaction was immediate and ugly. She was booed off the stage by her own party. She was called names and vilified for failing to toe the party line. The criticism intensified in the wake of the speech. One of her Republican colleagues swore at her in the legislature, telling her to "act like a ****ing Republican."

For some time, Beth had endured attacks from some elements in the GOP who had taken to calling her a RINO (Republican in Name Only) for her willingness to work across the aisle. Beth thought differently. Her mission, as she saw it, was to make progress for the people she represented. And in a lopsided legislature, that often meant working on a bipartisan basis. In 2013, she received a James Madison Memorial Fellowship from the Millennial Action Project for her capability for bipartisan work, and in February 2017, she was awarded an Aspen-Rodel Fellowship recognizing her ability to transcend partisan lines.

NO REGRETS

Despite the furor, Beth doesn't regret speaking out at what she believed was a wrong turn for the party, a turn that could not be reconciled with her own values. And it was the beginning of the end of her tenure with the Republican Party.

As she explained, "I thought a little bit about what the outcome would be, but more than anything else, I thought about what I could or couldn't live with." In conversation, Beth is open, articulate and thoughtful. When she speaks, it is easy to understand how, even at a young age, she defied the odds to win elections as a Republican in a Democratic state and how she has been able to transfer that leadership into other arenas.

In 2016 she wrote an op-ed for NBC News detailing how some of her colleagues judged her worthiness as a Republican by the extent and strength of her criticism of Democrats, whether she agreed with what they were proposing or not. She did not buy into being an extreme reactionary. She felt that according to this faction of the party, being a "real Republican" meant swearing that taxes are evil and guns are good, distrusting Muslims and rejecting Hispanic immigrants and refusing to compromise.

ALWAYS STAND UP TO BULLIES

At the Hawaii Women's March on January 21, 2017, Beth articulated her view of the essential values of any political party: vigorous debate on party policy and specific issues, and inclusivity and respect for all citizens, whether they are women, immigrants, LGBTQ, old or young.

The value that she strongly emphasized was being respectful, even when members disagreed. She spoke of how she explained the political landscape to her eight-year-old niece, who often accompanied Beth as she campaigned. "Sometimes people are angry and they don't know how to express it, so they treat other people badly. We explained to my niece that sometimes people are bullies, but that you should insist that they treat people with respect. We told her that you always stand up to bullies, no matter who they are."

Beth believed that her views were consistent with the Republican Party's own history and values, reflecting the style and principles of Abraham Lincoln, a Republican who encouraged debate, welcomed talented political foes into his cabinet and fought against slavery while remaining fiscally conservative. This century's adversarial, ultra-partisan approach — with overtones of exclusion — was the antithesis of that.

The final straw was the stand Trump took in refusing to condemn the internment of Japanese Americans during World War II, an act for which President Ronald Reagan had publicly apologized. According to the news and culture website the Outline, Beth was in a bar in Washington, D.C., where she was attending a conference with some fellow Republicans, when the topic of

Trump's "Muslim ban" came up. Her companions dismissed it as campaign rhetoric that could never actually happen, and Beth was outraged. She reminded them of the Japanese-American internment, and as she made the argument, a report came onto the bar's TV screen saying that Trump had refused to say that this internment violated American values.

SHE *HAD* TO SAY SOMETHING

Her Japanese-American heritage makes this an issue with great personal meaning for Beth. Her grandfather had narrowly escaped internment by removing and burying every Japanese item in his house. She found herself in a unique position to speak out and challenge what she saw as growing racist tendencies in the party.

"I was the only female Republican [in Hawaii] that was an ethnic minority. I *had* to say something," she recalled. "Otherwise, what am I here for? I can't say I've done that for every issue, but this [presidential nomination] is the first one that I looked around and realized that if I don't take a stand, there's nobody else to do it."

THE ACCIDENTAL POLITICIAN

Beth was born in Honolulu in 1985 and grew up in Mililani on the island of Oahu, part of the district she represented from 2012 to 2018. Despite her early ascent to public office, there was no inkling of a political future in her childhood or even by the time Beth went to college.

"Growing up, I didn't think about politics," she said. "[It] came out of necessity. I couldn't get a job." Her goal was to become a university professor, but when she finished her master's degree, there were no positions available. Instead, she found an opportunity at the Hawaii legislature, as a research clerk for the Republican Party, and she took the job.

It wasn't glamorous, but she was good at it and was soon promoted to director of research for the House Minority, the youngest woman ever in that role.

A RINGSIDE VIEW

As well as a living, this job gave Beth an inside look at politics. She saw how the state legislature worked and, ultimately, she began to see things she thought it could do better.

"I had a feeling that politicians were not representing my community," she said. "When I say community, I mean it super broadly — the people I grew up with, my neighbors and friends. It didn't seem like they had a voice … I looked at it and said to myself, we need new people to run for office."

The fact that the legislature was heavily weighted to Democrats also shaped her decision to run. In Hawaii, Democrats have a super-majority, which means they have control over the House and the Senate as well as the governorship. Beth considered herself a moderate and believed she could fit in with either party, but the overwhelming power Democrats held in the state helped sway her decision. She felt it wasn't good for government when power was too concentrated in one party, so she decided to join the Republican party.

So, what prompted her to take the leap and actually run?

Beth identified two factors that tipped the balance: role models and peer influence.

ROLE MODELS SHE COULD RELATE TO

"There were six people [in the Republican caucus]. Five of them were women, and they were mostly ethnic minorities. [Becoming a representative] seemed attainable … they were people I could identify with, and not just in ethnicity. They were feminine, they looked like me. The women in caucus were not that much older, but they had achieved what I never thought I could do." A couple of them suggested that Beth should run, and she started to see that as a real possibility.

And then there was the sense that she was not alone, that others she identified with were becoming involved as well.

"I do remember the moment I decided to put in the paperwork," she said. "A bunch of my friends were running too, other people about my age. They had all jumped in and I thought, we're going to do this as a team!"

Then she added with a laugh, "It never occurred to me until years later that they were all men, but we were all young."

NO LIMITATIONS

Beth credits her parents for building her confidence early. "I was raised to think there is no difference [in potential] between men and women. My dad was very involved and empowering in my upbringing. My mom is a very strong person and she runs her own business."

Equally helpful was being raised to take on challenges, not retreat from them. "Often when we read gender equity studies, you see that men are a lot less afraid of failing," she said. "I was raised to take chances." There was no expectation that she should be perfect, and she is very clear on that score. "There is no point in trying to be perfect. It won't happen."

When the moment came to file the papers to run, Beth found it exhilarating, not intimidating. "It should have felt scarier, but to me, it just felt exciting, this completely unknown thing I was about to do."

A SETBACK BUT NOT THE END

She first ran for office in 2010, vying to become the representative for the 37th District. She campaigned hard and had the full support of her family and friends. On Election Day, the polls showed her with a slim lead. But in the end, she came in second, 13 percent behind her opponent. What she had not taken into account was the absentee vote.

Beth said, "I won in some places but I didn't have the experience to know that [the campaign] had to peak earlier. I learned a lot." She had also submitted her papers at the last minute so did not have as much time to campaign as candidates who threw their hats in the ring earlier.

In 2012, she submitted her papers last minute again — just two days before the deadline — but she had the benefit of all she had learned in the previous election. She had mixed feelings. "I was definitely more hesitant the second time," she said, "but I knew that it was a good opportunity and I would regret letting it pass."

A lot had happened since the first time she ran, including her promotion to director of research for the House Minority. "I had met more people, I had a better network and a better name in the party," Beth said. "My personal life was going well. I was getting married, to someone who was also political, and I think all of that helped. Really, I had more maturity."

Beth campaigned on lower taxes and future increases only if there were improvements in services. She pushed for green, sustainable energy and the right for constituents to have a say in major development projects. She handily won the 2012 Republican primary with two-thirds of the votes and went on to win the general election by five points, earning 52.4 percent of the vote. Shortly after she was elected, she was named state House Minority floor leader.

Beth went from strength to strength, each win more convincing than the last. She won reelection in 2014 with 64.5 percent of the vote, and in 2016, she garnered just over two-thirds of the vote — 67.4 percent — in the general election. She served as Republican House Minority leader from 2015 until early 2017.

But despite her growing influence, there were bumps on the road.

CLASHING VALUES

"There were issues for a couple of years with the [Republican Party] and the different stances I took. I regularly said to my staff, 'They're not going to like this.' I felt I was constantly trying to thread the tiniest of needles," Beth said. Many of her votes were contrary to mainstream Republican positions. She supported a gun ownership registry, favored a rail tax to expand mass transit projects, voted to authorize a study on decriminalizing drugs and voted in favor of establishing a medical marijuana dispensary system.

In the aftermath of the 2016 general election, Beth had reached the point where she felt she had to speak out. She joined millions of women worldwide on January 21, 2017, participating in the Women's March to protest Donald Trump's inauguration as president. That was the catalyst for the GOP to remove her as House Minority leader in February 2017, by a narrow vote of 3–2 with one abstention.

A longtime representative who had participated in the Women's March with Beth was moved to tears by Beth's speech to the Hawaii House following the ouster. "I'm going to be there and continue that fight but, God, I am sorry to lose our minority leader, someone I so deeply, deeply respect — the face of Republicanism as it should be, but it won't be anymore," she said.

The time had come for Beth to move on, and she quit the Republican Party in February 2017.

But changing parties is not a simple matter. Although Beth describes herself as a progressive and often found herself aligned with Democrats on issues, she had to win acceptance to the Democratic Party. The process required her to obtain party approval at the county level by answering questions about her voting record and statements she made on key issues. She also consulted with her constituents.

It was a watershed moment. And it gave Beth the confidence and momentum to look at the next hurdle: running in the 2018 Democratic primary for U.S. Congress, representing Hawaii's First District.

CONGRESSIONAL RUN

Setting her sights beyond the state legislature was another major challenge and a new opportunity for Beth. She knew the odds were long, but she heeded her own advice about taking chances, and remained prepared to fail rather than taking the safer path.

This time, it was not to be. Beth lost the primary in a widely contested race, coming fifth out of seven candidates. She is philosophical about it. "It's the same way I felt in 2010. I know I started too late. [This time] I was able to assess it and when the ballots went out, I knew."

Past victories and defeats helped her put the setback in perspective. She said, "You know the [voters] are not determining whether they reject you as a person but assessing whether you are the right person for the role in terms of what you've been able to present them."

Beth is eager to share her experience with other women and help them navigate the obvious and more subtle challenges of running for the top offices. She said, "People were saying to me, 'You need to stop talking about gender issues and talk about more masculine topics' … The experience of running for Congress opened my eyes to the issues women face when trying to reach the top 10 percent of any career, and that hasn't been explored that much in politics … I want to take my experience and use it to train other women to run."

Because she ran in the congressional primary, Beth was not able to stand for reelection as a Hawaii State representative in 2018. But she has not ruled out running for office in the future. "I'm open to it if the right opportunity comes along."

As always, she will be ready to take her chances.

ADVICE FROM BETH

KNOW THE CHANGE YOU WANT TO MAKE

"The best advice anybody has given me — and I didn't follow it until later in politics — is to make sure you know who you are and what you are trying to do. Your career and outlet might be different. It could be journalism or politics, but know what change you are trying to make and why you are doing it. Knowing that about yourself is critical, and the sooner you figure it out the better and faster you are able to advance — with courage and integrity that comes with that foundation."

BE A ROLE MODEL FOR OTHERS

"What I most want to tell people, especially women, is that you don't have to feel ready to do things. You don't have to have everything perfect … not being perfect adds value to what you bring if you know how to apply it."

MAKE GOOD USE OF POWER

"You need to hold power lightly. That means having a support system around you that reminds you of who you are, and *all* of who you are, rather than just a politician. Too many politicians move away from that and they learn to enjoy the perks of being in office too much. You need people who are willing to tell you you're wrong … I know people who never had a Facebook account because they wanted to be president one day. When that has been your identity since you were a little kid, it's not easy knowing it's your job and not who you are. A lot of people are really afraid of being out of office and that has an impact."

THINK ABOUT RUNNING

"[It comes down to] what tools you have and whether you can live with not using them. [I know] a lot of people who regret not doing something when they had a chance to do it."

CHAPTER 16

SHAHARZAD AKBAR

A LEAP OF FAITH

Senior advisor to the president and high development councils, Afghanistan

SHAHARZAD AKBAR HAD THE perfect job at an organization she was passionate about. From 2014 to 2017, she was country director for Open Society Afghanistan, a not-for-profit group working to build a vibrant and tolerant society in Afghanistan after years of armed conflicts under successive regimes, including the fundamentalist Taliban.

She loved the job and the team she worked with. "I recruited them, I mentored them, we ate lunch together, we shared everything. We were a group of activists and journalists holding the torch, standing up for democratic rights and values," Shaharzad said. It was inspiring work and she was making a difference.

Then an unexpected offer came along in 2017. She was asked to become a change-maker from inside the government, as senior advisor to the president and high development councils. For someone devoted to making her country a better place, it was an incredible opportunity to help rebuild the nation from the inside.

But it caught her off guard. By then, Shaharzad had already packed a lot into her 30 years, and she was totally immersed in making change through activism, working outside of government. Women were participating in Afghanistan's appointed upper house and elected lower house, but that had not been an option she had considered in the six years since she had finished graduate school.

A TUMULTUOUS HISTORY

As the gateway between Europe and Asia, Afghanistan has faced a series of foreign invaders since ancient times, from Alexander the Great to Genghis Khan to Soviet occupation in the 1970s. Afghanistan has also been torn by ongoing war between ethnic factions within the country. What has all this meant for Afghan women?

In 1919, Afghan women were given the vote (a year earlier than women in the United States were granted the right). Within a few years, the first school for girls was opened, a women's hospital was established, child marriage was banned, equal rights for women were written into the country's first constitution, the legislature was created and women were given the right to choose their own husbands (which had previously been done by male relatives).

In 1929, tribal leaders, angered by the reforms that had been put in place in the previous decade, ousted the king and abolished most of the modernizations. Women lost the rights they had gained since 1919.

In the 1930s, a new period of modernization began and reforms were gradually reintroduced. By 1957, purdah (the separation of men and women) was banned. In 1959, state-enforced veiling was abolished. In 1964, a new constitution granted further rights, allowing women to enter into politics, go to university and participate in the workforce.

In 1973, while out of the country seeking medical treatment, King Zahir Shah — who had ruled the country for 40 years — was deposed in a bloodless coup. The new constitution was abolished and there were setbacks to freedoms.

By 1978, in a coup by the People's Democratic Party of Afghanistan, the religious and traditional laws were replaced by secularism following the Marxist-Leninist model. Burqas were banned and the minimum age for marriage was raised to 16. Women were encouraged to seek further education and take jobs. Photos from the era show women in western fashions, including miniskirts.

During the 1980s, Afghanistan was caught in the middle of a cold war struggle between the Soviets and the United States, with fundamentalist militia backed by the U.S. A civil war between the militia and the government forces had developed by the end of the decade.

By 1996, the Taliban was in power and women were required to wear burqas. They would face severe punishment if they showed even an inch of skin. During this period, women were banned from going to school, studying, working or leaving the house without a male chaperone. Residents of Kabul were ordered to cover their ground-floor and first-floor windows so women could not be seen from the street. Women faced severe physical punishment or even death for defying these restrictions.

In 2001, the Taliban was pushed from power and an interim government was formed. A new electoral system began in 2005, and since then, women in urban areas have regained many of their freedoms. The Taliban continues to battle for control in some regions of the country, where women are still subject to many restrictions.

A CHOICE

"Initially when I was approached to join government, I wasn't so excited," she confided. "I loved my job, I felt useful. And I had no prior experience in government." She told them she would consider their request and give her answer later.

Shaharzad's doubts grew the more she thought about government and the enormous challenges Afghanistan faced as it struggled to develop a fully democratic government after a long history of strife. Shaharzad would be walking into an administration facing major issues, moving forward but with halting steps. As Shaharzad explained, in Afghanistan, the government is in transition. The institutions haven't taken shape yet, and progress is slow and confusing. Sixty-eight of Afghanistan's 279 seats in Parliament are reserved for women, and in the 2018 elections, a record number of women candidates ran. However, much of the power still resides at the most senior government positions, which are entirely dominated by men.

And there was a sobering reality to face. Driving reform and modernization in Afghanistan is a dangerous business. The higher the profile, the greater the danger. It requires tremendous courage, whether running for election to the lower house, seeking appointment to the upper house or working within the civil service. Change is slow and the process can be frustrating.

A LEAP OF FAITH

But Shaharzad was determined to be part of the transformation, whether from inside or outside of government. As she thought beyond her own role, she began to warm to the idea of joining government. Although she would not be in an elected position, the role would give her tremendous potential to influence change at the highest level, working in concert with women elected to Parliament to move the equality agenda forward.

"If things are going to change, we need young people and we need women," she said. "Here there was an opportunity, not because of who my father is or my mother or which ethnic group I am from. I have been approached because I have skills that are useful."

When they called again to ask what she had decided, she said yes. "It was a leap of faith."

As senior advisor to the president, Shaharzad is at the center of the action, working at the Arg, the presidential palace in Kabul. Her role is to provide expert advice to the high councils, coordinating between the councils and different sectors. She works with ministers and the experts who brief them, communicating priorities from the president in the process.

LET'S NOT PLAY GAMES. LET'S GET THINGS DONE

Shaharzad is a trailblazer. She is a young woman in a position of considerable influence who also wants to see a new model for leadership. In her work with the higher councils, she has few women colleagues. "I am always sitting in rooms full of men," she said. "The important currency [with them] is power and symbols for what power is. I realize that a lot of people are fighting for bigger offices, more staff, a higher security clearance." People told her that if she wanted to be taken seriously, she had to play the same game, but she disagreed. She doesn't want to spend her energy on such things when there are more important tasks at hand. She admitted that she has moments when she doubts herself, but she concluded: "You can make your own way, without adopting things in contradiction to your values."

WHO'S IN THE PHOTO? A NEW VISION FOR LEADERSHIP

Shaharzad sees women evolving a new approach to politics and leadership. Twice she traveled with delegations to Washington, D.C., to engage with policy makers and think tanks. One group was made up of men and women, and the other with women only. She found the dynamics starkly different between the two groups. When men were in the group, there were displays of power. "What I saw time and again was [a focus on] who was sitting with who, who was in the photos. There is a lot of drama around this in mixed groups," she said. With the all-female group, it didn't matter who was sitting where. About the female group Shaharzad observed, "We met in Kabul, we prepared a lot. [In Washington] we kept referring to each other's work. No one was trying to undermine anyone else. In the end, it wasn't about 'what I did.' It was about 'this is what *we* did.'"

WOMEN MAKING THINGS BETTER FOR OTHER WOMEN

While women are playing a greater role than ever, Shaharzad has noticed continuing self-doubt in female colleagues. "There is more of a tendency to think 'maybe I'm not just made for politics, for public life,'" she said. "I find this with my friends as well. But then we think, maybe if there are enough of us, then public life doesn't have to be like this. It doesn't have to be about constant power displays, about undermining others. I think it can be better."

A CHANGING ROLE IN A CHANGING SOCIETY

Shaharzad is working in the government of Afghanistan at a time when the country is working toward expanding the rights and freedoms of women to be fully involved in all aspects of society. The treatment of women has varied throughout the years, with periods of advances and subsequent setbacks. Shaharzad was nine years old when the fundamentalist Muslim Taliban regime came to power in Afghanistan. During their reign, from 1996 to 2001, women who had previously been able to pursue careers were not allowed to work or to leave home unless escorted by a male relative. Women had to wear burqas (a garment of billowy material draped from the head to the ground) with small circles of mesh on the face to enable them to see out. Education for girls was outlawed. The consequences for defiance were harsh: women faced public amputation, stoning, imprisonment and torture. In 2011, Afghanistan was named the most dangerous country in the world for women.

Although things have improved since then, with continued efforts at modernization and reform, the transformation of the conservative cultural influences has taken time, and women in positions of power and influence are still underrepresented.

About the opportunities for women in Afghanistan, Shaharzad admitted, "It's definitely a work in progress. In some cases, I still feel like an outsider, despite being in the heart of power. My colleagues are all gracious, but sometimes as a woman, and someone who is used to different views of power, I feel I am watching as an anthropologist."

A TOLERANT FAMILY

Shaharzad's upbringing prepared her to understand the urgent work of helping to build a strong, democratic government. Tolerance was an important value in her family. She was very aware of the diversity of people in the world. In her family, education — including women's education — was important. Shaharzad's father had ambitions for all his children. She remembers the books he brought her — about female leaders in science, politics, art and literature. There were five girls and two boys in the family, and they all received an education. For girls at the time of the Taliban regime, that was not only unusual, it was also undertaken at the risk of harsh punishment or even death.

Shaharzad describes her father as unusual. He was a political activist, journalist and editor. He fought for modernization and wider freedoms for women. "He was part of a generation who tried to change Afghanistan for the better," she said. But they were unable to mobilize for lasting change.

Shaharzad's father was never taken in by the school of thought where many subscribed to a single point of view and never asked questions. He was thoughtful and looked for wisdom in books and in continuous learning. "To be useful to Afghanistan, he taught tolerance, and his own family was the start. That changed my life," Shaharzad said.

EDUCATED ON THE RUN

Growing up, Shaharzad's family moved often from district to district, dodging waves of armed conflict that engulfed the country and leaving the country for periods of time to escape Taliban-controlled areas where education was forbidden for girls.

"Despite the poverty and insecurity we faced, [my parents] never compromised the quality of our schools or our books."

When it wasn't safe to go out, they took refuge in reading. "If there was armed conflict in the street and helicopters flying overhead," she said, "I was inside reading Dickens, Dostoyevsky, Austen. That allowed me to see a much wider world where bigger things were possible. It was a tool of survival for me."

TITANIC IN THE TIME OF THE TALIBAN

For a few months, the family lived in Taliban-occupied territory and the girls couldn't go to school. Her father bought banned novels and history books, disguising them with religious book covers.

Shaharzad learned that even in desperate conditions, there could be resistance and hope. "People are so resilient and creative," she said. "We have this incredible power inside of us." Even with the Taliban prohibiting reading of all but religious texts and forbidding the watching of TV or films, people found a way to get around the rules. They watched television. The movie *Titanic* came out at that time, and Shaharzad said that even people in Kabul, where the Taliban had firm control, found a way to watch it. To her, this resourcefulness was profound. "This is keeping human civilization going forward. That sort of [repressive] operation is not sustainable."

After completing a year of high school following homeschooling, Shaharzad attended the Kabul University. But she became frustrated with the experience and dropped out. She felt that the university did not value her homeschooling, and she began to doubt her abilities as a student.

Shaharzad was working full-time for BBC Afghanistan when she met and befriended an American woman whose daughter had attended Smith College, a women's liberal arts college in the United States. When the daughter came to visit, she suggested that Smith, with its focus on women and gender equality, would be a good place for Shaharzad to study. She brought admissions forms with her and they filled them out together. The daughter took them back to Smith and Shaharzad was accepted, also qualifying for a financial aid package.

It was a wonderful opportunity but a difficult decision. "I was the primary breadwinner for the family at the time," she said. But her parents insisted that she take the opportunity for a first-rate college education. "They said, 'No, you go.'" Her parents had sacrificed so much already to educate their children, and they supported Shaharzad all the way. Although Shaharzad received a full scholarship, just scraping together enough money to get to Smith was a challenge in itself.

A NEW PERSPECTIVE

Going to Smith was eye-opening in unexpected ways. The university in Kabul emphasized technical subjects and didn't appreciate Shaharzad's deep knowledge of literature and other liberal arts disciplines. "When I went to Smith, I realized it was the [Kabul school] system, not me."

At Smith, Shaharzad discovered that she was better read than many of the students she met in America, and her confidence grew. "I started finding my voice and my conscience," she said.

And she got a glimpse into a much different world. "There were huge differences culturally," she said. The problems of young women at Smith were different from those of young women in Afghanistan. "At home, a young woman would be married and trying to navigate the household, the in-laws, motherhood. There [are] a lot of politics to manage." Her Smith classmates were worried about a whole different range of issues — schoolwork, diets and boyfriends. Shaharzad made the important realization that "context defines your priorities and challenges, and your resilience. The emphasis on women and women's ability to do anything was very empowering. It allowed me to rethink relationships with my mom and sisters and the bigger community of women."

BELONGING TO A GLOBAL MOVEMENT

It was the experience at Smith that gave Shaharzad a sense of "belonging to a global movement of women trying to change the world and make it more equal," she said. "The struggle [for women] in Afghanistan is the global struggle. There is a lot to be done everywhere. Women face difficulties with stereotypes. Even in the United States, it is very pronounced."

In her last year of undergraduate studies, Shaharzad applied to five different graduate schools, three in the United States and two in the United Kingdom. She was accepted at all five. She graduated cum laude from Smith with an anthropology degree and decided to pursue a master's of philosophy in international development at Oxford University, in large part because it had the best scholarship.

At Oxford, she noticed that "there were brilliant people who wanted to improve human knowledge — knowledge for the sake of knowledge," she said. That experience crystalized her concerns about translating academic learning into practical action. The challenge, Shaharzad discovered, was how to use knowledge in a relevant way to affect people's lives.

APPLYING THE LESSONS

Returning to Afghanistan in 2011, Shaharzad went to work as a senior analyst and reporter at the Free and Fair Election Forum of Afghanistan, which was dedicated to creating an open and equitable elections process. In 2005, just a few years before Shaharzard returned from her studies at Oxford, Afghanistan had held its first election in decades in which women could vote. There was still a lot of work to be done to nurture the electoral process. She cofounded and became a partner in a consulting firm, QARA, owned and run by young Afghans like her in Kabul, researching and consulting on issues such as the property rights of Afghan women, preventative health care and the causes of radicalization.

Then, in 2012, she cofounded Afghanistan 1400, a group of political activists who want to end the violence and civil strife. The Afghanistan 1400 movement was focused on bringing young leaders of all ethnic and religious backgrounds together to create a stable, safe society in which all girls can go to school, women can offer political opinions without being jailed and young people can be actively engaged in the democratic process. In addition, Afghanistan 1400 wanted to end the violence and bomb attacks that were still all too common in the country, a goal that became all the more meaningful in 2017 when one of the cofounders of the movement was killed in a Taliban bomb attack.

LOOKING TO A PROMISING FUTURE

Through her education and experiences working for change inside and outside of government, Shaharzad finds many reasons for optimism.

Afghanistan has a high birth rate, averaging more than five children per woman, and a low life expectancy of about 60 years, which skews the population younger. At 31, Shaharzad is older than about two-thirds of the population. "I see a generation of women younger than me. They are more assertive, they are more confident, they have a lot of dreams for Afghanistan," she said. "I see my colleagues in the government, and I see that we are developing a common language on development, on politics. We are redefining our vision for Afghanistan. I see that more and more people are interested in the politics of values, rather than the politics of ethnicity or religion … the government is being reformed from within, and it's actually becoming about service, rather than power." These changes give her hope and inspire her every day.

LEADING THE CHANGE: SHAHARZAD'S ADVICE FOR YOUNG WOMEN

INVEST IN THE SISTERHOOD

"One thing I would suggest to younger women: invest more in the sisterhood. I always in my life sought out mentors, women a few steps ahead, women who were older and wiser. But I wasn't planning to come to the government, so I hadn't engaged with women who were already [there]. It took me a while to build those connections to others who I agree with in values and principles. Since I've formed this circle, I have been more effective, I feel stronger, I feel that I have more power and resources because I have access to the other women. I also have male friends and allies, and that's important, too, because they have issues in common with women."

FIND YOUR VOICE AND EXERCISE YOUR POWER

"There are ways to creatively find your voice, to be a voice for your community. It starts at home for many of us. In your own family, in your own house, you start to recognize your voice as an equal human being. You stand up in family conversations and [are] unafraid of voicing your opinion. You won't always win, but it allows us to exercise our own voice. It took me a long time to realize I have a voice and I have to use it strategically."

GET STARTED ON A PERSONAL LEVEL

"Start with decisions that impact you. If you live in an apartment building, there are issues to address, like water distribution or the lift is broken or trash is not taken out. You don't have to wait for someone else to do something about it. Go knock on doors, ask, 'What should we do?' Say, 'If you are willing to accompany me, I am willing to go [to the authorities] and talk about it.' Your first act can be as simple as that."

BE OPTIMISTIC AND EMBRACE CHALLENGES

"I have no option but optimism. It has to work. There is no Plan B on a personal level. I am more realistic about the enormity of the challenges we face. Being in government [has] given me a view of the sacrifices and struggles needed to turn it around."

EMBRACE THE ESSENCE OF LEADERSHIP

"You have so many ideas, so many things to fix, you can [end up] running too far ahead. But leadership is about taking people and institutions along with you. A lot of us tend to forget that it requires a lot of patience."

RECOGNIZE THAT AUTHORITY CAN BE EARNED

"A signed paper doesn't give you authority. It's when people see you and trust you that you gain power."

BE PATIENT AND PICK YOUR BATTLES

"Good intentions will take you far, but they are not enough. You need wisdom and the skills to constantly assess the context and navigate it in a way that will make you a force for good. There are so many important issues, ones that have meaning, but if you want to fight every battle, you will lose every battle."

CHAPTER 17

ERIN MORAN

YOUNG AND UNSTOPPABLE

Board trustee, Waunakee village, Wisconsin, United States

WHEN ERIN MORAN DECIDED to run for the village board in her hometown, it was hard to get people to take her seriously at first. They asked her if she was doing it just to get attention. They thought that it was a stunt by a bored college student.

But they didn't know Erin very well.

In fact, anyone who has known Erin for a long time might have wondered what took her so long to enter politics.

When Erin was elected to the Village of Waunakee Board of Trustees, in Wisconsin in April 2018, she had just turned 21. When asked what had prompted her to run when most of her colleagues on the board would be at least double her age, Erin confided that running for office had been on her mind for some time.

DEEP ROOTS, STRONG CALLING

A strong sense of belonging encouraged Erin to find a way to give back to her community. Erin's roots in Waunakee — a community of 13 000 on the shores of Lake Mendota, just north of the city of Madison — go back for four generations. She even lives in a house that was built by her great-grandparents. "I think Waunakee is a special place," Erin said. "There are a lot of things I really love about it. There are great community initiatives, we have a creative economy and we also have a really strong school district."

Perhaps even more importantly, Erin sees the impact of having people who invest time and energy in the place where they live. "People are involved here," she said. "They care about each other and they take care of each other. If someone is injured or sick, they are looked after. It's a place where people support your accomplishments."

POSSIBILITIES AND INSPIRATIONS

Erin grew up thinking that she'd finish school, start a career and then — maybe after she'd had children — run for the local school board. But as she went through school, met a wider group of people and got involved in activities, she began to see more immediate possibilities in public life.

"I had a really influential teacher in high school who was the village president," she said. "He was passionate about it and I was inspired." This gave her a firsthand look at what the rewards could be; she saw in him the satisfaction that came from leading in the community. Sadly, her teacher passed away as Erin finished high school, but the example he set left a lasting impression.

As Erin read about elections happening elsewhere, she saw a growing number of role models that she could relate to and who played a major part in her decision to run. "Having Hillary [Clinton] on the 2016 ballot was a game-changer no matter the party, state or affiliation," she said. "Seeing someone who looks like you, has had to deal with the same problems as you and has to break through the same barriers as you is eye-opening. It makes the dream more accessible." Erin was also inspired by Shirley Chisholm, the first African-American congresswoman and the first African-American from a major party to run for presidential nomination, "[Shirley Chisholm] is quoted as saying 'I ran because somebody had to do it first,'" Erin said.

Closer to home, Erin was inspired by seeing a student on the school board. "I saw that they had done it, and I thought, it *is* possible. It is something that people like me do, so it's not so far out there."

I CAN DO THAT, TOO!

Erin also took inspiration from women leaders who weren't running for office, but who exemplified leadership in other ways. Two women she considers her mentors started a church mission trip called "Love Begins Here," which has grown to three different branches and trips that have expanded from one week to eight. Then there was Jennifer Braun, who taught at her school and who has multiple jobs, including director of a yoga studio. Erin has been encouraged by Waunakee Professional Women, an organization that supports entrepreneurship and brings together women business owners and women working in the area. And Erin was inspired by professors at college who introduced her to women who are leaders in their industries. Erin said, "You don't realize sometimes how rare it is to see a woman at the top level of things. [When you do] it makes it so much more attainable. I thought, I can do that, too!"

Then in late 2017, those thoughts of maybe-some-day-I'll-run began to take shape. Erin started wondering what it would be like if she ran for office, and the more she thought about it, the more the idea took hold. As Erin described it, it was almost like a calling.

GETTING AN EARLY START

In many ways, going into politics was a natural progression. Like many others who have run for public office, Erin showed early signs of leadership.

Erin started early, joining the student council at intermediate and middle school before being elected student council president at Waunakee High, a school with 1500 students. "I would be doing things like organizing fundraisers in my classroom in sixth grade for local flood victims; I was the captain of sports teams, and I was emcee at [church] retreats. From a young age I tried, to the best of my ability, to figure out why I often seemed to find myself in these roles as leader," she said. Through middle school and high school, she was also involved in an organization called Future Problem Solving, where students researched topics and followed a process to solve issues within the topic. "This truly changed the way I handled any problem I faced, and I often found that it worked with dealing with other people," she said.

For her junior year of high school, Erin attended an environmental semester school called Conserve School in northern Wisconsin. At Conserve School, there were many talks and learning experiences around leadership.

Erin realized that she liked to get people together and work with them to accomplish a goal, whether it was in the classroom, on the sports field or in a church or community organization. "As I got older," she said, "I realized, hey, there really is an art to this."

She said, "I've come to appreciate how these experiences have prepared me for bigger and more diverse roles within my life. I've often told my little sisters that saying yes to things that seem scary gets less scary the more things you let yourself try." Attending summer camps made it less "scary" for Erin to go to boarding school for a semester, which in turn made going away to college a much easier transition.

A MODEL TO FOLLOW: THE LEADER AS A SERVANT

Erin has always been an enthusiastic camper. She attended her first overnight session at Camp Gray, which is run by the Catholic Church, the summer before she entered first grade and went back every summer until her senior year in high school. Since the summer she was 19, she has been on staff at Camp Gray, first as the arts and crafts leader and then, in her second and third years, as the camp's photographer/videographer.

Camp was where Erin first encountered the concept of what she calls the "servant-leader," or someone whose leadership style is based on humility and focused on enabling others. Erin was impressed by codirector Rebecca Hoeben. As Erin elaborated, "She trusts the staff and doesn't micromanage." What also stood out for Erin is that Rebecca is composed and strong under pressure. "In a severe storm situation where we need to get campers and staff into safe shelter," Erin said, "[Rebecca] is always calm and makes smart decisions. That's the style of leadership that I want to exemplify."

Getting to see strong leaders in the servant-leader mold who weren't necessarily the oldest, strongest or most domineering sparked more than just admiration; it got Erin thinking about where else this leadership style could be effective. When she was on the high school student council, she thought, "Why can't the greatest be the youngest?" Erin tries to incorporate this way of serving and leading by example in her daily life, as well. "When I coach lacrosse, I try to teach [players] to do what they would want someone else to."

WHAT AM I GOOD AT? HOW CAN I CONTRIBUTE?

During her final year of high school, Erin focused on trying to decide what her college major should be. When she was younger, she had thought about natural resources and environmental sciences. But that didn't seem to be exactly the right fit any longer. Erin thought about what she wanted to do with her life and what she was good at. As she pondered these fundamental questions, she realized she was good at relating to people and good at organizing and rallying them. But how would you study that? she wondered. How could that be a career? It occurred to Erin then that she wanted to be a full-time student president. If only that were really a job.

When she began as an undergraduate at Edgewood College in Madison, she chose a course of study that would allow her to work with people and also put her planning and organizing skills to work. Her major is organizational communication, and she is also taking environmental studies and public relations classes.

It turned out to be a good choice, as Erin was able to put her studies to practical use during her campaign.

NOT YOUR USUAL VILLAGE BOARD CAMPAIGN

Erin set out to begin her campaign in an unusual way; she settled herself in a coffee shop as her campaign headquarters and used social media to let people know what she thought and where they could find her. "I didn't go door to door or have flyers, yard signs or buttons," she said. "I felt confident without them." Her main point of contact with voters was the local coffee shop. "It was my unofficial headquarters. It is two blocks from my house, right on Main Street." Erin went there frequently to study, and during the campaign she was there even more, combining school work with campaigning. "As I studied and got my work done, I had conversations with other visitors and reached out to them to make sure they knew that I was an option and why I was running." She also posted online about when she would be there.

Running a campaign also put her problem-solving and time-management skills to the test: "I was constantly figuring it out, constantly wondering, how can I make sure I am meeting the right people and being authentic?" Between school, work, family and social life, she had to carefully watch her time. "I made sure I was in Waunakee as much as possible. Just being visible helped me reach more people."

Erin played to her strengths and used the communications tools that had become second nature to her. "Social media was huge" in her campaign, she said. "I studied PR, so I was familiar with using it."

She explains her strategy. "I would schedule my posts to run regularly and check messages every chance I got. I would tag local businesses that I was at and reach out to people to ask them to share what I had posted." She also searched for relevant articles or blog posts that she could share on Facebook and Instagram.

Erin took pride in her ability to have fun and be creative with her social media sites. "I used fun short videos, a variety of posts like food at local restaurants, flowers from the Waunakee floral shop, and used unique features from the sites," she said. One day, on her walk to class, she went on Facebook Live and gave information about absentee voting. "I knew that followers would potentially get a notification that I was live-streaming," she explained, "so the reach could be higher." She used her own personal pages to share the content she had created and encouraged others to do the same within posts

She was savvy about leveraging the coverage on other media. "As I was interviewed by newspapers and media, I directed them to my Facebook page for more information. I used some of Instagram's and Facebook's tools to gain more reach within posts, so if I posted a picture, I set the location as Waunakee, Wisconsin, so people who were searching and in that location could also see the post."

As a young woman, still a student, who had no idea what she would be doing when she graduated, Erin was in a very different life stage than the four men she was running against. "I decided to use that to my advantage rather than feel ashamed or less than them because I am in a different stage of my life. I highlighted that in my posts." She believes her age also made it easier for younger voters to relate to her.

FACING DOWN THE DOUBTERS

Her strategies worked. There were three spots to fill on the village board, and five candidates ran (including the three incumbents who ran for reelection). Erin came in second, only 122 votes behind the first-place finisher and well ahead of the third-place candidate.

Asked what the biggest surprise of the campaign was, Erin said she had expected more negative criticism, until she realized that many people just didn't want to tell her directly that they wouldn't be voting for her. "I was humbled by the support I did get from people I hardly knew, [and] from old friends or acquaintances," she said.

While people may have been shocked that she was running at such a young age, Erin believes they knew her well enough to understand why. "I am very involved in things. People know that, and they would say, 'I'm very glad young people are running.' Other people said they just thought it was cool."

There was one other reaction that surprised her. People asked Erin if running for office was "just a résumé thing" or whether she was doing it because she wanted to be a congresswoman or senator in 10 years.

Erin knew exactly why she ran. "I am interested and excited about [being on the board] because I care about it. Maybe it will be a stepping stone or maybe not. I've realized that the whole point behind the political world is to figure out the best plan to serve the most amount of people in the best way. Senator? State senator? Maybe. I'm not writing it off."

CHAPTER 18

EVA AARIAK

ONE WOMAN, ONE MISSION

Former premier of Nunavut territory, Canada

IN OCTOBER 2008, WHEN Eva Aariak was elected to government in Canada's Arctic territory of Nunavut, she was the only woman in the 19-seat legislature.

It was just the third territorial election in the newly formed jurisdiction, and Eva won the seat for Iqaluit East, in a community on Baffin Island (formerly known as Frobisher Bay). Then, less than a month after being elected as a member of the Legislative Assembly (MLA), Eva was elected premier of Nunavut. She was only the fifth woman in the history of Canada to become leader of a province or territory.

When the announcement was made that Eva had been voted in by her peers, she was given a standing ovation by many of her fellow MLAs. Eva gave her first address in Inuktitut (an Inuit language) before the MLAs proceeded with the next order of business — electing a speaker and the cabinet.

SHAPING A YOUNG GOVERNMENT

When Eva was elected, Nunavut was only nine years old. It had been created in 1999 when the eastern portion of Canada's Northwest Territories was carved out for a new territory with Indigenous self-government.

Nunavut was the outcome of the Nunavut Land Claims Agreement (NLCA), the largest Indigenous land claim in Canadian history, after two decades of campaigning by Inuit for a separate territory with greater rights over land use.

One-fifth the size of Canada, Nunavut is one of the most sparsely populated regions in the world. If it were an independent country, it would have the twelfth-largest area of any nation, yet with a population of only 36 000 people. In Nunavut, 84 percent of the population are Indigenous people — Inuit — and one of the main concerns in creating the new territory was to protect their culture and language.

When Eva was elected, the government was still very much in its formative stages. Under the NLCA, the proportion of Inuit in government must match their proportion in the territory, but meeting that goal was a stretch. Eva's administration focused on major policy initiatives that would build strength for Inuit society in the future. Her mission was urgent. "Many Nunavummiut [people of Nunavut] are moving away from their interests in government," she said in an address to the legislature. "Others are moving away from their personal hopes and dreams. Too many are moving away from their responsibilities." She felt that some of the energy and enthusiasm that spurred the creation of Nunavut had "apparently gone missing." To bolster the new territory, she focused much of her efforts on youth and around health and education. One of Eva's key goals was to ensure that all children in the territory were able to receive instruction in Inuktitut. It was a huge challenge, for many reasons. With a low rate of high school graduation, recruiting teachers who were proficient in Inuktitut was difficult. In addition, Canada's history of residential schools — with its policy of forbidding Indigenous children from speaking or writing in their native tongue — left an entire generation struggling in their own language.

Eva fought hard to engage the community in shaping their future. She initiated the Qanukkanniq (meaning "What's next?"), which were extensive independent surveys to determine the concerns and wishes of the people before her government set its mandate.

Eva was also vocal in fighting for Nunavut's share of the resources and infrastructure enjoyed by other provinces. She bargained hard with the federal government, extracting a promise from the prime minister to open negotiations on transferring control over Crown lands and resources to the territory.

THE LANGUAGE IS THE PEOPLE

In some ways, becoming premier was just an extension of Eva's abiding commitment to Inuit culture, language, education and economic development — as well as her support for the full participation of women in all aspects of life in Nunavut.

Before joining the legislature, Eva was Nunavut's first language commissioner, which meant that she had the opportunity to further the development and understanding of Inuit languages. During her term, she was instrumental in making Inuktitut and Inuinnaqtun the working languages of the territorial government and laid the groundwork for the bills that became the Official Languages Act and Inuit Language Protection Act in 2008.

"TRAVELING THROUGH LAYERS"

It was in this capacity that Eva made a unique contribution. To bring the modern world of technology to her people in their own language, Microsoft software interfaces had to be translated into syllabics, the system of writing used by Inuit. There was no existing word for *internet.* It was up to Eva to come up with something appropriate, and she did. Throughout the North where they speak Inuktitut, the word for *internet* is now *ikiaqqivik.*

Literally translated, ikiaqqivik means "traveling through layers" and refers to the traditional powers of Inuit shamans.

"The idea is that when shamans are in their trance, they can go anywhere around the world, including the moon," Eva explained to HuffPost. To Inuit elders, going to the moon was old news because shamans have always been able to travel anywhere in a trance in order to see family who are far away and know how they were faring. Like the shamans, those who use the internet travel through layers of meaning and experience.

STRONG WOMEN SETTING AN EXAMPLE

Eva was born in Arctic Bay, a tiny community in the Far North on Baffin Island. At 73 degrees latitude, it lies well north of the Arctic Circle. Eva's father, Eric Mitchell, worked for Canadian Arctic Producers as an art buyer. Although Eva and her six siblings were raised by her adoptive father, Aliguq Joseph, Eva developed and nurtured a relationship with her biological father later in life.

Aliguq worked for the Hudson's Bay Company, and Eva's mother, Kautaq, who spoke English and Inuktitut, worked in the local nursing station as a translator. Learning English had come at a high price for Kautaq, the result of two lengthy stays in sanitariums for treatment of tuberculosis, where both the conditions and the treatment of Indigenous peoples were dire.

Eva credits her mother, and many of the other women in the community, with showing her that strong women contribute to advancing the community as well as their families. Her mother taught her traditional Inuit life skills and not to be afraid to take risks.

Never one to shy away from physical labor, Eva's mother was the one to pick up a hammer and start a new project — her dad would come along later to help. She was unstoppable.

When Eva was in her late teens, she became a member of the Arctic Bay recreation committee. She introduced a motion to ban smoking in a community center where children and others gathered. It was a radical notion, given the sky-high rates of smoking in the community, but it had an impact. Eva was surprised to see that the smokers quickly found other places to smoke, away from the children. She realized in that instant that one person really could make a difference.

A WAY OF LIFE DISAPPEARS

The world that Eva was born into in 1955 was at the cusp of change. The traditional, nomadic Inuit life of hunting and fishing had begun to give way to a Western-influenced, sedentary lifestyle with permanent settlements and a reliance on modern commercial goods. Once, Inuit had traveled from place to place by dogsled, living in igloos, animal skin tents or *qarmaq* (a hybrid igloo-tent), depending on the season. In the twentieth century, they started living in permanent wooden structures, even though all wood above the tree line in the Arctic tundra has to be imported. Self-sufficiency was replaced by a dependence on cloth, guns and tools.

With the introduction of snowmobiles in the 1960s came widespread resource exploration and an influx of people from the south. But the most traumatic — and tragic — impact on Inuit society was the Canadian government's education policy, known as the residential school system, in which Inuit and other Indigenous children were taken from their parents and placed in government-owned "residential schools." Abuse of all kinds was rampant, and many of the students were treated so badly they died. The children were forced to give up their language and culture; they had to learn to speak English or French and exchange their Inuit clothing for Western-style Canadian clothing and adopt Western practices.

Spending the school year away from home for years at a time both traumatized children and estranged them from their families. In turn, this caused widespread deterioration of Inuit social structure, which had been developed on a foundation of kinship and close extended families. The impact is still being felt today, long after residential schooling has ended, with high rates of substance dependence and suicide.

WE ARE SORRY: AN APOLOGY FROM THE GOVERNMENT OF CANADA

In 2008, Prime Minister Stephen Harper apologized to Inuit and First Nations people for the systematic damage caused by the residential school system. Here is an excerpt: "To the approximately 80 000 living former students, and all family members and communities, the government of Canada now recognizes that it was wrong to forcibly remove children from their homes and we apologize for having done this. We now recognize that it was wrong to separate children from rich and vibrant cultures and traditions, that it created a void in many lives and communities, and we apologize for having done this. We now recognize that, in separating children from their families, we undermined the ability of many to adequately parent their own children and sowed the seeds for generations to follow, and we apologize for having done this. We now recognize that, far too often, these institutions gave rise to abuse or neglect and were inadequately controlled, and we apologize for failing to protect you. Not only did you suffer these abuses as children, but as you became parents, you were powerless to protect your own children from suffering the same experience, and for this we are sorry."

NUNAVUT NEEDS MORE WOMEN LIKE EVA

Eva was one of the lucky ones in that first wave of children to receive a Western-style education because she emerged from the experience able to function and supported by the family she returned to. She later completed high school in Ottawa, where she boarded with a family she remains close to even today. It was unusual for Inuk (singular of Inuit) of that period to continue education after high school. Eva went on to earn post-secondary certificates in both business management and teaching.

THE DESIRE TO LEAD COLLIDES WITH PRACTICAL REALITIES

With the devastating effects of the residential schools, and with few attaining post-secondary degrees, the women of Nunavut do not always seek elected office.

The 2017 election marked the first time that Nunavut has ranked higher than last or second to last among Canada's provinces and territories for female membership in the legislature, electing 6 women out of 22 seats, representing almost 28 percent of the legislature.

Despite this record number, Eva admits she was still disappointed in the proportion of women. "I was really hoping there would be many more women in the 2017 election," Eva told the CBC. "There are just not enough yet."

The issue isn't a lack of women with the chops to lead; Eva believes there are a lot of women who have great experience leading in the community and are now ready to tackle Canadian territorial politics. In fact, it's the depth of community experience that may be holding some back from higher levels; they are so entrenched in community activities and leadership, it may be hard to lure them away to the territorial legislature.

Eva acknowledges that there are risks that come with standing for election, but she is adamant in her belief that the risks are well worth it and the only way to get past the concern about running is to just do it.

For her own campaigns, Eva focused on the issues that she is close to and those that the people of Iqaluit said are important to them. As an educator and a passionate advocate for Inuit languages, education is right near the top of the list, especially early childhood education, which leads to better outcomes later in life.

Eva believes that improving childcare capacity and quality is important, not just in enabling women to work but also in encouraging them to enter politics.

A SYSTEM OF GOVERNMENT UNIQUELY SUITED TO INUIT

Nunavut is governed by what is known as the consensus system, in which politicians decide issue by issue how they are going to vote rather than voting in blocks based on political parties or ideology. Political parties exist in Nunavut only to facilitate the support of candidates in federal elections. This structure is significant because it reflects the Inuit process of decision-making and culture.

Though the consensus system does not always require unanimity in reaching decisions, it does favor cooperation. In 2018, Paul Quassa, then premier of Nunavut, was recalled — ousted — after only seven months in office in a vote of nonconfidence. The reason? His style of leading was not in keeping with the Inuit model.

"Reducing licensing barriers for home childcare as well as including training opportunities for childcare advisors are ideas that need to be addressed," she told *Nunatsiaq News*, adding that a complete review of the Education Act is essential.

Eva believes that women are an integral part of the Inuit style of leading, which is based on equality and balance. Women's knowledge and strength have helped Inuit to survive and thrive under often challenging conditions. She sees women as the backbone of Inuit community today; grounded in Inuit culture and values and having a solid understanding of where they come from.

TAKE THE RISK, YOU CAN DO IT

Since leaving the legislature in 2013 — losing her seat in the election by 43 votes — Eva has continued the push to convince more women to stand for office. She knows that women need to see a range of examples of what female leadership can look like so that they can gain the courage to run themselves.

The best way to get started, she advises, is to begin at the community level.

But the trick is not to stop there. Eva advises young women to start off small and then work their way up so that they gain confidence as they gain responsibility.

Eva Aariak is optimistic.

She continues to support women getting into higher levels of politics, and she believes it is important to encourage women to run not just in Nunavut, but the rest of Canada and the world. Eva is confident that women who want to run are already out there and ready for the challenge — they just need to stand up and be counted.

CHAPTER 19

CORI BUSH

WHAT MAKES CORI RUN?

Candidate and former candidate for U.S. Congress, United States

Cori Bush is a woman on a mission. She is running to represent the First Congressional District of Missouri in 2020, taking on a seat that has been held by the same family, Bill Clay and his son William Lacy Clay, since 1969. That takes guts. But the prospect of political glory is not what drives her on. Cori is aiming for public office to improve the well-being of constituents and literally save lives, right now. She is determined to put an end to the disproportionate number of young black men shot to death by the police, deaths that she says wouldn't happen if police were trained to de-escalate, instead of using increasing — and often deadly — force.

And she knows firsthand about de-escalation.

GIVE ME YOUR GUN

The acclaimed documentary *Knock Down the House*, directed by Rachel Lears, is about first-time candidates running for the House of Representatives in 2018 — including Cori Bush, in her last (and unsuccessful) campaign. In one of the film's highlights, Cori criticizes her opponent's acceptance of the status quo and directly challenges the notion that the routine use of deadly force is necessary for police officers.

"The person I'm running against is complacent, but I'm not," she said in the film, pausing to make her point. "If I myself can de-escalate a person with a gun, and I'm not a police officer … I wonder how come they can't do it."

More than once, she's had to rely on her own wits and courage to head off a potentially lethal situation. She recounted an incident several years ago when she found herself facing a man armed with a handgun outside her workplace. "[He] said, 'I have a gun and I want to use it.'" The man told Cori he was getting ready to kill a member of his family. When he ran away, Cori ran after him for five blocks because she was afraid that if police were called in to stop him, it could easily have led to the man being shot.

Politics is a natural progression for Cori, the latest step in her long continuum of caring and change.

Cori was born and raised in St. Louis, Missouri, where her mother was a computer analyst and her father was a politician and activist who took his children with him on marches and boycotts. Early on, she learned the value of taking action on issues that matter.

A graduate of Harris-Stowe State University and the Lutheran School of Nursing, Cori's career has focused on delivering mental health care to the most vulnerable citizens of St. Louis, including homeless people and people with no or minimal insurance. She supervises nursing at numerous mental health facilities in the city. Cori is a single mother with two teenaged children, a son and a daughter.

She is also an ordained pastor with a deep commitment to her faith and its community.

In her roles as nurse and pastor, Cori has had a firsthand view of how political action — or the lack of action — affects people across a wide spectrum of experiences.

Cori ran on a platform that emphasized the need for criminal justice and police reform, a living wage for workers and affordable, reliable health care and coverage for all. She has seen many of these obstacles and issues firsthand.

A TRAGIC TURNING POINT

Her road to politics began when Cori took to the streets in 2014, protesting the fatal police shooting of unarmed black teenager Michael Brown, in Ferguson, Missouri. Michael was an 18-year-old walking down the middle of a street late at night when an interaction with a police officer went from a scuffle to a confrontation that ended in a hail of bullets.

Michael's death sparked widespread waves of protests in Ferguson and marked the beginning of Cori's public activism. She became one of the protest movement's leaders, not only because she was outraged that yet another unarmed young black man had died at the hands of police, but also because it hit home on a personal level.

"It was the idea that my son, who is now 19 — he's a tall, big guy — that it could happen to him," Cori said in a 2019 interview. "[I felt] the moment I closed my mouth, this could happen to someone else because I didn't speak up." Cori began attending protests to support the physical and mental well-being of activists, according to the *Brandeis Hoot* community newspaper. Soon, however, she was participating as a protester herself.

Today Cori is part of the Justice Democrats, a progressive movement within the Democratic Party that seeks to engage ordinary citizens in running for office and to counter the influence of corporations in political campaigns. Cori was the first candidate to be endorsed by the organization for the 2020 election, and she is part of a growing cadre of women changing the face of political candidacy — younger, more women of color, more grassroots.

TENACITY AND COURAGE

The 2020 campaign is Cori's third attempt to win public office. In 2016 she ran for the U.S. Senate and lost. In 2018 she ran for U.S. Congress and lost.

Where others might have been too discouraged to keep trying, Cori doesn't give up easily.

Going into her third campaign, she is undaunted and energized, gaining strength and resolve as support for her candidacy grows. She knows she is facing a steep uphill battle in trying for the second time to defeat her solidly entrenched, dynastic opponent, but she is not afraid to push out of her comfort zone, even if that means she might fail. She believes higher goals are at stake.

"I have learned," she said, "that if you are comfortable, you are not making change. I was out of my comfort zone [in 2016] but I went for it. Even though I didn't win, during my campaign I went all over the state and talked about the issues — racial inequality, police brutality, wage inequality." While she would have liked to win, Cori believes strongly that her candidacy in itself achieved some important goals. "By doing that [campaigning], I changed the conversation."

This accomplishment did not come without a price, and she has learned some hard lessons along the way. To start with, going from activist to politician turned out to be a more difficult transition than she had anticipated. When asked how it went, she had one word: "Rough."

"When they [Justice Democrats] asked me to run, first I said no. No!" As often happens with people who run for public office, especially women, other people recognized her political potential before Cori did. She resisted, but then her attitude started to soften. "The more I said no, the more I felt the yes inside me growing. I knew in my heart I had to do it."

She soon got on board with the idea of running but wasn't prepared for the reaction of her fellow activists, who saw her candidacy as a betrayal. It was painful. "They turned on me," she recalled. "They said, 'You will become what we are fighting against. You are selling out.'" The saving grace was when another activist also decided to run for political office. The two teamed up to support each another as first-time political candidates.

A STEEP PRICE TO PAY

Becoming an activist and aspiring politician has tested Cori's courage and resolve. From the time she became involved in the Ferguson protests, she has faced hostility and violence. "All the times I was in Ferguson, I suffered a lot of violence, harassment, intimidation. I was shot at, my daughter was shot at, my car was vandalized, I had death threats."

But there was worse to come. In 2016, after she lost the Senate rate, she was violently raped, on the same day that one of the Ferguson protesters was shot to death and burned in a car. "I was turned upside down for four months," she confided. "I was completely incapacitated." There was no conviction in the case.

Ultimately, that only hardened Cori's resolve. She said, "If I didn't advocate, this could happen to others. I knew I had to [keep going]. The people in power who could do something didn't do anything."

YOU CAN'T COME HERE

As she began her first political campaign in 2016, she encountered the ugly remnants of the Jim Crow era, when segregation and overt racism were the order of the day in large parts of the United States. She was told there were communities and places she could not go to because she is a black person — so-called "sundown" towns or municipalities that overtly ban black people from entering or staying after dark and in which people of color are generally not welcome.

She didn't let that stop her.

"I got into areas that blacks don't get into," she recounted. "They [representatives of the town] said, 'Let her know she can't come here. This is a sundown town.' One time, police put up a blockade to stop us from going into a town." Cori got out of her car and walked.

This bravery and persistence paid off. "What I learned was that once I spoke, by the time I'd finished a speech, I'd won a lot of them over," she said. In some cases, that meant changing perceptions that had lasted a lifetime. "One person came up to me and said, 'I've never seen a black person before, only on TV.'"

A LEGACY TO BE PROUD OF

Even though she has yet to win a political race, Cori is confident that she has already left a legacy in her community. "I believe by not backing down, by remaining vigilant, people see that it's okay to be you and to stand up, even if you have to do it alone."

Through the events and protests she's organized, she is convinced lives were saved. "I don't know how many, but by raising awareness, we may have stopped a police officer [from shooting] or made the police think about what they are doing."

BECOMING BULLY PROOF

With all the obstacles and danger Cori faces, it's hard not to wonder what keeps her going. But the answer is simple.

"My desire to change is greater than my fear of what they could do to me," she explained. She worried more about what would happen if she didn't act. "It's my faith," she added. "This is my mission in life. What I fear is my people not

CORI'S ADVICE FOR YOUNG WOMEN THINKING OF RUNNING FOR OFFICE

ON KNOWING YOURSELF

"Remember who you are before you make that leap, even if you have been thinking about it for a long time. Your character, your strengths and your weaknesses will be highlighted. Know your weaknesses and get support or work on them. With your strengths, know what you can tap into."

ON IDENTIFYING AND FOCUSING ON YOUR GOALS IN RUNNING FOR OFFICE

"Know why you are doing it!"

ON MAKING A DIFFERENCE AS A WOMAN

"We [women] are great enough. We are great. We are able to do the work. No one can take that from us. We are told we don't have what it takes, we're too emotional. But we can do it."

PARTING WORDS

"You don't have to have it all together to run. You need the heart, the passion, the drive."

As for herself, she says, "I'm just loud enough, bold enough and weird enough to do it!"

getting what they need. I fear the violence against them, I fear for those who do not have the strength to advocate. But I'm not afraid [for me]."

No matter what her opponents or detractors throw at her, there is no chance their tactics of intimidation will stop her. Cori has become bully proof.

When asked about her thoughts going into the 2020 campaign, she doesn't hesitate.

"I can do this," she said. "The fact that supporters are still there, that we are gaining, not losing, supporters, that the people who fought with us last time are still there, I can't let them down. I haven't accomplished [what I set out to]. The issues I am fighting for have not been addressed. There are people living in conditions that I would not wish on anyone."

Taking a second run at the First Congressional District, Cori is not daunted but encouraged. She sees people who weren't interested in politics before suddenly wanting to be involved. "It's amazing in my campaign the amount of people who want to help out," she said. "They are telling me, 'This is the one!'"

So, to Cori, an electoral defeat is not the end, it is merely a step along the way.

PART 2

THE PLAYBOOK

SECTION 1.0

GETTING YOURSELF PREPARED

Now that you've had a chance to read all those inspirational profiles, are you ready to get to work on your own leadership and ambitions?

Running for office will allow you to have a real effect on your community, but your ultimate impact will depend, in part, on the preparations you make before you even throw your hat into the ring. You'll want to begin a campaign with clear goals, strong supports and a full toolbox. By laying this groundwork, you will reap benefits for your campaign as well as for your life as an involved citizen.

The Playbook is meant to help you explore your options and reach the level of preparedness that you want and need in order to make a difference through elected office. And even if you don't run, the Playbook can help prepare you for other goals you set — or challenges you face — in life. It will guide you to be clear about your intentions and realize your ambitions.

How do you know when you're ready to put yourself forward as a candidate for election (or for a job, a promotion, a scholarship, an award)? Do you have to tick all the boxes and be 100 percent of what makes an ideal candidate?

The answer is no! But as a female, you may be more likely to answer yes. There's research to back that up. An internal study by Hewlett Packard showed that men will put themselves forward as long as they can meet about 60 percent of the qualifications, but women want to meet 100 percent of them before they feel entitled to apply. When men aren't able to tick a box, they will lobby for the job anyway and talk about how they will acquire the skills they are missing.

What does this mean for you? It means that you don't have to be perfect to go forward.

WHAT'S YOUR GOAL?

Do you aim for excellence or perfection? Here's a quiz to find out. Jot down your answers — yes or no — on a piece of paper to calculate your score:

1. I prioritize my to-do list and focus on the most important tasks to ensure that I get the most out of my efforts. I know some tasks won't get done.
2. I don't ever stop until I finish everything on my to-do list. It's important to finish everything you start.
3. I try to achieve maximum impact with everything on my list. I never give less than 100 percent.
4. I am focused on overall impact, not on each task. I know that 80 percent of results come from 20 percent of effort.
5. When a new job or project comes up that I'm interested in, I put my name forward if I can meet more than half the criteria. I need challenges and "stretch assignments" to grow.
6. I need to meet 100 percent of the criteria before I will apply for a position or a project. I won't put myself forward unless I'm fully qualified.
7. If I am able to get agreement on almost all the issues I put forward at a meeting, I feel great!
8. If I wasn't able to get agreement on all the items I put forward, I'll wonder what I did wrong.

Score one point for each yes you answered on questions 2, 3, 6 and 8. Deduct one point for each yes you answered on questions 1, 4, 5 and 7.

If you scored 0, you don't let perfectionism hold you back.

If you scored between 1 and 3, you may be seeking perfection too often, but you are able to go forward nonetheless.

If you scored 4, think about whether you need to improve your effectiveness or whether it's really perfectionism that is holding you back.

SETTING REALISTIC EXPECTATIONS

The key to success is to focus on your goals, not your mistakes. When mistakes happen — and they do for everyone — learn from them and move on. Once you accept this, you can set achievable expectations.

What is the difference between excellence and perfection? Excellence is setting a high standard for yourself and delivering on it.

When you focus on excellence, you are concentrating on the process, on what you can control and how you will go about being the best you can be. If you seek perfection, you are focused only on a specific outcome, one that may be impossible to attain.

Achieving excellence makes you feel proud and confident, and that means taking on new challenges — stretching and embracing risks — will be easier. But perfectionism, on the other hand, is setting impossible and unsustainable standards. It's all or nothing. And no one achieves 100 percent success all the time. Getting perfect results 9 times out of 10 shouldn't make you feel like a failure just because one time didn't go exactly as planned.

People who are insecure may feel the need to be perfect and therefore above criticism, but it doesn't work that way — no one can get it right all the time. Perfectionism erodes confidence; striving for excellence builds it up.

ASSESSING YOUR STRENGTHS AND WEAKNESSES

Before getting into the competitive political arena, you'll need to do some self-reflection. This will help you understand how you lead (your leadership style), how you approach working with people, how best to pace your work and how you respond to rules set by others.

There are no good or bad answers and there is no "particular profile" that you have to worry about fitting into. But the greater your insight into your own unique style, the better you will be able to prepare yourself to meet your goals.

For example, if you are a 100-mile-an-hour talker, you may need to slow down and focus more on listening. If you have trouble remembering names, you may need to push yourself to meet people and practice. Having a good understanding of yourself will help you identify strengths you can use to your best advantage and challenges you will need to work through.

KNOW YOURSELF!

A self-assessment provides useful insights you can act on. Answer these basic questions, adding details and examples, to create a thumbnail sketch of what makes you *you*.

PLANNING AND ORGANIZATION

Do you like to plan and prioritize tasks and finish them one at a time? Or do you like having a variety of tasks on the go, rolling with it when things change last minute?

PEOPLE STYLE

Are you energized by meeting people? Do you enjoy large meetings and conferences? Or do you need to be alone to recharge your energy after meeting people or being in crowds?

ATTITUDE TO RULES

Do you feel strongly that there's a right way to do things? Do you like to follow those rules and pay attention to details? Or do you feel there should be flexibility in how things get done?

DECISION-MAKING

Do you like to "think big" and feel that if it hasn't been done before, you don't mind being the first? Or do you prefer to think things through and make decisions carefully, avoiding unnecessary risks?

In the Deep Dive section, you will find information and links to some of the best online tools that you can use for more thorough self-assessment.

MAKING A PERSONAL SUPPORT PLAN

Although you are just one person, politics is a team sport. And you're the captain of two teams — your campaign team and your personal support team.

The importance of your campaign team may seem obvious, but your personal support team is equally important. To be at your best, it's smart and strategic to make sure you aren't operating on your own — or feeling alone — when you run.

An athlete has a coach, a physiotherapist, a nutritionist and likely many others who help her achieve her goals. She also relies on family and friends to keep her upbeat and help her get through challenging times.

The good news is that your support team can come from almost anywhere. Here are some of the kinds of people you might consider adding to your support team (it's okay if you can't cover them all):

1. A really close friend or relative you can confide anything to, who won't judge you if you are struggling or unsure and who will also help you keep your feet on the ground when you need a reality check.

2. A romantic or life partner who is behind you and ready to support you in your campaign.

3. Your family members — parents, siblings, cousins, aunts, uncles — who understand you.

4. A circle of three or more friends or relatives you respect, who have different areas of experience and skill and who you can call on for advice. (This is sometimes called a "personal advisory board" or a "kitchen cabinet.")

5. If you're in school, a supportive teacher, advisor or guidance counselor.

6. A boss who supports you with some work flexibility or time off. Or if you work for yourself, you might have backup support so you can spend time on the campaign without harming your business.

7. An organization you have found or joined with a track record of supporting women who run for office.

DEVELOPING RESILIENCY

Things don't always go as smoothly as we would like. In fact, it's rare to take on a major challenge like an election campaign without experiencing setbacks. That's why resiliency is such an important factor in success. But what is resiliency and how do you get it?

A simple way to think of it is the capacity to "bounce back." It's not just being tenacious and slogging on grimly; it's also being able to regain your sense of optimism and well-being after you've been through a difficult period. Resiliency also entails a sense of proportion, allowing you to put negative events in the proper context.

How does resiliency relate to election campaigns? Here are two scenarios to consider:

SCENARIO 1: You've just received the results of a recent poll that shows you trailing your opponent by a wide margin. It's early in the campaign, but the gap between you and the leader is daunting. You've worked hard and you are understandably discouraged. What happens next?

	RESILIENT	NON-RESILIENT
Tactical response	I'll analyze the results to look for factors contributing to the gap and develop plans with my team to counteract them.	Maybe it's best to cut my losses instead of trying to win. Maybe the goal is to stop the opponent from a landslide victory.
Emotional response	This is bad news, but it gives me important information about where to focus to make up the difference in support.	Wow, I think this may be hopeless. Why did I ever think this was a good idea?

SCENARIO 2: You've been in the first of three all-candidates' debates. It wasn't your finest hour. One of the moderator's questions took you by surprise. Your opponent pounced on your misstep and scored a lot of points. The consensus of your team and the local newspaper is that your opponent won the debate.

	RESILIENT	NON-RESILIENT
Tactical response	I know I can do better. She outdueled me this time, but I have two more debates to win people over. I'll do more research, and now that I know how she operates, I will be ready for the next time we debate.	I am going to rethink whether to participate in the next debate. There's no point in trying to defend myself after this.
Emotional response	This feels awful. But I've been through worse and it's something I can recover from. It's all part of the process and I am learning a lot.	This is humiliating. I've completely let down the whole team. I don't know how I can go on.

USING EMOTIONS TO HELP YOU

You can prepare for a lot of things, but there is no way to anticipate every possible situation you may find yourself in. When there are no obvious rules and no previous experiences to go by, you need to rely on what you might call your "gut instinct" or "sixth sense" to make decisions.

Have you ever found yourself in a situation where you were feeling very certain about a decision or a direction to take, but you didn't know exactly why you felt that way? That's your subconscious at work, giving you the cumulative benefit of everything you've experienced, learned and felt before your conscious mind can sort it all through and retrieve the facts. That's why it's important to heed those feelings and take them into account.

In what kinds of situations do you need to pay attention to your gut? Ask yourself these questions about something you are confronting:

1. Does making this decision keep me awake at night or preoccupy me during the day?

2. Do I get a sick feeling in the pit of my stomach when I think about it?

3. Am I showing any other physical signs of stress when I think about the situation?

4. Does my anxiety level rise when I think about it?

5. Am I reluctant to make a decision or move forward despite logical reasons for going ahead?

If you answered yes to one of these, you may just be nervous about the decision or a situation, but if you answered yes to several or all of them, your gut is telling you there may be a bigger problem. Talk to a trusted advisor or mentor before moving forward.

The same holds true for positive feelings. Sometimes you can't find the evidence, but you just have a very strong feeling that you're on the right track. That's also your gut instinct, and it's something that you should pay attention to as well.

These feelings are part of your emotional "toolkit." Women are sometimes labeled "too emotional," as if emotion is a shortcoming. But emotion is a powerful force that can be harnessed to help you succeed. It includes your instincts for decision-making, your passion for a cause and your optimism in creating change. It can also constructively include anger that inspires you to act when you see injustice or wrongdoing.

Politics has been described as a series of compromises. It can mean balancing party discipline with voting according to your conscience. Paying attention to your gut and acknowledging your emotions can help you be true to yourself and warn you when you are at risk of going against your moral compass.

TRAINING FOR COMBAT

Politics at its core is adversarial. You are competing for voters' time, attention and loyalty. You "run" against your opponents in a "race." In many political systems, the party not in power is called the "official opposition."

Developing a thick skin is one of the most common recommendations for women considering running for election. It's good advice for anyone — nearly everyone is sensitive to criticism to some degree. But how do you function in an adversarial environment where scoring points off an opponent's weaknesses is often a sport?

There are several ways to take political sparring in stride:

- Manage your expectations of the experience. You're not in politics to win friends and be liked by everyone; you are there to represent your constituents and give them a voice. Former U.S. president Harry S. Truman famously said, "If you want a true friend in Washington, get a dog."

- Try not to take attacks on your policies and positions personally. Adversarial exchanges are part of the game.

- As Kathleen Wynne, former premier of Ontario (Canada's largest province), advises, "Develop a thick skin, but make sure it's porous." What she means is that you have to be able to withstand criticism while also hearing what your constituents are telling you.

After Canadian cabinet minister Rona Ambrose faced a barrage of criticism for her actions as environment minister and was demoted to a less contentious portfolio, she joked she was going to start her own cosmetics line, featuring a body cream for women going into politics. The label would say to use liberally, because "the more you put on, the thicker your skin gets."

BUILDING CONFIDENCE: FROM "WHO, ME?" TO "WHY NOT ME?"

Both women and men deal with self-doubt. The real issue is the gap between the level of self-doubt women face compared to men, and the effect that can have on the way women approach their lives and their careers.

During my 15-plus years as head of an organization promoting the career advancement of women, I have heard this consistently — from young women, mature women, women starting their careers, women promoted to their first management position, women who were executives and board directors.

No matter how accomplished or how outwardly assured they seem, when the time comes for frank discussion about challenges, accomplishments, fears and triumphs, most women admit to suffering from self-doubt and lack of confidence. Before you get started planning your run for office, it's a good idea to do a confidence check and bolster your self-esteem.

Your view of yourself, where you think you belong and your level of confidence all affect the choices you make and the goals you set for yourself.

Lack of confidence can prevent women from reaching their potential — they may be capable of more but are reluctant to take the risks that come with putting themselves forward, whether for a job, a promotion or a spot on the ballot.

Let me share an example. I have had the happy responsibility of calling the winner of my former organization's Woman of the Year Award. One year, the recipient reacted with dismay, not delight. She was hesitant to accept the award because it would draw attention to her. She had long felt that, as a woman, the safest way to approach her career was to fly under the radar, not make waves, and stay out of the spotlight. That way, no one would challenge the legitimacy of her increasingly senior roles or decide she was a threat and try to take her down a peg. I was shocked that a woman of such accomplishment would feel that way. I knew the story of a man who canceled a trip to the Olympics just to accept a lesser award.

When looking at career choices and assessing whether you might throw your hat in the ring for an elected position, keep in mind that doubts are normal and having doubts should not be taken as a sign that you're not cut out to run for election. You may wonder, *Can I do it? Am I the right person? Will anyone listen to me?* These questions should be the starting line, not the end point.

All too often, the insistent voice of doubt drowns out the voice of possibility, the one that asks, *Why not? What have I got to lose? What's the worst that can happen?*

Listen for the voice of possibility that also says, *Maybe I don't know, but I can learn. I'm good at achieving my goals. I know how to work hard.* Then you can hear the voice that says, *This matters enough that I need to try.*

It's possible to reframe each one of our fears so that we are realistic without being self-limiting. Whatever you decide, don't rule yourself out of the race before you even get to the stadium, let alone step up to the starting line. Each attempt, regardless of outcome, will give you confidence to push harder and aim higher.

NEGOTIATING WITH CONFIDENCE

It is not uncommon for women to be reluctant to negotiate on their own behalf. One woman, a highly successful chief executive officer (CEO) of a large regional company, told me she had never, not once, negotiated her salary until she became CEO. The position was structured to require a CEO to negotiate her own compensation package. Previously, this woman had simply taken whatever was offered.

This doesn't mean that all women avoid negotiating — many women are excellent negotiators. But studies have shown that women negotiate far less than men do. And since negotiation plays a huge role in business and politics, it's something you need to be conscious of when you are pursuing your goals.

It also means that if you've been hesitant to negotiate or felt unsure about how hard you can push before it could backfire, you're not alone.

THE DISADVANTAGEOUS DISCOUNT

Understanding that you are more likely to sell yourself short as a woman isn't something to be discouraged about — but you need to be aware of it. Once you see that you are applying an automatic discount to your capabilities, you can learn instead to give yourself full credit for your skills and accomplishments.

When you look at leaders — in school, at work or in the public sphere — try to envision yourself in one of those roles. Don't think, *Who, me?* Instead, believe, *Why not me!*

FAKE IT TILL YOU MAKE IT

You may have heard this expression. It means that sometimes you have to act confident to feel confident. Smiling even if you don't feel totally happy makes you feel happier. It works! When you focus on visualizing the outcome you want, you will unconsciously start working toward that goal. It is important to understand how your thoughts affect the direction your life will take. Keep moving ahead. You will learn and solve problems as you go.

Very early in my career, just out of journalism school, I was looking for freelance writing assignments. I noticed that the free magazine at movie theaters was edited by an alumna of my school. I called and asked if she used freelancers. She said yes, but had no assignments at the moment, so I asked if I could call back in six weeks. This went on for almost a year, until one day, she said she had an assignment and asked if I was interested. Of course I was. When she explained what she was looking for, my knees started shaking. It was a full-length article featuring two well-known movie stars who were in Toronto to shoot a movie. One of the stars, Glenda Jackson, was famously intolerant of journalists who asked stupid questions. I didn't have a lot of experience, but I was a quick study and determined to do whatever it took to succeed at this assignment. I said yes in a confident voice and then buried myself in research, compiling a long list of carefully framed questions. I felt prepared, but I was so nervous during the interview with Jackson that at one point, I realized I couldn't feel my legs and wondered if they would support me when I stood up. They did, and I survived the interview without any major gaffes. I wrote (and rewrote) the piece and had it published. Glenda Jackson went on to become a member of Parliament in England, only recently returning to the stage. I learned a great deal from the experience.

Is there something you're interested in doing but not sure if you're qualified or confident enough to try? Here's a guide to help you decide if you're ready to "fake it till you make it":

EXPERIENCE VS. CONFIDENCE: THE MAGIC FORMULA	
High experience **Low confidence** You've got the skills and experience. Fake the confidence — it'll come over time.	**High experience** **High confidence** You're ready — go for it!
Low experience **Low confidence** Work on gaining some more experience.	**Low experience** **High confidence** This is a calculated risk. If there's time to learn on the job, especially if the challenges play to your strengths, do it!

It takes courage to be ambitious, to take the leap to run for election. You can condition yourself to feel entitled to take risks, to put yourself forward, to try and to feel it's not the end of the world if you fail.

IT'S POSITIVELY DESTINY!

Positive thoughts → Self-encouragement → Actions → Habits → Character → Destiny

Positive thoughts become words of self-encouragement. These in turn lead to actions and guide the way we respond to challenges. Over time, these actions become habits. Habits, good or bad, ultimately serve to define our character. Finally, our character — the values we have internalized and the sense of optimism or pessimism with which we approach the opportunities and challenges that come to us in life — becomes our destiny. This is what "fake it till you make it" means. The better you understand the process, the more you can gain the power to guide your own destiny!

LACK OF CONFIDENCE OR REALITY CHECK

Some feelings of doubt you ought to push through, but at other times, those feelings arise as a red flag. Not all ideas are good ones and not every opportunity is a good fit. Here are some questions to help you decide whether to push ahead or not when you have feelings of doubt.

1. **What will I achieve if it works out?**

   Imagine achieving your goal and then take the time to list the positive things that will come once the goal is achieved.

2. **Is that outcome important to me and my goals?**

   You want to be able to answer yes to this question. You are going to work hard, and that hard work should count for something you believe in. If your answer is no, rethink the plan or adjust it so that its outcome is more in line with your priorities and interests.

3. **What will happen if I mess it up?**

   Failure is a part of learning and growing. Exploring the consequences of a bad outcome is important to do before you make a decision. But once you act, be prepared to face any mistakes head on, learn from them and move on with confidence.

4. **How can I recover from a bad outcome?**

   Develop one or two scenarios of how you would deal with each possible bad outcome. Think about what could go wrong and try to visualize how you would deal with it. Making mistakes or experiencing failure teaches us a lot. Learning to deal with things that go wrong is one of the most important ways we develop strength and resilience. Something that feels like a disaster may actually be a huge opportunity to grow. It's a bit like lifting weights to become fit. There's a lot of sweating and struggling at the time, but you do get stronger, and the next time you have to lift something, you can lift with confidence.

   If you are stuck and can't visualize how to recover from a bad outcome, ask a close friend to help you brainstorm and develop possible responses to potential pitfalls. When you face what could go wrong and develop strategies to deal with it, it can keep the fear of failure from getting in your way.

5. **How big is the upside compared to the downside? (How does the size of the risk compare to the size of the reward?)**

   Part of the calculation in a calculated risk is deciding if the reward for success is worth the risk of failure. It's not a matter of the number of positives compared to negatives. There could be lots of negatives and only one positive, but that positive could be so huge that it outweighs a whole bunch of smaller risks. The reverse can also be true.

   An effective and often-used way to do this is to make a list of "pros" (the rewards if you succeed) in one column and "cons" (the risks and possible adverse results) in the other. Seeing it in writing will help you analyze the situation and come to the decision that is right for you.

6. **What will I learn by trying, whether I succeed or fail?**

   Try to identify what you will gain from the process, regardless of whether you win or lose. Some of the things you might consider putting on this list are: learning to articulate my points of view, learning more about the community, making a wide range of contacts, developing relationships with people involved in politics, becoming better known in the community, and learning the ropes for a future run or role as a campaign team member. Many benefits may come out of a run for office.

Without exception, women who have both succeeded and failed in their bids for election have told me that just going through the process itself was worth the whole effort because they gained so much.

7. **Will I gain important skills or experiences?**

   If your answer is yes, take time to jot down the most important ones you think would come out of running for office. Then try to pinpoint one aspect that would be the most significant. As you go through your campaign, being mindful of this one point will heighten your sense of achievement.

   If the potential learning and growth you identify is *not* important to you, you might want to think about what made you consider running in the first place or look at a different direction that would provide a more valuable experience.

8. **Why am I feeling uncomfortable about making this decision?**

   Try to analyze what exactly is making you feel hesitant or uncomfortable about making the decision to run or not to run. Each person will have different thoughts on this, but here are some common ones:

   - I'm nervous because it's new and I can't tell by past experience whether I'm likely to succeed or if I might fail.
   - I'm not sure I have the skill set to succeed.
   - I don't meet the required criteria. (If you meet fewer than half, analyze the gaps and work out a plan to overcome them.)
   - Something feels "off" about this situation. (If you believe there is something unethical involved, listen to your gut.)
   - I'm not sure how I feel about the people involved. (If it is because you don't know them, don't let this stop you. If it is because you know them and don't like, respect or want to work with them, this might not be the right situation for you.)

FINDING YOUR CONFIDENT INNER VOICE

To be effective, you need to have a confident inner voice. This means having an informed perspective and, when faced with a difficult or intimidating situation, speaking up and defending your position.

Imagine you have worked hard, competing against dozens of other applicants, to become the sole intern at a company. You are attending a meeting where you're the youngest person in the room by far. The topic is developing a new marketing strategy, and you are listening intently to everything that is being said. The company's target market is consumers between the ages of 15 and 30. This is a group you know a lot about! Someone suggests a social media campaign on a platform you know is past its peak and losing credibility quickly among your friends. The marketing executive in charge seems very keen on the strategy being discussed. But you feel very sure that its chances will be hampered by the wrong platform. You're the youngest and least experienced person at the meeting. Do you speak up and share your thoughts?

THE DOUBTING INNER VOICE

This voice might say, *I think they're on the wrong track. I should say something. But these people know what they are doing and they have more experience than I do. What if I'm wrong? I will look so stupid. Why would they listen to me anyway? What if they think I am being difficult and they won't want me back as an intern next year? Maybe I should just listen some more and see where this goes.*

This is your doubting inner voice. Listening to it will hold you back.

THE CONFIDENT INNER VOICE

A confident voice says, *I have something to add here. They may not realize how quickly this platform is being left behind by users my age. I'll just point out what I've been observing. What if they've already thought about it? That's okay, at least it will show I am paying attention.*

This confident inner voice gives you the ability to venture out of your comfort zone and find a way to move ahead. It gives you the resilience to recover if you make a mistake — which everyone does. Keep your ears open for the confident inner voice — it will guide you to success.

SITUATION	DOUBTING VOICE	CONFIDENT VOICE
This is a sensitive issue. Should I speak up?	No, I'm not 100 percent sure I'm right. Suppose I'm wrong?	Yes, I've thought this through. I'll be tactful.
No one has raised this issue yet. Should I say something?	Maybe there's something I'm not getting. I'll keep quiet and see if it comes up.	It's relevant and needs to be on the table so I am going to raise it.
This is complicated. Maybe I'm in over my head.	I'll just see how the conversation goes and hope it's explained in the discussion.	I need to ask a question so I can get clarification and make sure I understand.
This is important, but everyone who has spoken has an opposite view to mine. Should I still put my ideas forward?	No, I must have missed something. Maybe it doesn't matter that much anyway.	Yes. I've given it a lot of thought. I'll explain how I came to this conclusion. Maybe others agree with me but haven't spoken yet.
I've been accused of being obstructive because I don't agree on an important issue.	I know this is important, but maybe I shouldn't take up any more of people's time. I don't think I can win everyone over so maybe I will defer to the group.	I've considered other points of view, and I still think mine is valid. This is an issue I feel strongly about. I'll restate my opinion and come at it another way. If there's still no agreement, I will ask that my view go on the record and suggest that we move on.

GETTING A HAND UP – FINDING MENTORS TO GUIDE YOU

Mentorship has always been a major factor in helping people achieve. Mentorship happens when someone takes another person "under their wing," such as a veteran team member encouraging and advising a rookie. Mentorship is also when corporations groom employees for leadership. The concept has its origins in ancient Greece, when Odysseus went off to battle and asked his trusted friend Mentor to guide and advise his son Telemachus while he was away. Since then, the word *mentor* has referred to anyone who plays a guiding advisory role; the person who receives this guidance is called a mentee.

A mentor is a combination of many things — advisor, role model, sounding board, cheerleader and thoughtful critic. They are someone who shares their insights and hard-won wisdom, who takes an interest in your development, who encourages you, lifts you up when you are down, gives you a push when you're stalled, helps you correct course if you veer off and gives you advice when you need a different point of view. Whether or not you are considering running for office, it's a wise move to keep your eyes open for potential mentoring relationships.

FINDING MENTORS

There is no "one size fits all" mentor. Mentors offer different lessons and different kinds of support, and you will find more than one person who can be a mentor to you. For example, one person may have direct campaign experience and be able to help with tactical aspects of running for office. Another may have an area of expertise that will help you on policy issues as you develop your platform. Yet another may model leadership skills and even coach you on becoming more resilient.

HOW DO I FIND MENTORS? OR DO THEY FIND ME?

Ideally, mentorships develop from existing relationships. If you find someone you are comfortable turning to for advice, someone who seems happy to listen to you and answer your questions, then that person may already be filling a mentoring role. If you want to be sure this person is on board, you can ask,

"Do you mind if I call you again and ask for advice?" If she welcomes the notion, you are on your way. You may ask for advice once or twice or stay in touch with your mentor for a few weeks or a few months. In rare cases, the relationship can last for several years, and by that time, it is likely to be a friendship as well as a mentorship.

Here's a scenario that illustrates the progression from connection to acquaintance to confidante/advisor to mentor:

You decide to volunteer at a campaign office of a candidate you support. You meet a woman who is the volunteer organizer, and she gives you a list of names and phone numbers to call. Your assignment is to canvass the electorate and ask the people on your list if they have decided who to vote for, and if so, if they will tell you their chosen candidate's name. It's a tedious task but essential information to gather for the candidate. While the volunteer coordinator is explaining what to do, you get into a conversation about the election, the issues and the candidate's chances. You discuss how the trend toward populist politics could affect the race. You connect and enjoy the conversation.

The next time you go to the campaign office, the same volunteer coordinator is there and you have another interesting conversation. On the way out after completing your task, you notice that the volunteer coordinator is packing up to leave. You ask if she would like to go for a coffee sometime and continue the conversation.

When you meet, you buy the coffee because it was your invitation. You mention that you have thought about running to be the student representative on your college's board of directors. The volunteer coordinator reacts enthusiastically and says she might have some advice that would be helpful. You tell her you would really appreciate that and ask if she would meet you for coffee again.

You meet again (and again, you buy the coffee). After you meet, you ask if she would be open to you contacting her again and she says yes. After a while, you feel comfortable calling on your new connection from time to time to ask questions about preparing for your campaign.

Then you notice that your candidate's campaign office is short of volunteers to work the phones. It's a chance for you to return the favor for your new acquaintance. You offer to recruit some of your friends to join the campaign, and you can tell that the volunteer coordinator really appreciates the gesture. You meet and chat from time to time. You have just acquired a mentor.

WHAT A MENTOR IS AND WHAT A MENTOR IS NOT

Mentors guide you and support you, but they do not work magic or do the work to make you a success. They care about your progress and success, but they are not responsible for you. They can open doors of all sorts, but you have to walk through them.

A MENTOR DOES	A MENTOR DOES NOT
Guide you	Work magic
Support you	Make you successful
Care about your progress	Take responsibility for you
Open doors for you	Do the work for you

HOW DO I FIND MENTORS AND ASK THEM FOR HELP?

There are times when you may need or want to be more direct and ask someone to be a mentor. In this case, be prepared to explain what you hope to get from your mentor so they know what's expected and can assess whether or not they have the time or expertise to mentor you.

MENTEE DOS AND DON'TS

DO	DON'T
Be considerate of your mentor's time and set limits on how much of it you ask for: 10 to 15 minutes if it's just a question, or 30 to 60 minutes if you want to go through a more complicated situation.	Be late or overrun your allotted meeting time.
Show appreciation: send a handwritten note or treat your mentor to a coffee, a drink or a lunch.	Take your mentor for granted and assume they are happy to give you an unlimited amount of time or attention.
Make it a two-way street: think of ways you can return the favor. Ask if there's something *you* can do to help and be a "reverse mentor."	Think of it as a tap you turn on and it's there for you whenever you want. Having a mentor is a privilege.
Develop a relationship before you decide if you want someone to be a mentor. Tell them why you think mentoring would help you and why they would be a good fit for what you want to accomplish.	Ask people you've never met or had contact with to be your mentor. If they have indicated — in a presentation, a blog or in some other way — that they are open to such mentoring requests, reference that when you make contact.
Keep your mentor up to date with your progress and tell them how their advice was helpful.	Wait for your mentor to contact you and ask how things are going.

A TWO-WAY STREET

A mentor is generally older and more experienced than the mentee. Reaching out to give a hand up is satisfying, but often, it also provides an

MATCH ME!

If you are having trouble finding mentors on your own, there are programs that will match you with a mentor. These are typically offered by professional associations, business organizations or sometimes civic engagement charities or not-for-profits. Programs usually include an application process to identify your goals, your expectations and your suitability for the program. The process may also involve online training, sometimes as a prerequisite for participating in a mentoring program. In these instances, the mentoring relationship will be in effect over a specified period of time, often for a year, and the organization will provide guidelines on the number of meetings and responsibilities of the mentee and the mentor. See the Deep Dive for tips on researching mentoring programs.

opportunity for the mentor to widen their own understanding of another company, industry or function. If you work in an industry or have experiences of interest to your mentor, you may have skills and training that your mentor is interested in. Are you a social media maven? Do you have an extensive network that you can tap to assist your mentor in something they're working on? Remember to offer your mentor help in an area that you are good at and love to do.

FINDING YOUR PASSION — WHAT DRIVES YOU?

Are you ready to look for leadership opportunities? Good! Then it's time to figure out two or three issues or areas that will become your focus. These are areas that will move you to action.

As a career coach in my own practice and as a coach for Challenge Factory, a company that focuses on the future of work, I helped clients figure out "what's next." Challenge Factory designed a series of exercises to help people find their passions, and I have adapted it for this book.

PASSION PREDICTOR

This exercise helps you find out where you are interested in making an impact by noticing which news stories compel you to read to the end.

1. Buy a newspaper on three different days. (This exercise doesn't work with online versions.)

2. Read all the headlines.

3. Track which articles you read all the way through. Write down the topic of each article in one or two sentences. Then write down what it was that made you read to the end.

   Review the headlines again and look for common areas of interest. Then look at your lists of topics those articles covered. These are your areas of interest. Then try to figure out what it was that made each headline and article so compelling for you. Was there a problem to solve? Do you identify with it in some way? Were you simply curious about the topic?

   As you analyze these articles, think about who solves these problems or creates these opportunities. Are these issues of local, regional, state, federal or national interest? Keep these areas of interest in mind as you think about which level of public office you aspire to.

THINK BIG!

Imagine you could devote the next two years to working on solving any problem or achieving any goal that you feel is worthy of your time — without any other considerations. No barriers to qualification, no one competing for the same role and no obstacles to volunteering because you don't have to earn a salary. All your day-to-day needs are taken care of.

Make a list of three issues you would like to work on — whether local, national or international — and write down what your role would be. Start with very general issues, things such as fairness, equality, environmental sustainability. Then dig deeper and consider what kinds of actions your three chosen issues might require.

For example, when considering the concept of fairness, you could look at fairness in local tax structures: Who decides on policy and how do they arrive at it? Or fairness in educational policies may be your interest, and that could mean primary, secondary or university-level education. Fair access to education might be a focus, or addressing bias in school curriculums. You could also examine your country's criminal justice system or the international justice system for issues of fairness. You can come at the question of fairness from many directions.

KNOW THE PLAYERS

Research your three most compelling topics. Find out more about politicians who are working on these issues and which positions in government relate to them. Look into the issues at the national or local level. Find out more about politics in your town or region of the country and who is responsible for these issues. Or you can think about international roles in different regions of the world or countries that interest you.

DIG DEEPER

Of the three issues you've identified, narrow down to one that most stands out for you.

Is this an issue that is dealt with at the local, national or international level of government? Once you've identified the level of government involved, research three elected positions related to this issue.

As an example, you may have identified the fairness of the judicial system as your wider area of interest. When you drill down, you may discover that the local level, with the role of justice of the peace, holds the most interest. Are justices of the peace elected? What are the qualifications? What is the breadth of responsibility? Likewise, you may go the other way and look at the bigger picture. You might want to learn more about the role of the department of justice. You can see there are many different avenues to explore within one area of interest, in this case, fairness.

FIND THE WAY IN

There are more than 500 000 elected offices in the United States alone. That represents a lot of opportunities to enter public office and advance. The distribution of local, regional and national elected offices looks much like a pyramid, with the local level providing the broadest base and highest number of opportunities narrowing to the fewest and most specialized positions at the federal level. Here's a small sample of roles that fall under various levels of government:

LOCAL	REGIONAL, STATE, PROVINCIAL	NATIONAL
city councillor, animal control officer, public health official, traffic safety commissioner, local road authority, school trustee, justice of the peace, district attorney, judge	governor, lieutenant governor, education policy advisor, health care advisor, highway commissioner, public account/state comptroller, state treasurer, agriculture commissioner, railroad commissioner, attorney general, insurance commissioner, state superintendent of public instruction	Congressional representative, senator, member of Parliament

VOLUNTEERING — GET INVOLVED!

Now that you have an idea of some of the issues you're passionate about, it's time to get involved. One of the most essential ways to prepare for a run for office is to volunteer on a campaign. It's an invaluable opportunity to see up close how things work. It's also a great way to learn the whole process. A key aspect of campaigning — and an area where volunteers are always in great need — is knocking on doors and speaking to people about the campaign. This may seem simple, but repetition is key to learning how to be effective. The same goes for making phone calls and putting up posters and lawn signs. Volunteers who do take on these tasks get to practice making a pitch for the candidate. They also see how the tasks and campaign workers are organized — and they get a good campaign education!

SHOW UP!

When it comes to volunteering for a political party or campaign at any level, the most important thing is to show up. It's really that simple. Campaigns are always looking for assistance, and you will almost certainly be welcomed with open arms. And while you are giving your time to a candidate's campaign, you will meet and connect with people who share your interests and approach to life.

The people you volunteer for will appreciate it, and you'll gain great strategic and tactical information about campaigning.

To find opportunities in your area, do some research. Find out what elections are coming up in your class, student government, athletic society, community or electoral district (for regional, state, provincial or national elections).

In addition to knocking on doors and making calls, there are other ways to get involved. Have you worked on a campaign of any kind before? You may have been the social media manager for your best friend's campaign to become class president. Or you may have been the volunteer scheduler for a friend who ran for election to head the local business improvement council. Don't discount these experiences — they are important stepping stones and confidence builders.

To get involved in a bigger campaign covering a broader area, you can match these experiences and your skills and interests with the roles and tasks that are part of campaigns.

VOLUNTEER-CAMPAIGN MATCHUP

YOUR INTERESTS	YOUR SKILLS	CAMPAIGN ROLE OR AREA
Organizing	You love to organize and plan, you are on time and you get things done. You prioritize tasks, pay your bills on time and keep good files.	SCHEDULER Every campaign needs a really strong scheduler, someone who handles requests for meetings and appearances.
Being active on social media	You are a strong writer, comfortable with different media and love to post on your favorite platforms (and you do it well).	SOCIAL MEDIA MANAGER **Messaging Leader:** Your job is to create the messages, finding new ways to express the key points. **Advertising/Publicity Leader:** Your job is to craft messages for online ads.

Working with people	You are the person who gets chatting to the people on the bus, in the grocery line, in a waiting room. You stay in touch with the people you met on vacation. You are interested to hear what people have to say.	**CANVASSER** Your job is to do the door-knocking that is so essential to a campaign. You may canvass on your own, with a team or with the candidate.
Fundraising	When someone is in need, you are the one who will pass the hat or create a crowdfunding campaign for a cause.	**FUNDRAISER** You use your pitching skills to raise money for the campaign. You will be welcomed with open arms if you have any fundraising experience at all.
Numbers and accounting	You are good at math and love keeping track of money. Your life is organized into spreadsheets and you follow the rules.	**ACCOUNTANT** Your job is to track all donations to ensure they comply with the rules, that money is accounted for and that it is spent on eligible expenses. There's a lot for an accountant to do.
Networking	You have tons of friends and lots of people you stay in touch with, in person and through social media. You are active in the community.	**NETWORKER** Grab the opportunity to leverage your network to spread the word about the candidate and lay the foundation for fundraising. Networking will be essential for politics.

Managing people and projects	You have a detailed study schedule, and you stick to it. You know what to finish when, and you have each step marked on a calendar.	**VOLUNTEER MANAGER** You are the person to take charge of a team of volunteers and keep them on task, making sure teams get out canvassing all areas and that there is follow-up. You will be popular at any campaign headquarters.
Marketing and promotion	You know how to persuade people and get them interested in a product or a service.	**COPYWRITER/GRAPHIC DESIGNER** Every campaign needs materials — slogans, signs, pamphlets, buttons — and you can ensure that the communications are eye-catching, clear and effective.
Following the fine print	Rules and regulations are second nature to you. You never leave a stone unturned.	**COMPLIANCE MANAGER** Chances are your expertise is needed in a variety of areas, including campaign finance and compliance with electoral rules.
Examining the issues	Issues interest you. You might be a news junkie. You read in-depth articles on topics you are interested in. You always want to know why. You go deep, digging out facts and figures to support a point of view.	**POLICY ANALYST** You will help develop the campaign platform. You'll advise which issues to focus on and what approach to take with each.

Researching	For you, nothing is more fun than researching a topic, drilling down into the references and digging out facts and figures to support a point of view.	**RESEARCHER** A researcher's skills will be welcomed when the candidate is preparing for debates, writing articles and developing the policy platform.
Knowing your demographic	You've studied statistics and you really enjoyed it. You know how important it is to tailor your approach to appeal to different groups when you are presenting your case.	**POLLSTER** Polling is an essential part of electoral campaigns. Your understanding of trends and your ability to interpret demographic information will help with campaign strategy and tracking the candidate's position against competitors.
Using technology	You know how every phone model works and how to write and debug computer programs. You also know all the features and capabilities of different programs and platforms.	**TECHNOLOGY MANAGER** Maximizing technology to run a strong and sophisticated campaign is essential. You can be instrumental in giving your candidate the edge.
Strategizing	Chess is your second life. You love making strategies and staying two steps ahead of your opponent. Maybe you have studied business and are involved in writing business plans and strategies through your studies.	**STRATEGIST** You work with the campaign manager and policy analyst to advise on campaign strategy at the beginning of the campaign and as issues arise.

Taking charge	When you're with a group, you're the one who pushes for a decision, gets the group heading in the same direction and feels comfortable taking responsibility. You're thoughtful but unfazed at the prospect of making a mistake. You'll learn and move on.	**CAMPAIGN MANAGER** You are the captain of the team. You make sure that everyone has a responsibility, and you set up a system to ensure they are accountable for getting their tasks done. You are comfortable with strategy but you also focus on execution.

JOIN A PARTY

Getting involved with a local party chapter or organization is a great way to get close to politics, hone your leadership skills and get to know like-minded and influential people. In Canada, for example, each major party (Liberal, Conservative, New Democratic Party, Green Party) has an electoral district association for each federal and provincial riding. In the U.S., there are two major parties (Democratic, Republican) and numerous minor parties (e.g., Libertarian, Green). These parties will likewise have local, state or provincial, and regional associations or offices. The role of the local party organization is to liaise with the national and regional party organizations, recruit members, and oversee the nominations, primary elections and election processes for the area. These groups are run by a local board or executive committee. In larger cities, there may be neighborhood groups, as well.

Identify which areas on the Volunteer–Campaign Matchup chart interest you, then approach the local electoral association and offer your services in those areas. If there is no election campaign in progress, there may still be a need for volunteers. Even between elections, there are ongoing efforts to raise funds, recruit members, publicize the party's policy platform and update members on news, events and ongoing policy development.

COMMUNICATING WITH SKILL

Being good at communicating is not magic. It is the disciplined use of a few basic methods and concepts put into practice over and over. Clear, compelling messages are the primary tool — *what* you communicate. Equally important is *how* you communicate — the words you choose and the platform or medium you use to distribute your message. Strong communication skills will help you deliver the information your voters need to know to understand who you are, what you care about and how your being elected will affect those issues.

It's never too early to start building your communication skills. But it's never too late, either. There are three key ways to build your presence and develop a high profile: networking, social media and public speaking.

NETWORKING

Networking is getting to know people. That sounds easy, and often it is, especially if you are naturally outgoing. But in a campaign context, it's also a strategic necessity. Networking works on multiple levels — personal, professional, political and local — and in an election campaign, you will use them all.

Personal: Chances are you have already developed a sizable personal network through your friendships and social media platforms. Your network will comprise your friends, family, acquaintances, friends of friends and neighbors.

Professional: If you work during the school year or over the summer, or if you are already into your career, you will be developing a professional network of people, including coworkers, clients, suppliers and other business contacts.

Political: If you have volunteered on a political campaign or joined a party (you should!), you will establish a political network and build a strong base of support for whatever kind of elected position you aspire to. Your political network will include people with experience in political strategy and campaign tactics. You might eventually draw a good part of your campaign team from this network.

Local: If you've ever volunteered at your local community center, participated in a neighborhood program or a local initiative, joined a campaign to save historic homes or attended a local place of worship, then you are also developing a community network.

Effective networking means building relationships, not just collecting names, likes and social media connections (although those are good, too). It's about connecting in person and engaging in conversations at events. People you meet through networking will not all become your best friends, but many friendships do develop out of networking.

Are there rules for networking? Here are some guidelines to help you excel at networking, as well as some pitfalls.

NETWORKING DOS AND DON'TS

Do:

- take a genuine interest in the people you meet
- ask questions
- listen carefully to find areas of common ground
- offer to make appropriate connections or follow up with information of interest to the other person
- follow through on any promises you make to call, send information or make an introduction
- find a way to reach out to your connections once in a while to say hello, pass news along or send a link to something interesting
- ask for connections or information to help you achieve your goals

Don't:

- nod at someone speaking to you while you scan the room looking for people you want to meet
- talk nonstop about yourself and your needs
- jump in to make a point every time there is a pause
- ask for favors without ever offering to help in return
- promise what you can't — or aren't planning to — deliver; it's better for your personal reputation not to offer than to offer and fail to deliver
- expect someone you have met or connected with only once or twice to do you a favor years later
- bombard your contacts with requests for introductions or information, or reach out only when you want something

Building and maintaining a network takes some organization and effort, but you can develop a few habits to make it easier. Whatever platform you choose, review it regularly. When you see an article you think might interest one of your friends or contacts, send them a quick note with a link. Touch base with people from time to time. Let them know when something important happens in your life or career, or ask how they are doing or how a project is coming along.

While all this is useful for politics, it will enrich your life and broaden your horizons, too.

SOCIAL MEDIA

The social media skills you use to keep in touch with your friends can be put to good use in building your profile ahead of or during an election campaign.

Many experts recommend that you create multiple pages on social media platforms: a private one for your usual personal updates to friends and family and a more measured and thoughtful public channel to show the world your thoughts and ideas about your community and the world around you.

But even if you do this, there is a hitch: everything you put on social media is public and can be shared with the world. So, if you have political aspirations, review your personal social media strategy. Don't post photos, information or opinions that you don't want the whole world to know about.

Here are some of the many things you do want on your public platform:

- links to articles on issues you care about
- posts on issues you find interesting
- insightful shares and comments on important issues
- updates on political events, community meetings or talks you attended
- requests for feedback on key issues

The pace at which you initially post sets expectations for those who are following you. So, if you think you can manage to contribute something to your profile once a week, start there rather than opening with a flurry of activity that dwindles to nothing. And when you choose to post or comment on something, it's important to maintain a presence once you start.

PUBLIC SPEAKING

Is it possible to be more afraid of public speaking than dying? Not really, but it may feel like that sometimes, so let's look at how to master this important personal communication skill.

Public speaking is an essential form of communication in election campaigns. Throughout a campaign, you will speak to groups of supporters and potential voters. Once you are in government, there are specific times when you debate bills publicly or question the government on issues. And there are often media interviews, as well.

Good public speaking can be learned, even if you are shy or not a natural. And even if you are a rookie speaker, with a few tips and a little practice, you will get better and find it more enjoyable. After all, you speak in front of others all the time. When you answer questions in class or ask a question at a community meeting, that is a form of public speaking. When you are asked your opinion at the dinner table or when you say something about a friend at her birthday party, propose a toast to someone or plan a play strategy with your soccer teammates, those are also forms of public speaking. So you've already had some practice.

There are many different kinds of public speaking, but they all use the same basic principles.

EIGHT PRINCIPLES OF PUBLIC SPEAKING

1. Understand your audience. Before the day of your speech, find out who you will be speaking to. How many people will there be? Are they expecting a formal speech, a casual chat or an opportunity to ask questions? Why are they coming to hear you speak? What are their main interests and concerns, and how can you best address them?

2. Focus on a maximum of three messages that speak to your audience. People can't generally absorb more than three main ideas in one sitting. Use plenty of examples to illustrate each message, and spend time building up to them.

3. Less is more. Attention spans are short and people get distracted during a long speech. Don't overstay your welcome on the podium.

4. Storytelling is an effective way to illustrate key messages. Use statistics

sparingly and only when they are needed to illustrate a point. For example, talking about a young boy who has a permanent disability because he didn't have access to proper health care in the rural area where he lives will be far more memorable than quoting statistics about the ratio of physicians to population size.

5. Be authentic. You can tailor your message to your audience, but you shouldn't try to change who you are. Don't adopt the speech patterns or dialect of you audience, and don't pretend to be someone you're not. You can relate to people without becoming whatever you think the audience wants.

6. If you feel nervous, focus on your message, not on your delivery. If you stumble, don't dwell on it, just carry on. The less attention you pay to a mispronounced word or a hesitation, the less the audience will pay attention.

7. Don't rush! If time is short, shorten your remarks, but don't speed talk. And don't be afraid to pause confidently. This can be very effective as the audience will wait attentively to hear what you are about to say.

8. Practice your speech aloud several times. Reword any bits that you consistently stumble on. Record it and play it back to yourself to see how it sounds. Does it flow or are there awkward spots? Or practice it with a trusted friend or mentor.

THREE ELEMENTS TO A SPEECH OR PRESENTATION

Whether you are giving a formal presentation with a detailed, written speech or an informal address from brief notes, you will likely use the same three elements: introduction, messaging and conclusion.

1. **Introduction:** Thank the person who introduced you and the event organizer (a person or organization). Address the audience and acknowledge any important people in the audience. (Find out who will be there in advance and be sure to use the correct form of address for members of government, such as *Honorable*, *Right Honorable*, *Minister*, *Senator*, *Congresswoman*.) Include a remark that is specific to the audience or location you are addressing.

STRUCTURE THE MESSAGING

Many public speakers follow this simple format for the messaging part of their speech:

1. Tell them what you are going to tell them. Briefly outline your key messages.
2. Tell them what you want to tell them. Explain those messages in detail.
3. Tell them what you just told them. Recap your message in a brief summary.

SCENARIO:

Imagine you are speaking to a group of seniors in your electoral district. You have a policy in your platform that directly affects them. Here is how you might get across one of your messages:

1. Tell them what you are going to tell them: "I'd like to speak to you today about an important issue that stands at the center of my platform and that is increasing the supply of affordable seniors' housing by 10 percent within three years."
2. Tell them your message: "Anna is 89 years old and worked all her life, paying taxes and contributing to the pension plan. She never married, lived frugally and saved all she could. But now, while she is in good health for her age, she lives in a tiny rundown apartment and cannot afford the necessities of life. She often doesn't have enough to eat. Anna doesn't need the support services of a nursing home, she can't afford a private retirement residence and she doesn't have enough money to properly house and feed herself independently, so she lives in poverty. If I am elected, I will [outline details of your policy] to address the issue. No one in our society who has made that kind of contribution should be left to wither in poverty in their final years."
3. Tell them what you just told them: "We need to take action on affordable housing for seniors now, and if elected, I will increase affordable housing for seniors by 10 percent within three years."

2. **Messaging:** Present your three main messages. You may begin this way: "There are three important things I want to talk about today: 1._____ 2._____ and 3._____." Then you start on your first message. When you have finished delivering your first message, repeat your main point briefly. Do the same for the second and third messages. (See "Structure the Messaging" sidebar for more tips.)

3. **Conclusion:** Wrap up your speech. Remind the audience why your messages are important. You may want to do a brief recap. Be sure to thank the organizers again and the audience for their attention. And finally, make your "ask." What is an "ask"? Here is an example: "On Election Day, I encourage all of you to come out and vote. And when you decide whose name you will put an X beside, choose the candidate who stands for affordable housing. You can count on me and I hope I can count on you on [date of election]."

WRITTEN SCRIPT OR BULLET POINTS?

Some speakers work from a written speech and deliver it word for word, and others speak from a few notes or a list of key points, more like an outline. Work with the format you are most comfortable with. You might choose different options for different settings. These guidelines will help you assess which approach makes the most sense for different people, comfort levels and situations.

Use a written script when ...

- time is tightly managed. Sticking to a script helps you be more exact with your timing.
- the presentation is long, especially if it is a formal occasion. Scripting a long address will help you keep things in proper sequence and ensure details aren't lost.

Use bullet points when ...

- you have some leeway with the time and you know your material well enough that you can tailor your remarks to fit the time slot.
- the presentation is short or the situation is informal, and you can remember the details and keep the presentation in order.

- you are a fluent reader and stumble less when you read a script.
- your speech is on a topic that is new or not familiar. You want a structured presentation to ensure you get it right.
- you find that with practice, you can make your speech seem fresh and it's not obvious that you are reading.

- you have trouble reading fluently and might stumble when you have to try to stick to exact wording.
- the speech topic is in your wheelhouse and you are totally comfortable with the material. Using bullet points helps you keep your delivery fresh.
- you find that no matter how much you try, your delivery is a bit stiff when you speak from a written script.

IF YOU STUMBLE, CARRY ON

Canadian senator Pamela Wallin, formerly a national television news anchor, shared an experience that proves the value of just carrying on. When she was hosting the national news, she mispronounced German chancellor Helmut Schmidt's name, leaving out the *m* as the show was about to go to a commercial break. The instant the red light went off, indicating they were off air, she collapsed, stricken, convinced that her career as a journalist and broadcaster was over. Then she realized the cameraman and other members of the crew were laughing uproariously. They all assured her that her career was still intact and that she should just carry on with the newscast. And her boss told her that no one would believe that she had cursed on air. It turned out that listeners, expecting her to say "Schmidt," didn't believe their own ears and assumed she had pronounced his last name correctly. It was a complete nonissue and an important lesson learned about carrying on.

BEING AUTHENTIC

We know being authentic is important, but how do you know if you are doing it? Here are some examples of how being authentic and inauthentic can look:

Authentic	**Inauthentic**
Regardless of where or to whom you're speaking, you deliver your messages in a way that is natural to you, in language you are comfortable with. You are relevant to the audience in terms of what you say, not by changing your presentation or speaking style.	When speaking to an audience that intimidates you — perhaps a room filled with academics and experts — you use lots of long and unusual words. You end up trying to convince the audience you are as smart as they are, instead of communicating your message.
You wear an outfit that reflects your style, makes you feel confident and is appropriate for the occasion.	You don't like suits, but you read that "power suits" will make you look like a powerful person, so you wear one. But it doesn't feel like you.
You're one of those people who gestures with your hands when you talk — a lot. It's natural. Be mindful that you don't knock anything over while you are at the podium, but don't try to lock your arms at your sides or change the way you gesture to make a point.	You choreograph every hand gesture you are going to use to emphasize precise points in your speech or presentation. You think this will make you look more professional. But it doesn't look natural to the audience, and you end up being distracted by trying to get every motion exactly right.
You stand naturally and don't pose at the podium. Over the years, family members and teachers may have told you to stand up straight. They have a point — slouching can convey a lack of confidence. But don't be stiff and unnatural.	You think walking with confidence means standing tall, thrusting your shoulders back and striding up to the podium. If this isn't your natural walk, you may look more like a drill sergeant closing in on a misbehaving cadet than an inviting speaker with an interesting message.

SECTION 2.0

GETTING STARTED

YOUR 12-STEP CAMPAIGN PLAN WORKBOOK

STEP 1

ASSESS AND BUILD YOUR SUPPORT SYSTEM

DECIDE YOU'RE INTERESTED IN RUNNING!

This is the most important step of all. You feel ready and confident. You've thought it through and now you're ready to go!

FIND A TRUSTED SUPPORTER

Now that you've decided to run, you need someone you can trust, someone who really supports you and believes in you as a candidate, to help you figure out some important next steps. It could be a close friend, a member of your family or someone you have met through your community activities or campaign volunteering. This person should be someone you can be honest with in moments of doubt as well as when things are going well. Pick someone who will be honest with you, too — who will push you when you need a nudge and encourage you when the going gets tough. This is the person you will lean on, particularly as you get started. You can be casual about the arrangement and ask if they would mind being a sounding board for you as you develop your ideas and run your campaign, as needed. Or you could make it a more structured arrangement and ask if they would be an advisor and meet with you regularly.

FIND AN ORGANIZATION THAT SUPPORTS WOMEN CANDIDATES (AND FIRST-TIME CANDIDATES)

There are organizations that provide campaign training, coaching and mentors. If you can't find one in your area, excellent training programs are available online. Check the list of organizations and programs in the Deep Dive section.

STEP 2

IDENTIFY THE ISSUES THAT MATTER MOST TO YOU

DECIDE WHAT TO RUN FOR

There are several steps to deciding what office to run for and making sure you have all the necessary information.

1. Here's an expanded list of functions and areas of interest to help you define your political focus. Build on the information you developed in the earlier section "Finding Your Passion — What Drives You?"

    - Agriculture
    - Animal welfare
    - Anti-terrorism
    - Arts
    - Business
    - Childcare
    - Democratic engagement
    - Democratic reform
    - Education (quality, accessibility, curriculum)
    - Elder care and aging
    - Energy policy
    - Entrepreneurship
    - Environmental policy
    - Environmental programs
    - Financial management
    - Fiscal policy (government)
    - Food safety
    - Food supply
    - Gender rights/gender identity
    - Health care delivery
    - Homelessness
    - Housing policy
    - Human rights
    - Inclusiveness
    - International relations
    - Justice
    - Legal reform
    - LGBTQ issues
    - Military defense/security
    - Military strategy
    - Privacy and security
    - Public health policy
    - Racial equality

- Road traffic
- Scientific research and advancement
- Student rights
- Technology
- Transportation
- Urban planning/renewal
- Violence against women
- Water safety and supply
- Women's rights/advancement

2. Once you've reviewed the list, write down the top five areas of interest in order of priority. If considering running for government, research which level (local, regional or national) oversees each of those areas. Determine which level of government gives you the best opportunity to have an impact on the issues you are most passionate about.

    If you are running for a school position, find the issues that are relevant to the student population or school board. The issues will be fewer. Pick one or two that are relevant and that you are interested in.

3. Is there a jurisdiction that controls more than one of your key interests? If so, what level of government is it?

4. When is the next election for the district/jurisdiction you are interested in? Is there an upcoming election, a special election or by-election (held to fill a vacancy that has arisen since the last election)?

5. How much lead time do you realistically need for this election? If you're not sure, research how much time other candidates for similar elections spent campaigning and when they announced that they were running.

    If you don't feel you have enough lead time, consider picking another top area of interest within a different jurisdiction and determine the timing of that election process. Look for the best match between an area of interest and the timing of the election process.

CONCLUSION

Write down your goal: I will run for ______________________________ (office) in ______________________________ (jurisdiction).

Now you know what office you will be running for!

STEP 3

LEARN THE LOCAL RULES AND REGULATIONS

MAKE SURE YOU QUALIFY

Some jurisdictions may have restrictions on who can run, so check to make sure you can be a candidate. Requirements may cover:

- citizenship
- age
- residency (you may need to live in the jurisdiction)
- financial status (bankruptcies and debt issues)
- party affiliation (length of time as a party member)

In the Deep Dive, you will find a list of electoral bodies and commissions that will list the specific qualifications you need to meet in order to run. Sometimes this information is also available on the government website for the jurisdiction you are interested in.

STEP 4

CONSIDER YOUR FUNDING

KNOW THE RULES ABOUT CAMPAIGNING FINANCES

Before you start campaigning and fundraising in a jurisdiction, find out what the rules are about:

- accounting (candidates may need to use a professionally accredited accountant)
- individual donation limits
- corporate donation regulations
- conflict of interest issues

Will you need to create and register your campaign as a legal entity for banking, compliance and reporting? Check with the local electoral body to find out. If you do need to do this and you need assistance or advice, organizations that support first-time or women candidates may be able to help. (See the Deep Dive for recommendations.)

STEP 5

LEARN ABOUT THE OFFICE AND JURISDICTION

SCAN THE POLITICAL ENVIRONMENT

Identify who won the position you are seeking in the last three elections. Study their campaigns and identify the main factors that got them elected. What do media reports say? What do your politically active connections tell you? Write up your analysis.

Does a particular political party or orientation (left, right, center, independent) prevail in the jurisdiction you are interested in? If so, what does that trend tell you? Does it align with your perspective on the issues you're interested in building your platform on? If yes, that makes your path easier. But if no, don't be put off. You *can* buck the trend and unseat an incumbent if you run a strong campaign. But if you'd rather not enter a partisan battle right off the bat, look for other options for running that might align more closely with your views. Then consider which opportunity you want to focus on.

STEP 6

LEARN ABOUT THE VOTERS

IDENTIFY THE VOTERS

If you are running for public office, you can get a voter list for the district from the applicable electoral commission or government website. In some areas, these will be available for free, but in others, you may have to pay for the list. If it's not free, you could ask a candidate from a previous election for their list. You may also purchase the voter list from a company that specializes in lists and voter demographics. These voter lists will provide useful information, such as:

- demographic make-up of the electorate (age, gender, occupation, ideology, religion, ethnicity, socio-economic status)
- voter turnout rates (percentage of eligible voters to cast a vote in the last election)

The people who actually vote are the people you need to target first. Then work on the people you need to convince to come out and vote.

For school elections, much of the campaigning will be done directly during school hours, but speak to the principal or administrative office to find out if there is a student list that you are permitted to have access to.

STEP 7

LEARN ABOUT THE POLITICAL VIPs

IDENTIFY THE INFLUENCERS AND DECISION MAKERS

To win a campaign, you need to have as many influential voters on your side as possible. They can only vote once, but their impact is multiplied by the influence they have on circles within the community. They can even lead a voting trend.

HOW TO IDENTIFY INFLUENCERS

Identifying influencers involves a similar process, whatever and wherever the race. Influencers are the people whose names come up in conversation and in news reports, those whom other people refer to, who blog, write articles or letters to the editor, who start committees, who are leaders in your school, community or electoral district. These influencers may be leaders of the local chapter of a political party, municipal officials, riding or electoral district heads or political committee leaders. They might also be local business leaders or media personalities (e.g., journalists, DJs or news anchors) or politically active local celebrities or religious leaders. Younger influencers will have many followers on Facebook, Twitter, Instagram and other platforms.

Find out who is active locally and in political parties. Who has managed election campaigns before? The best way to do that is to speak to people you know who are politically connected or to research candidates whose campaigns you were impressed by. The names of campaign managers will often be included in news reports.

Also, find out who has a history of making political contributions in your area or to your party. In most jurisdictions, campaigns are required to file a list of donors above a minimum threshold (which will vary by jurisdiction) so you can see who gives how much to whom. This information can be found at the electoral commission of your municipality, region, state, province or country, or on the government website for the jurisdiction you are interested in.

Keep a list of as many influencers as you can identify, and include people you've only heard about as well as those you may already know.

STEP 8

ASSEMBLE YOUR TEAM

PUT TOGETHER THE "KITCHEN CABINET"

By this point, you have already found one key person who you can confide in. Now it's time to add a few more people to your trusted inner circle. Of course, you want these to be people who you trust. But they should also have experience and skills that complement yours. These are the people in whom you can confide your hopes and fears, the people you can ask for second opinions on strategy, and with whom you can discuss your platform before you make any final decisions with your whole campaign team.

BUILD YOUR CORE CAMPAIGN TEAM

If you are running for a school position or a community organization, you may only need a small group of volunteers to help you, with each person taking on multiple responsibilities. However, most campaigns will require a larger, well-structured team, with each person given specific responsibilities. There are many ways to organize this kind of team, but it will include the following key roles, with additional roles required for larger campaigns.

CAMPAIGN MANAGER

If you only have one person devoted to your campaign, this is who you need. A campaign manager oversees all the operations — administration, coordination, compliance with rules — to ensure the candidate can focus on being the face of the campaign and connecting with voters. On large campaigns, the campaign manager will be supported by:

- a deputy campaign manager, who acts as second-in-command to the campaign manager, and
- a field director, who obtains voter lists and does advance work in preparation for the candidate's voter outreach.

On a regional or national campaign with multiple offices, a field director also will run the local offices.

VOLUNTEER MANAGER

The volunteer manager recruits and organizes volunteers. Making sure the canvassers are out door-knocking, while campaign signs are hammered in the ground and phones are kept busy.

FUNDRAISER AND ACCOUNTANT

Finance and fundraising are two separate functions but they are often grouped together in smaller campaigns. The fundraiser's job is to manage the process of fundraising, set goals, and recruit and manage additional fundraisers. Finance entails ensuring that campaign donations are recorded and records are submitted as required by local election rules. Other roles in this area may include:

- a finance committee in charge of securing major corporate donations,
- an accountant to track donations and expenditures, and
- legal advisors to ensure compliance with all campaign donation laws, who work with the fundraising team, meet information filing deadlines, and are responsible for adherence to campaigning and voting rules.

TECHNOLOGY MANAGER

The technology manager (sometimes called the chief information officer) makes sure information systems are in place and that they work. When there are multiple offices and tens of thousands or even hundreds of thousands of voters, effective use of technology keeps the campaign on course, tracks voter outreach and efficiently shares information within the campaign. Even in small campaigns, it is useful to have someone to set up and troubleshoot computer software and equipment.

ANALYST, RESEARCHER, STRATEGIST, POLLSTER

In big campaigns, managers are often hired to develop policy and strategy. In smaller campaigns, a candidate may huddle with a key advisor and assign volunteers to research key campaign issues.

COMMUNICATIONS MANAGER

From campaign flyers and door hangers to social media posts, blogs, ads, policy statements and speeches, there is a lot of writing to be done on any campaign! The communications manager will write, or oversee the writing of, all the material produced for your campaign.

Larger campaigns will also have a press secretary or public relations manager who is responsible for ensuring that the candidate is always presented in a good light. This person looks for publicity opportunities, handles interview requests and manages press conferences.

ELECTION AGENT

In almost all political campaigns, no matter how you organize your team, you or someone you appoint will need to file information on election expenses. In Canada, the U.K., India, Australia and New Zealand, this is called an official agent. In the U.S., the candidate appoints someone within the campaign team to cover these tasks.

STEP 9

BUILD YOUR CAMPAIGN PLATFORM

UNDERSTAND THE NEEDS OF YOUR VOTERS

List at least three of the most important issues in the area where you want to run (school, community or district).

Now, compare your areas of highest interest from Step 2 with the issues most important to your voters. Where are the similarities? Make a list matching your areas of interest with important campaign issues.

Use what you have just learned to identify three problems you want to solve in the school, community or district. State the strategies you could use to solve each problem, with a list of specific tactics (within the power of the office you are running for).

DEVELOP A PLATFORM

Example:

1. **State the issue:**

   The cafeteria does not manage the issue of food allergies.

2. **Develop your position in a short paper:**

   Specify the problems around food allergies (e.g., not having a nut-free prep area creates risk of contamination; not labeling products for common allergens, like gluten or lactose, reduces food options). Tell a story about a student who had a serious allergic reaction to illustrate the danger. Explain the impact this has by indicating how many students have allergies (or use rates in the general population). Tell how the school administration has not done anything about it. Emphasize the need to go beyond school officials to get results. Communicate your goal: to improve food safety for students with food allergies.

   (Identify for yourself what emotion your argument appeals to, e.g., the desire for safety and well-being.)

3. **Outline your three strategies:**

   Strategy #1: Put pressure on the food-service company.

   Tactics:

   a) Research the food service company so you have all the facts.
   b) Contact the company directly and outline the deficiencies.
   c) Start a social media campaign highlighting the potentially deadly consequences and estimate the number at risk.
   d) Propose improvements.

Strategy #2: Put pressure on the school board.

Tactics:

a) Research the board's responsibilities.
b) Write a formal letter of complaint to the board, explaining the deficiencies in the cafeteria and urging it to uphold its responsibility to provide a safe environment for students with food allergies.
c) Support the letter of complaint with social media posts.

Strategy #3: Mobilize students to complain and protest.

Tactics:

a) Discuss the issue with students, especially those affected.
b) Hand out pamphlets explaining how food service needs to be improved.
c) Organize a rally (and livestream, blog or post photos about it).
d) Urge students to write letters to the food company and the school board.
e) Start an online petition.

Your articulation of the issues and how you propose to deal with them essentially form your campaign platform. You won't necessarily talk about all these strategies and tactics in detail every time you make a speech or reach out to people, but you have thought them through, so that when questioned, you will be confident and knowledgeable in your answers. Voters will see your competence.

STEP 10

FRAME YOUR CORE MESSAGES

CREATE YOUR CORE CAMPAIGN MESSAGES

Great core campaign messages are simple to understand, relate to your campaign platform and appeal to voters' emotions. They also make you stand out from your opponent.

Core messages not only tell voters *what* you stand for but compellingly tell them *why* they should vote for you. And to have the greatest chance of convincing them that you are the best candidate, your messages must appeal to emotions, which most affect voter preference. These messages and how you deliver them will create a perception about you, and it's that perception that will drive voter decisions.

For instance, during his first campaign for the U.S. presidency, one of Barack Obama's core campaign messages was "Yes we can."

Underlying that slogan was a message of hope, that life could be better under his leadership. There were specific policies in his campaign platform that explained how he proposed to achieve a better, more inclusive future, including universal health care and a move toward energy independence.

USING VALUES AND EMOTIONS TO SHAPE YOUR MESSAGE

To frame your core messages, consider the values and emotions you want to appeal to. No matter what issue you are addressing, you will want to appeal to at least one of these feelings:

1. Safety and security: People want to feel free from harm, whether it's harm caused by other people (e.g., violence) or the environment (e.g., unsafe drinking water, pollution or uncontrolled wildfires).

2. Financial well-being: This means the ability to earn a living, have reasonable

job security and save sufficiently for education, family and retirement.

3. Physical and emotional health: This means access to health care and an adequate supply of food and water to support good nutrition. It also includes programs such as government health insurance.

4. A belief in integrity of others: The ethical beliefs of politicians and the actions that those beliefs inform give voters confidence that their leaders will take the jurisdiction in a defensible direction.

5. Hope: Believing in a better future is one of the most powerful emotions. It speaks both to your own life and to that of your children and grandchildren.

A NOTE ABOUT FEAR

A discouraging but important reality is that negative emotions — like anger and fear — are often more motivating than positive emotions. Anger about an issue will prompt voters to look for more information, get more engaged. This could be anger over increased taxes, reduced school funding, a cut in social services to the disabled or the watering down of environmental protection regulations.

Some candidates blast a constant stream of fear-inciting messages to engage voters. Be aware of this and decide how and when to use negative emotions in your core messages.

USING PRACTICAL AND EMOTION-BASED MESSAGES

Here is an example of how a core message in a run for city councillor might be framed. Increased pedestrian safety is a key part of the candidate's platform.

Issue: A busy road is a danger to pedestrians, especially children going to and from school. Traffic tie-ups are almost constant.

Proposed action: To install pedestrian crossings at high-accident locations.

Opponent's position: To improve commuting times by upgrading traffic signals.

Practical message: I, [candidate name], will take action to keep your family safe by putting in pedestrian crossings where children need them.

Positive emotion–based message: I, [candidate name], care about you and your children, and I will be the one who keeps you safe.

Negative emotion–based message: Children have been injured and killed walking to school. Don't let this happen to your child.

How the message differentiates the candidate from their opponent(s): The other candidate is focused on easing the traffic congestion, making commutes faster, not on safety.

Now look at some issues that are important to you and choose one. Think about how you might craft your messages and how those messages would play out in a campaign by following these steps:

a) Write down the issue.

b) Propose an action in response.

c) Identify your opponent's position.

d) Craft your message. Include a:
   - practical message
   - positive emotion–based message
   - negative emotion–based message

e) Relate your message to your platform.

f) Differentiate your message from that of the other candidate(s).

A useful tool to develop your core messages is called a "message box." It can help you and your team see issues from different perspectives.

To make your message box, draw a large square on a sheet of paper and draw vertical and horizontal lines to create four quadrants.

Take the issue of road safety for children described above. Here's how you might fill out the message box to develop a core message. This method allows you to consider your messaging from your own angle as well as that of your opponent(s). That's how you know it will stand up to scrutiny when you use it.

PERSPECTIVE 1	PERSPECTIVE 2
***Our* view on *our* position** We are the ones who care about the safety of children by proposing new crossings so that children are protected when crossing busy streets.	***Their* view on *their* position** We are taking the practical approach to road safety. Fewer stops means less frustration and safer driving habits. That is what keeps children safe.
PERSPECTIVE 3	**PERSPECTIVE 4**
***Our* view on *their* position** They care about cars and drivers and are willing to sacrifice the safety of children to reduce commute times.	***Their* view on *our* position** They are just going to make your commute longer with unnecessary and ineffective traffic stops for crossings. We are attacking the root of the problem — driver frustration.

Now it's your turn. Start with one issue. Fill in the first quadrant (Perspective 1) in the message box by writing a few short, clear phrases or ideas. Review the quadrant and only keep the phrases or ideas that you feel best reflect its perspective.

Shift perspective now and think about what your opponent is saying about her or his campaign (Perspective 2). Then think about what you would say about their campaign (Perspective 3). And finally think about what your opponent would say about your campaign (Perspective 4). This helps you spot strengths and weaknesses in your messaging and your opponent's messaging.

For each of your own messages, identify the platform items or campaign promises that support the message. Now, reframe your core message three ways so that you appeal to each of these states:

1. hope, security, happiness, optimism, etc. (positive emotions)

2. anger, fear, insecurity, pessimism, etc. (negative emotions)

3. fairness, integrity, peace and harmony, social and environmental responsibility, etc. (social values)

You now have your core messages and have created different ways to communicate them.

STEP 11

HANDLE THE FINANCES

FUNDRAISING PAPERWORK AND PROCESS

Before you ask for or accept your first campaign contribution, make sure you have all the paperwork in place to handle campaign funds.

A political campaign finances checklist:

☑ Set up a separate bank account. You'll need to keep campaign funds apart from your personal money.

☑ Find a professional accountant or bookkeeper skilled at accounting to track donations and expenditures. Depending on the election laws where you are running, you'll need to file this information with an election commission or be prepared to produce it when asked.

☑ Decide whether you will handle banking yourself or authorize someone to act on your behalf. Larger campaigns have staff handling all financial and fundraising matters.

BEGIN FUNDRAISING

As soon as you have the paperwork set up, begin fundraising. Start with close friends and family, as they are most likely to support you. Plus, you can practice your pitch on them to gain confidence for larger asks.

DETERMINE HOW MUCH MONEY YOU NEED

This is a big question and vital to your success. The candidate who raises and spends the most money doesn't necessarily win, but you do need to raise enough money to be competitive. And that means you need to estimate your expenses. To start, find out what is typical in your area for the type of election you are considering.

TYPE OF ELECTION	NATIONAL/FEDERAL	PRESIDENTIAL/PRIME MINISTERIAL CAMPAIGN COST
U.S.	Average of all House of Representatives races: $202 338 Senate $569 846[1] Top 10 House of Representatives avg. $9.5 million each Top 10 Senate campaigns avg. $13.1 million each[2]	2016 election: $768 million Hillary Clinton; $398 million Donald Trump[1] When spending by parties and others is added, the figures are $1.2 billion and $647 million respectively.[2]
U.K.	2017 election: $45 214 USD average for Conservatives and Labour[3]	
Canada	$55 334–$65 000 USD[4]	2015 election: $99 900 USD Campaign for Justin Trudeau's seat in Papineau, QC[4]
France	Candidates for National Assembly are limited to around $45 000 USD plus around $0.17 per inhabitant in the district.[5]	$25.6 million USD max.[5]
Germany	Parties pay campaign costs. Total campaign costs of approx. $83 million USD, averaging $138 000 USD per seat.[6]	
New Zealand	Limit of $36 372 (half from candidate, half from the party)[7]	

All figures in U.S. dollars

1. www.opensecrets.org/overview/index.php?cycle=2016&type=A&display=A
2. www.opensecrets.org
3. www.electoralcommission.org.uk
4. www.elections.ca
5. www.assemblee-nationale.fr
6. www.theatlantic.com/international/archive/2013/09/why-germany-s-politics-are-much-saner-cheaper-and-nicer-than-ours/280081/
7. www.parliament.nz

STACKING UP THE COSTS: HOW MUCH MONEY DOES A CAMPAIGN NEED?

Costs vary. You can begin your research on campaign spending for different types of elections by following the instructions below.

United States

Federal elections

To find out how much was spent by a previous candidate:

- Go to Federal Election Commission (www.fec.gov)
- Click on menu at left of screen at the top
- Choose "Campaign finance data"
- Under "Explore all data," click "Spending"
- Under "Browse data," click "Candidates"
- Choose the category you wish to explore: "All Candidates," "Presidential Candidates," "Senate Candidates," "House of Representatives Candidates," "Most Recent Statements of Candidacy (Form 2)"
- Search for the candidate you are interested in and you will be given choices about what kind of information you wish to explore

State elections

Open Secrets, the website for the Center for Responsive Government, provides information on money raised by candidates and outside organizations. It can help you get an accurate idea of how much in total has been spent to elect a candidate. To search for expenditures and funds raised through www.opensecrets.org:

- Go to the home page.
- Enter jurisdiction in search window, i.e., Ohio.
- Then choose which election cycle you want to look at, and it will list the candidates and how much money they raised.

Some states have their own elections information websites. For example, if you want to find out how much money was raised by a candidate in New York State, you could search the state website. It will have information that includes county elections in addition to Senate and Congress elections:

- Go to www.elections.ny.gov and see the wide range of information available from the Campaign Finance FAQs, Treasurer/Candidate Duties, Handbook, Forms and Publications sections.

Canada

Elections Canada has all the spending reports for federal candidates (www.elections.ca). For local elections, you can identify the location you are interested in and go to the website for that town or electoral district. There should be several years of records for you to search.

In most cases, information is available to the public on how much was spent on campaigns in your local community or region and on larger (e.g., national) campaigns.

School campaigns

For school campaigns, the money required should be minimal and will probably be limited to copying pamphlets and perhaps a campaign button or a few signs.

How do campaign costs compare?

In Canada: In the 2015 election, the average cost of a campaign to become a federal member of Parliament ranged from $12 642 for Green Party candidates up to $90 665 for Conservative candidates. The party that won a majority, the Liberals, spent an average of $71 660 per campaign while third-place NDP candidates spent an average of $54 404. — CBC News

In the U.K. as of 2015, the cost to run for member of Parliament runs upward of 30 000 GBP, while a 2006 study of Conservative candidates pegged the average for that party as 42 000 GBP. — *New Statesman*

The U.S. tops the list when it comes to how much you need to spend to get elected. The average cost of running for U.S. Senate in 2016 was more than $10 million and can run as high as $50 million. For the House of Representatives, it was more than $1.5 million. And that doesn't include spending by outside groups, known as PACs (political action committees) or super PACs. — OpenSecrets.org

Besides fundraising, how can I finance my campaign?

In some jurisdictions, there may be money available to subsidize campaigns. This could include:

- tax credits where citizens who donate to a political campaign or party can get a full or partial tax refund
- programs in which each citizen in the electorate receives a voucher they can give to any candidate and which the candidate then redeems for campaign funds
- grants that provide a lump sum for political campaigns, often limiting the campaign spending to that amount
- small donor matching programs that match the money donated to a campaign by individuals, often in ratios of up to 6:1 (e.g., New York City), whereby a $10 donation from an individual to the campaign triggers a $600 donation from a public fund

UNDERSTAND WHERE THE MONEY COMES FROM AND YOUR FINANCIAL OBLIGATIONS

WHOSE MONEY IS IT? DO I HAVE TO PERSONALLY GUARANTEE THE MONEY? DO I NEED TO USE MY HOUSE, CAR OR OTHER ASSETS AS SECURITY?

The answers vary from jurisdiction to jurisdiction. You can find out what the rules are from your local political party association or someone in your political network. However, the general principle is that you raise money from donations and from loans from your associated party or party association. In some cases, your party or supporters will be allowed to cosign a loan, which helps you get the money from financial institutions without using your house or other assets as collateral, and it motivates your cosigner to help you raise the funds to pay it back. But it's still a loan, and you are still responsible to repay it. Fundraising will often continue after the election to pay off campaign debts, even for unsuccessful candidates, so the election is not always the end of the effort.

Some candidates contribute their own funds, but that is not necessary in most cases (and in some jurisdictions, it is not allowed). If you cannot afford to put your own money into the campaign, work with experienced fundraisers to put you on solid footing financially.

CAMPAIGN ON YOUR BUDGET

With your campaign manager, work out how much your campaign budget will be, how you will raise funds (from a list of potential donors, loans, etc.) and what you are going to spend it on. Ensure that the campaign manager or finance manager tracks and keeps the campaign on budget.

Here's a sample of the kinds of expenses that are typically part of a political campaign, though you will not need to incur all of these costs if you are running a smaller, less complex campaign. Check out the Deep Dive for links to budget templates you can download.

OPERATIONS: funds to keep your campaign office going

EXPENSE	MONTH	YEAR TO DATE	DETAILS
Office supplies			
Rent, internet, utilities			
Salaries			
Vehicles (gas and maintenance)			
Bank fees			
Website (domain and hosting)			
Cell phones and plans			

OUTREACH: funds spent on connecting with voters

EXPENSE	MONTH	YEAR TO DATE	DETAILS
Voter lists, files and databases			
Mailers to households			
Newspaper ad space			
Newspaper ad production			
Radio and TV ad placement fees			
Radio and TV ad production			
Digital ad placement fees			
Digital ad production			
Yard signs			
Large signs (road signs and billboards)			
Posters, tape and zip ties			
Automated call service			
Volunteer expenses (gas, transit reimbursement)			
Canvassing door-to-door expenses (gas, pamphlets)			
Community meetings			
Getting out the vote (getting registered voters to the polls) (gas, honorariums or wages, etc.)			

FUNDRAISING: costs that you incur to raise campaign funds

EXPENSE	MONTH	YEAR TO DATE	DETAILS
Event costs (venue, catering)			
Printing (direct mail pieces, donation cards, letterhead, envelopes)			
Postage			
Email management systems for electronically soliciting donations (Mailchimp, etc.)			
TOTAL CAMPAIGN COSTS			

STEP 12

WRITE YOUR CAMPAIGN PLAN

PLAN FOR THE RUN

Congratulations! You've now created the foundation of a campaign plan. When you start an actual campaign for office, get a big binder that can hold your detailed campaign plan. This will include the main elements of the work that you've done here. It will take into account your preparation; include the research you and your team have done on the issues and voter demographics; and assign responsibilities for each aspect of the campaign to your team members. It will include a campaign budget, fundraising goals and timelines, as well as a communications plan, community engagement plan and a GOTV (Get Out the Vote) plan.

PART 3

THE DEEP DIVE

BROWSE. READ. EXPLORE. CONNECT.

The Deep Dive is the final item in your toolkit for running, or preparing to run, for office. Here you will find a broad sampling of information, including places to find out more about making a run for office, resources to help you on your journey, websites to visit and books and articles to read.

I. **Finding Support and Learning How: Organizations Supporting Women Candidates**
II. **Essential Information**
III. **Campaign Basics: Learning the Ropes**
IV. **Campaign Costs: Raising and Handling Campaign Funds**
V. **Books and Articles That Inspire and Inform**
VI. **Live Viewing of Government Proceedings**

I. FINDING SUPPORT AND LEARNING HOW: ORGANIZATIONS SUPPORTING WOMEN CANDIDATES

There are numerous organizations set up specifically to help women enter into politics and run for office. Some of them run programs that provide training and advice, provide tips on raising campaign funds and include online communities where you can learn and share your ideas. Here are some you might want to check out.

Center for American Women and Politics (CAWP) (U.S.)
cawp.rutgers.edu | @CAWP_RU
Research on women's participation in politics and government, and training for women candidates, including the Ready to Run campaign training program for women.

Emerge America (U.S.)
www.emergeamerica.org | #emergenow | @EmergeAmerica
Mission is to increase the number of Democratic women leaders from diverse backgrounds in public office through recruitment and training and by providing a powerful network.

EMILY's List (U.S.)
www.emilyslist.org | @emilyslist

Online community of more than five million helping pro-choice women get elected to office. Includes the Run to Win training program for women candidates and those who want to support them.

Equal Voice (Canada)
www.equalvoice.ca | @EqualVoiceCA
Advocates for gender-balanced political offices and runs programs to support women candidates, including events and initiatives for young women.

Getting to the Gate (Canada)
gettingtothegate.com
Equal Voice Canada's online campaign school for Canadian candidates.

Higher Heights (U.S.)
www.higherheightsforamerica.org | #BlackWomenLead | @HigherHeights
Founded in 2011 to harness the power of black women as voters, organizers and candidates, through online, grassroots and national initiatives. Offers webinar training.

IGNITE (U.S.)
www.ignitenational.org | #WriteTheRules | @IGNITE_National
A movement to engage young women, with chapters in California, Texas and Colorado. You can declare your intention to run on the website.

Off the Sidelines (U.S.)
offthesidelines.org | #offthesidelines | @getots
Encourages women to make their voices heard and to run for office. Includes opportunities to make donations to women's campaigns. Features blogs, book clubs, chats, podcasts, videos and links to related organizations.

Parliament (U.K.)
www.parliament.uk/get-involved | @YourUKParl
Provides guidance on how to run as a candidate for the House of Commons, from getting the nomination for a riding to running a campaign for member of Parliament.

Run for Something (U.S.)
runforsomething.net | @runforsomething
Works with progressive millennials who are running for local office for the first or second time.

Running Start (U.S.)
runningstart.org | @runningstart
A nonpartisan movement geared toward bringing young women to politics through training and mentorship. An annual week-long Young Women's Political Leadership program introduces high school girls to political leadership, and the ElectHer program offers one-day sessions to train college women to run for student government.

Run Women Run (U.S.)
www.runwomenrun.org | #RWR | @runwomenrun
A nonpartisan organization that inspires, recruits and trains qualified, pro-choice women to seek elected and appointed office.

She Should Run (U.S.)
www.sheshouldrun.org | @SheShouldRun
An incubator course for parents and mentors to inspire the next generation of leaders by helping young girls see their own possibility and promise. It includes tools and activities to talk to a girl in your life about the ways she can become a leader — and the obstacles she'll probably face.

Women's Campaign Fund (U.S.)
www.wcfonline.org | @WCFonline
A nonpartisan organization aiming to achieve 50 percent representation of women in U.S. elected office. Focuses on collaborative problem-solving skills and candidates' viability for election. Includes information on issues, campaigns and endorsements of women's campaigns.

The Campaign School at Yale University (Global)
www.tcsyale.org | @TCSYale
An issue-neutral leadership program whose mission is to increase the number and influence of women in elected and appointed office in the United States and around the globe.

II. ESSENTIAL INFORMATION

Find the information that is essential when you are considering running for office. This section covers electoral commissions, where you can find important information about elections, such as how to qualify as a candidate and how to handle campaign expenses. There's also guidance on where to get information on campaign costs.

Afghanistan
Independent Election Committee of Afghanistan
www.iec.org.af

Australia
Australian Electoral Commission
www.aec.gov.au

Canada
Elections Canada
www.elections.ca

Candidate information from Elections Canada

Information and guidance on running provincially can be found by searching the name of the province or territory and "elections" and "candidacy." Links are also provided below.

- British Columbia
  www.elections.bc.ca/docs/guidebooks/856-Guide-for-Candidates.pdf
- Alberta
  www.elections.ab.ca/parties-and-candidates/candidates/
- Saskatchewan
  www.elections.sk.ca/candidates-political-parties/candidates/
- Manitoba
  www.electionsmanitoba.ca/en/Political_Participation
- Ontario
  www.elections.on.ca/en/political-entities-in-ontario/candidates.html
- Quebec
  www.electionsquebec.qc.ca/english/municipal/candidate/how-to-run-as-a-candidate.php
- New Brunswick
  www.electionsnb.ca/content/enb/en/representatives/provincial-candidates.html
- Nova Scotia
  www.electionsnovascotia.ca
- Prince Edward Island
  www.electionspei.ca
- Newfoundland and Labrador
  www.elections.gov.nl.ca/elections/candidates/nomination.html
- Yukon
  www.electionsyk.ca/en/parties
- Northwest Territories
  www.electionsnwt.ca/en/guides-and-forms
- Nunavut
  www.elections.nu.ca/sites/default/files/documents/guide-nunavut-elections-act-14-en.pdf

France
Electoral Code
Search "Code electoral legifrance," and select "Translate this page" after the URL.

Germany
The Federal Returning Officer
bundeswahlleiter.de (click on the English tab)

Israel
Central Elections Committee
bechirot21.bechirot.gov.il/election (click on the English tab)

Malawi
Electoral Commission
www.mec.org.mw

New Zealand
Electoral Commission
elections.nz

Northern Ireland
Electoral Commission
www.electoralcommission.org.uk

Scotland
Electoral Commission
www.electoralcommission.org.uk

South Africa
Electoral Commission of South Africa
www.elections.org.za

United Kingdom
Electoral Commission
www.electoralcommission.org.uk

United States
Federal Election Commission
www.fec.gov

Ballotpedia
www.ballotpedia.org | @ballotpedia
This website is an online encyclopedia of American politics and elections, providing accurate and objective information for all levels of government. To find

information on your state, go to the website and type "How to run for office" in the search bar. A drop-down menu of states will appear.

VoteSmart
votesmart.org | @VoteSmart
A website where you can look up information on political candidates so you can make sure you are informed when it's time to vote.

Wales
Electoral Commission
www.electoralcommission.org.uk

III. CAMPAIGN BASICS: LEARNING THE ROPES

The decision to run for office may be overwhelming. Luckily, there are many resources to help you along the way. This section provides different websites and blog posts filled with information about political parties and their candidates, and templates to help you build your own campaign. Don't be surprised to see that some of the organizations are regional; the information is useful regardless of where you are running.

Election Handbook (Alabama)
http://lsa.alabama.gov/PDF/ALI/election_handbook/Alabama_Election_Handbook_18th_edition.pdf
A good source of general campaign information.

Handbook for Candidate (India)
eci.gov.in/files/file/9435-handbook-for-candidate-feb-2019/
A good source of general campaign information specific to India.

Hootsuite
"9 Social Media Templates to Save You Hours of Work"
blog.hootsuite.com/social-media-templates/
"19 Social Media Metrics That Really Matter — And How to Track Them"
blog.hootsuite.com/social-media-metrics/

Political Campaign Planning Manual (Malaysia)
ndi.org/sites/default/files/Political_Campaign_Planning_Manual_Malaysia_0.pdf
A good source of general campaign information.

St. John's, Newfoundland, Candidate's Handbook
stjohns.ca/sites/default/files/files/publication/Candidates%20Handbook_2017.pdf
A good source of general information as well as information specific to St. John's.

Local Victory
"The 9 Crucial Components of a Successful Political Campaign Plan"
www.localvictory.com/strategy/political-campaign-plan
Local Victory has advice for building a campaign for local office.

Utah Policy
"Campaign Guru: The Basic Elements of a Politcal Campaign"
https://utahpolicy.com/index.php/topics/campaign-guru/70-campaign-guru-the-basic-elements-of-a-political-campaign
Utahpolicy.com publishes an informative checklist to help you write a campaign plan.

IV. CAMPAIGN COSTS: RAISING AND HANDLING CAMPAIGN FUNDS

Election Campaign Costs
Open Secrets: Center for Responsive Politics
www.opensecrets.org/overview/cost.php
Information on the costs of election campaigns in the U.S.

Handling Campaign Contributions (Elections Canada)
On Elections.ca, go to "Political Participants," then "Tools for Candidates," then "Manuals." At that point, you can open the Political Financing Handbook for Candidates and Official Agents.

Small Donor Fundraising (U.S. Municipal)
callhub.io/city-council-small-donor-fundraising/

V. BOOKS AND ARTICLES THAT INSPIRE AND INFORM

Books

A Good Time to Be a Girl: Don't Lean In, Change the System by Helena Morrissey (William Collins, 2018)

The Confidence Code: The Science and Art of Self-Assurance — What Women Should Know by Katty Kay and Claire Shipman (HarperBusiness, 2014)

The Confidence Code for Girls: Taking Risks, Messing Up, and Becoming Your Amazingly Imperfect, Totally Powerful Self by Katty Kay and Claire Shipman (HarperCollins, 2018)

Run for Something: A Real-Talk Guide to Fixing the System Yourself by Amanda Litman (Atria Books, 2017)

Tragedy in the Commons: Former Members of Parliament Speak Out About Canada's Failing Democracy by Alison Loat and Michael MacMillan (Random House Canada, 2014)

Unite and Conquer: How to Build Coalitions That Win — and Last by Kyrsten Sinema (Berrett-Koehler Publishers, 2009)

Articles

"3 Young, Female MPs On Life in Parliament" by Samantha Magnus (Refinery29, August 10, 2017) (U.K.)
www.refinery29.com/en-gb/2017/08/167058/female-mps-2017

"Ask a Woman to Run" (U.S.)
www.sheshouldrun.org/ask

"Calling More Women: Nunavut's 1st Woman Premier Says Equal Representation a Work in Progress" by Walter Strong (CBC.ca, October 4, 2017) (Canada)
www.cbc.ca/news/canada/north/eva-aariak-female-candidates-needed-1.4321450

"Donald Trump's Presidency Has Inspired 11 000 Women to Run for Office" by Rebecca Shapiro (HuffPost U.S., April 24, 2017)
www.huffingtonpost.com/entry/donald-trumps-presidency-has-inspired-11000-women-to-run-for-office_us_58fd863ae4b06b9cb917d111

"Girls Just Wanna Not Run: The Gender Gap in Young Americans' Political Ambition" by Jennifer L. Lawless and Richard L. Fox (American University School of Public Affairs, Washington, D.C., March 2013) (U.S.)
www.american.edu/spa/wpi/upload/Girls-Just-Wanna-Not-Run_Policy-Report.pdf

"The Hidden Power in Trusting Your Gut Instincts" by Liz Funk (*Fast Company*, April 7, 2016) (U.S.)
www.fastcompany.com/3058609/the-hidden-power-in-trusting-your-gut-instincts

"How to Run for Mayor (Yes, Really!)" by Sarah Climenhaga (*The Kit*, March 7, 2018) (Canada)
www.thekit.ca/life/how-to-run-for-mayor/

"Vanishing Point: Why Women, Minorities Get Squeezed Out of the Political Race" by Sabrina Nanji (*Toronto Star*, September 30, 2017) (Canada)
www.pressreader.com/canada/toronto-star/20170930/281509341385224

"Why Are Women in Politics Less Authoritative on Twitter? Because Men Are

Less Likely to Retweet and Follow Them" by Mary Ann Sieghart (*New Statesman America*, December 5, 2017) (U.S.)
newstatesman.com/politics/feminism/2017/12/why-are-women-politics-less-authoritative-twitter-because-men-are-less

"More Women Are Signing Up to Run for Office, but Will They Succeed?" by Kelly Wallace (CNN.com, June 21, 2017) (U.S.)
www.cnn.com/2017/06/20/health/women-running-elected-office-win/index.html

"The New Wave of Local Candidates Running for Office" by Sarah Holder (Citylab.com, November 6, 2017) (U.S.)
www.citylab.com/life/2017/11/new-wave-of-local-candidates/544853/

VI. LIVE VIEWING OF GOVERNMENT PROCEEDINGS

In many jurisdictions, unedited and live coverage of government proceedings is available on television and by live-streaming on the internet. Included here are links to many of the countries of the women profiled in Part 1: The Journey, plus a number of other key countries. It is by no means an exhaustive list so there's a lot more to explore.

- Afghanistan
  www.parliament.af
- Australia
  www.aph.gov.au
- Canada
  www.cpac.ca
- European Parliament
  www.europarltv.europa.eu
- France
  www.lcp.fr (Lower House)
  www.publicsenat.fr (Senate)
- Germany
  www.bundestag.de
- Ireland
  www.oireachtas.ie
- Israel
  www.knesset.gov.il
- Mexico [Spanish language only]
  www.canaldelcongreso.gob.mx
- New Zealand
  www.parliament.nz
- Northern Ireland
  www.niassembly.tv
- Scotland
  www.scottishparliament.tv
- South Africa
  www.parliament.gov.za
- United Kingdom
  www.parliamentlive.tv/Commons
- United States
  www.c-span.org
- Wales
  www.senedd.tv

SOURCES

PART 1: THE JOURNEY

Chapter 1: Michelle Stilwell

"2013 Voting Results by Voting Area." Elections BC, May 14, 2013. https://elections.bc.ca/resources/voting-results/provincial-general-elections-results/2013-ge-results/

Aylward, Brendan. "Biomechanics of Push-Rim Wheelchair Racing." Unified Health and Performance (blog), May 2, 2019. https://unifiedhp.com/blog/2019/5/2/biomechanics-of-push-rim-wheelchair-racing

"Canadian Track Star Stilwell Takes 2nd Paralympic Gold." CBC Sports, September 15, 2008. https://www.cbc.ca/sports/2.720/canadian-track-star-stilwell-takes-2nd-paralympic-gold-1.716905

Girard, Daniel. "Michelle Stilwell Wheeling Toward Perfection." *Toronto Star*, June 2, 2012. https://www.thestar.com/sports/olympics/2012/06/02/michelle_stilwell_wheeling_toward_perfection.html

Kingston, Gary. "MLA Michelle Stilwell Sets World Wheelchair Record." *Vancouver Sun*, July 25, 2013. http://www.vancouversun.com/sports/michelle+stilwell+sets+world+wheelchair+record/8709320/story.html

"Michelle Stilwell Announces Retirement." Athletics Canada, February 8, 2017. https://athletics.ca/michelle-stilwell-announces-retirement/

Mikey Stilwell (website). http://www.mikeystilwell.com

"Paralympian, Former Winnipegger Stilwell Wins B.C. Seat." *Winnipeg Free Press*, May 15, 2013. https://www.winnipegfreepress.com/local/Paralympian-former-Winnipegger-Stilwell-wins-BC-seat-207545691.html

Spencer, Donna. "B.C. Wheelchair Sprinter Michelle Stilwell Primed for Paralympic Glory." *Globe and Mail*, August 27, 2012. https://www.theglobeandmail.com/sports/olympics/bc-wheelchair-sprinter-michelle-stilwell-primed-for-paralympic-glory/article4504088/

"Wheelchair Basketball Skills: Beginner." BC Wheelchair Basketball Society. Last accessed on October 29, 2019. http://bcwbs.ca/sites/default/files/users/documents/pdfs/Wheelchair_Basketball_Skills-Beginner.pdf

Zussman, Richard. "World Record-Setter Politician Aims for Paralympic Gold." CBC News, September 5, 2016. https://www.cbc.ca/news/canada/british-columbia/world-record-setter-politician-aims-for-paralympic-gold-1.3732900

Chapter 2: Kyrsten Sinema

"Arizona Senate Election Results: Martha McSally vs. Kyrsten Sinema." *New York Times*, January 28, 2018. https://www.nytimes.com/elections/results/arizona-senate

Bradner, Eric. "Democrats Flip Arizona US Senate Seat with Sinema Victory." CNN, November 13, 2018. https://www.cnn.com/2018/11/12/politics/sinema-arizona-senate-race/index.html

Dresser, Michael, and Carrie Wells. "With Same-Sex Marriage Now Available, State to End Benefits for Domestic Partners." *Baltimore Sun*, May 3, 2013. https://www.baltimoresun.com/news/bs-xpm-2013-05-03-bal-with-samesex-marriage-now-available-state-to-end-benefits-for-domestic-partners-20130506-story.html

Farzan, Antonia Noori. "The Arizona Senate Race Is Now a Total Clu$terf*ck (Unless You're Kyrsten Sinema)." *Phoenix New Times*, January 10, 2018. http://www.phoenixnewtimes.com/news/arizona-senate-race-total-clusterfuck-unless-kyrsten-sinema-10026823

Friedman, Ann. "America's Most Colorful Congresswoman: Kyrsten Sinema." *Elle*, May 22, 2013. https://www.elle.com/culture/career-politics/a12563/arizona-congresswoman-kyrsten-sinema-profile/

"Kyrsten Sinema." Ballotpedia. Last accessed on October 29, 2019. https://ballotpedia.org/Kyrsten_Sinema

Kyrsten Sinema for Arizona U.S. Senate (website). https://www.kyrstensinema.com

Romero, Simon. "Kyrsten Sinema Declared Winner in Arizona Senate Race." *New York Times*, November 12, 2018. https://www.nytimes.com/2018/11/12/us/kyrsten-sinema-arizona-senator.html

Sanders, Rebekah L. "The Congresswoman Who Grew Up in a Gas Station." azcentral, January 30, 2016. https://www.azcentral.com/story/news/arizona/politics/2016/01/30/congresswoman-who-grew-up-gas-station/79206952/

Sunnucks, Mike. "20 Things to Know about Arizona's U.S. Senate Race with Kyrsten Sinema in against Trump Foe Jeff Flake, Kelli Ward." *Phoenix Business Journal*, September 29, 2017. https://www.bizjournals.com/phoenix/news/2017/09/29/20-things-to-know-about-arizona-s-u-s-senate-race.html

Zhou, Li. "Democrat Kyrsten Sinema Widens Lead in Arizona Senate Race." Vox, November 8, 2018. https://www.vox.com/2018/11/8/18075478/midterm-elections-arizona-vote-count-mcsally-sinema

Chapter 3: Juliana Lunguzi

"Court Stops MCP Recognizing MP Lunguzi as Dedza East' May Elections Torch Bearer." Maravi Post, January 7, 2019. http://www.maravipost.com/court

-stops-mcp-recognizing-mp-lunguzi-as-dedza-east-may-elections-torch-bearer/

"Current Members of Parliament." Parliament of Malawi. Last accessed on October 29, 2019. http://www.parliament.gov.mw/#/legislators

"Juliana Lunguzi Dubs Govt Conduct Strange." Afriem, June 1, 2015. http://www.afriem.org/2015/06/juliana-lunguzi-dubs-govt-conduct-strange/

"Juliana Lunguzi" (speaker profile). Women Deliver's 4th Global Conference. Last accessed on October 29, 2019. http://wd2016.org/speaker/juliana-lunguzi/

Kawale, John. "I Am Bold for Change as I Just Do It." MamaYe! (blog), March 8, 2017. https://mamaye.org/blog/i-am-bold-change-i-just-do-it

Khamula, Owen. "Chakwera Confused, Lost Voter Registration Card: Lunguzi Shocked Over Missing Name." *Nyasa Times*, May 21, 2019. https://www.nyasa times.com/chakwera-confused-lost-voter-registration-card-lunguzi-shocked-over -missing-name/

Kondowe, Russell. "MCP Excludes Juliana Lunguzi." *Malawi24*, November 8, 2018. https://malawi24.com/2018/11/08/mcp-excludes-julianna-lunguzi/

Mapeto, Chikondi. "Lunguzi Accuses Dedza District Council of Sidelining Her, Council Says She Always Gives Excuses." Malawi News Agency (MANA) Online, September 17, 2018. http://www.manaonline.gov.mw/index.php/national/ politics/item/10626-lunguzi-accuses-dedza-district-council-of-sidelining-her -council-says-she-always-gives-excuses

Ngwira, Robert. "Bandawe Obtains Court Injunction Restraining MCP from Declaring Lunguzi Winner of Dedza East Primaries." Face of Malawi, January 7, 2019. http://www.faceofmalawi.com/2019/01/bandawe-obtains-court-injunction -restraining-mcp-from-declaring-lunguzi-winner-of-dedza-east-primaries/

Nyondo, Andrew. "Juliana Lunguzi Gets Last Laugh." *The Nation* (Malawi), November 27, 2018. https://mwnation.com/juliana-lunguzi-gets-last-laugh/

"Vantage Point: An interview with Hon. Juliana Lunguzi — Co-Chair of Malawi Caucus on Population and Development." The African Institute for Development Policy (AFIDEP), May 31, 2017. https://www.afidep.org/vantage-point-interview -hon-juliana-lunguzi-co-chair-malawi-caucus-population-development/

Chapter 4: Catherine McKenna

Beeby, Dean. "Canadian Charities Feel 'Chill' as Tax Audits Widen into Political Activities." *Toronto Star*, July 10, 2014. https://www.thestar.com/news /canada/2014/07/10/canadian_charities_feel_chill_as_tax_audits_widen_into _political_activities.html

Commisso, Christina. "Environment Minister Looking for 'Ambitious' Deal at Climate Summit." CTVNews.ca, November 13, 2015. https://www.ctvnews.ca/politics/

environment-minister-looking-for-ambitious-deal-at-climate-summit-1.2657005

"Federal Election Results 2015: Justin Trudeau's Liberals to Form Majority Government." Canada Votes, CBC News. Last updated October 20, 2015. https://www.cbc.ca/news2/interactives/results-2015/

Helmer, Aedan. "Catherine McKenna Scores Huge Victory in NDP Stronghold." *Ottawa Sun*, October 20, 2015. https://ottawasun.com/2015/10/20/catherine-mckenna-scores-huge-victory-in-ndp-stronghold/wcm/54c49c63-a585-4d5c-90b6-30747140a2bb

"The Honourable Catherine McKenna MP." Government of Canada (website). Last updated December 6, 2018. https://www.canada.ca/en/government/ministers/catherine-mckenna.html

Ibbitson, John. "How Harper Transformed Canada's Foreign Policy." *Globe and Mail*, January 31, 2014. https://www.theglobeandmail.com/news/politics/how-harper-transformed-canadas-foreign-policy/article16626348/

Taylor-Vaisey, Nick. "An Escalator Pitch from Catherine McKenna on Canada in 2020." *Maclean's*, October 3, 2014. https://www.macleans.ca/news/canada/an-escalator-pitch-from-catherine-mckenna-on-canada-in-2020/

Voski, Anaïs, and Robert Sibley. "McKenna Upsets Dewar in Ottawa Centre." *Ottawa Citizen*, October 20, 2015. https://ottawacitizen.com/news/politics/ottawa-centre-saw-a-vigorous-campaign

Zimonjic, Peter. "Catherine McKenna Demands Reporter's Outlet Stop Calling Her 'Climate Barbie' in Terse Exchange." CBC News, November 3, 2017. https://www.cbc.ca/news/politics/catherine-mckenna-rebel-media-exchange-1.4387510

Chapter 5: Michelle Wu

Abazorius, Greg, and Zoe Gregoric. "Michelle Wu Stresses Perseverance." Wentworth Institute of Technology, March 22, 2016. https://wit.edu/news/michelle-wu-stresses-perseverance

Bernstein, David S. "City Council Candidate Chat: Michelle Wu." *Boston* magazine, August 9, 2013. https://www.bostonmagazine.com/news/2013/08/09/candidate-chat-michelle-wu/

"Boston's Outstanding Young Leader." Boston Consulting Group, June 8, 2017. https://www.bcg.com/alumni/boston-outstanding-young-leader-michelle-wu.aspx

Chen, Sizhong. "After Two Years as Boston City Council President, Michelle Wu Steps Down to Focus on Policy." Boston University News Service, January 24, 2018. http://bunewsservice.com/michelle-wu-steps-down-to-focus-on-policy/

Dwinell, Joe. "ICE Agents Blaming Sanctuary Cities for Enabling Criminals." *Boston Herald*, October 6, 2018. http://www.bostonherald.com/news/local_coverage

/2018/10/06/ice_agents_blaming_sanctuary_cities_for_enabling_criminals

Jiang, Hezi. "Quiet Leader Runs Boston's City Council." *China Daily USA*, March 25, 2016. http://usa.chinadaily.com.cn/epaper/2016-03/25/content_24094749.htm

Kim, Young Jin. "Michelle Wu, Boston Official, Marches Toward a 'New Boston.'" NBC News, May 19, 2016. https://www.nbcnews.com/news/asian-america/michelle-wu-boston-official-marches-toward-new-boston-n562781

Leung, Shirley. "Visibility Key for Asian-Americans." *Boston Globe*, November 11, 2015. https://www.bostonglobe.com/business/2015/11/10/michelle-run-for-city-council-president-highlights-need-for-asian-americans-power/MrQNnJUWnEYlXrFyikwVsM/story.html

"Michelle Wu." Ballotpedia. Last accessed on October 29, 2019. https://ballotpedia.org/Michelle_Wu

Michelle Wu for Boston City Councilor At-Large (website). http://michelleforboston.com

Rattner, Rebecca. "Counsel from a Councilor: An Interview with Michelle Wu '12." *Harvard Law Today*, March 23, 2016. https://today.law.harvard.edu/some-counsel-from-a-city-council-president-an-interview-with-michelle-wu-12/

Swenson, Sally. "JP and City Councilor Michelle Wu." *JP and Me Blog*. Jamaica Plain Neighborhood Development Corp. (JPNDC), May 25, 2017. https://jpndc.org/jp-and-city-councilor-michelle-wu/

Ustundag, Ezgi. "Michelle Wu — 2003 Scholar." U.S. Presidential Scholars Foundation, April 18, 2017. http://www.presidentialscholars.org/notable-scholars-1/2017/4/18/michelle-wu-2003-scholar

Walker, Adrian. "Michelle Wu Shows Promise for City's Future." *Boston Globe*, April 3, 2013. https://www.bostonglobe.com/metro/2013/04/02/meet-michelle-city-council-candidate-who-wants-help-shape-boston-future/Gzym6U189B3Cm1TMRxMTEN/story.html

Walker, Alissa. "How Multimodal City Councilor Michelle Wu Gets around Boston." Curbed, May 9, 2018. https://www.curbed.com/2018/5/9/17332048/boston-transit-michelle-wu-kids

Wong, Ling-Mei. "Asian American Local Politicians Work to Overcome Stereotypes." *Sampan* (Boston), January 8, 2016. https://sampan.org/2016/01/asian-american-local-politicians-work-to-overcome-stereotypes/

Wong, Ling-Mei. "First Chinese-American City Councilor in Boston: Michelle Wu." *Sampan* (Boston), May 9, 2014. https://sampan.org/2014/05/first-chinese-american-city-councilor-in-boston-michelle-wu/

Wu, Michelle. "Love Thy Neighbor." *Boston* magazine, March 13, 2018. https://www.bostonmagazine.com/education/2018/03/13/harvard-university-broken/#Michelle

Chapter 6: Hala Lattouf

"The Government." Embassy of the Hashemite Kingdom of Jordan. Last accessed on October 29, 2019. http://www.jordanembassynicosia.com/The-Government

"Hala Bsaisu Lattouf." Aya for Consultancy and Development. Last accessed on October 29, 2019. http://www.ayaconsultants.org/about6.php

"Hala Lattouf: Jordan's Minister of Social Development."MEED, November 18, 2010. https://www.meed.com/hala-lattouf-jordans-minister-of-social-development/

Husseini, Rana. "Gov't-Civil Society Collaboration Vital for Women Empowerment — Lattouf." *Jordan Times*, October 26, 2017. http://www.jordantimes.com/news/local/gov%E2%80%99t-civil-society-collaboration-vital-women-empowerment-%E2%80%94-lattouf

Husseini, Rana. "Safety, Security of Abused Women Top Priority — Lattouf." *Jordan Times*, July 31, 2018. http://www.jordantimes.com/news/local/safety-security-abused-women-top-priority-—-lattouf

Lattouf, Hala. "Gender Equality: A Matter of Social Justice." In *Visions and Actions to Promote Gender Equality in the Mediterranean*, 18–19. Barcelona: Union for the Mediterranean, November 2017. https://ufmsecretariat.org/gender-equality-matter-social-justice-hala-lattouf/

Lattouf, Hala. "Supporting Jordan's Youth: For the Greater Good." *YOUth* magazine, Summer 2010, 16–18. International Youth Foundation. https://www.iyfnet.org/sites/default/files/library/YOUth10_PolicyMatters.pdf

"Minister of Social Development: Daycare Centers' By-Law Revised." National Council for Family Affairs, November 14, 2017. http://ncfa.org.jo:85/NCFA/en/content/Minister-Social-Development-Daycare-Centers-law-revised

"Minister of Social Development Visits UN Women's Resilience and Empowerment Centers." UN Women, Jordan, May 10, 2018. https://jordan.unwomen.org/en/news/stories/2018/may/minister-of-social-development-visits-un-womens-resilience-and-empowerment-centers

Chapter 7: Kim Campbell

Alary, Bryan. "Former PM to Lead the Way at Peter Lougheed Leadership College." Folio, April 15, 2014. University of Alberta. https://www.folio.ca/former-pm-to-lead-the-way-at-peter-lougheed-leadership-college/

The Canadian Press. "Kim Campbell to Chair Supreme Court Advisory

Board." *Maclean's*, August 2, 2016. https://www.macleans.ca/politics/ottawa/kim-campbell-to-chair-supreme-court-advisory-board/

The editors of Encyclopaedia Britannica. "Kim Campbell, Prime Minister of Canada." *Encyclopaedia Britannica*, July 28, 1999. Last updated October 15, 2019. https://www.britannica.com/biography/Kim-Campbell

"Ex-PM Kim Campbell Speaks at Canadian Museum for Human Rights." CBC News, January 27, 2016. https://www.cbc.ca/news/canada/manitoba/kim-campbell-cmhr-1.3422477

"Former Prime Minister Kim Campbell Advocates a Greater Role for Women Leaders." The Ismaili, November 15, 2014. https://the.ismaili/ismailicentres/culture-diversity/burnaby/former-prime-minister-kim-campbell-advocates-greater-role

"Keynote Moderator: The Right Honourable Kim Campbell, 19th Prime Minister of Canada." ILA's 21st Annual Global Conference website, International Leadership Association. Last accessed October 30, 2019. https://ilaglobalconference.org/kim-campbell-bio-2/?gclid=EAIaIQobChMIhtX7nMiz5AIVCMDICh0KMQE5EAAYASAAEgKVSPD_BwE

"Kim Campbell to Deliver Keynote on Eve of 100th Anniversary of Women's Vote: From Suffragists to the Prime Minister's Office." Canadian Museum for Human Rights, January 27, 2016. https://humanrights.ca/news/kim-campbell-to-deliver-keynote-on-eve-of-100th-anniversary-of-womens-vote-from-suffragists-to

McCullough, J. J. "Kim Campbell." In "History: Prime Ministers" in The Canada Guide. Last accessed on October 30, 2019. http://www.thecanadaguide.com/history/prime-ministers/kim-campbell/

McKerrow, Graham. "Bill Clinton and Nelson Mandela Promise to Lead Peer Education among Political Leaders as World Looks for $10 Billion a Year to Fight HIV/AIDS." HIV Treatment Bulletin (HTB), September 11, 2002. HIV i-Base. http://i-base.info/htb/6776

The Right Honourable Kim Campbell, Canada's 19th Prime Minister (website) http://www.kimcampbell.com

Wallin, Pamela, host, and Joe Schlesinger, reporter. "Kim Campbell the Candidate." CBC Prime Time News. CBC Television. Aired March 24, 1993. https://www.cbc.ca/archives/entry/kim-campbell-the-candidate

Chapter 8: Jacinda Ardern

Fisk, Robert. "Ardern's Response to Christchurch Has Put Other Leaders to Shame — but Not for Its Compassion Alone." *The Independent*, March 21,

2019. https://www.independent.co.uk/voices/jacinda-ardern-new-zealand-shooting-christchurch-donald-trump-erdogan-turkey-a8833156.html

Gessen, Masha. "Jacinda Ardern Has Rewritten the Script for How a Nation Grieves After a Terrorist Attack." *New Yorker*, March 22, 2019. https://www.newyorker.com/news/our-columnists/jacinda-ardern-has-rewritten-the-script-for-how-a-nation-grieves-after-a-terrorist-attack

Hehir, Liam. "Prime Minister Jacinda Ardern's Response to Christchurch Mosque Shootings Pitch Perfect." Stuff, March 25, 2019. https://www.stuff.co.nz/national/christchurch-shooting/111515320/prime-minister-jacinda-arderns-response-to-christchurch-mosque-shootings-pitch-perfect

"Jacinda Ardern's Speech at Christchurch Memorial — Full Transcript." *The Guardian*, March 28, 2019. https://www.theguardian.com/world/2019/mar/29/jacinda-arderns-speech-at-christchurch-memorial-full-transcript

Lester, Amelia. "The Roots of Jacinda Ardern's Extraordinary Leadership After Christchurch." *New Yorker*, March 23, 2019. https://www.newyorker.com/culture/culture-desk/what-jacinda-arderns-leadership-means-to-new-zealand-and-to-the-world

Tharoor, Ishaan. "New Zealand Shooting: The World Is Praising Jacinda Ardern's Response to Terrorist Attack." *The Independent*, March 20, 2019. https://www.independent.co.uk/news/world/australasia/new-zealand-shooting-jacinda-ardern-video-reaction-world-praise-a8832186.html

Tharoor, Ishaan. "The World Is Watching New Zealand's Jacinda Ardern." *Washington Post*, March 18, 2019. https://www.washingtonpost.com/world/2019/03/19/world-is-watching-new-zealands-jacinda-ardern/?utm_term=.7ec6edcbe81c

Wiggins, Amy. "Ardern's Pledge to Decriminalise Abortion Sparks Controversy." *NZ Herald*, September 5, 2017. https://www.nzherald.co.nz/nz/news/article.cfm?c_id=1&objectid=11917231

Williams, Jennifer. "New Zealanders Have Sent a Clear Message to the Mosque Shooter: You Will Not Divide Us." Vox, March 22, 2019. https://www.vox.com/world/2019/3/22/18277189/new-zealand-call-to-prayer-headscarf-haka-christchurch-hagley-park

Chapter 9: Kirsten Gillibrand

Burns, Alexander. "Gillibrand Drops Out of 2020 Democratic Presidential Race." *New York Times*, August 28, 2019. https://www.nytimes.com/2019/08/28/us/politics/kirsten-gillibrand-2020-drop-out.html

Chartock, Alan. "Sen. Kirsten Gillibrand Drops Out." *Berkshire Edge*,

September 3, 2019. https://theberkshireedge.com/alan-chartock-33/

Chu, Jeff. "Kirsten Gillibrand Talks Work and Family and Why 'Women Are Often Selfless.'" *Fast Company*, September 10, 2014. https://www.fastcompany.com/3035537/interview-kirsten-gillibrand-talks-work-family-and-why-women-are-often-selfless

Cramer, Ruby. "Quietly, Gillibrand Raises Big Money for Female Candidates." BuzzFeed News, October 1, 2012. https://www.buzzfeednews.com/article/rubycramer/quietly-gillibrand-raises-big-money-for-female-ca

Fast Company staff. "Secrets of the Most Productive People." *Fast Company*, November 18, 2014. https://www.fastcompany.com/3038214/secrets-of-the-most-productive-people

Forbes, Moira. "Sen. Kirsten Gillibrand on Why Ambition Is Not a Dirty Word." *Forbes*, November 12, 2014. https://www.forbes.com/sites/moiraforbes/2014/11/12/sen-kirsten-gillibrand-on-why-ambition-is-not-a-dirty-word/#16116f3273f0

Gillibrand, Kirsten. Chap. 1 in *Off the Sidelines: Speak Up, Be Fearless, and Change Your World.* New York: Ballantine Books, 2014. https://www.penguinrandomhouse.ca/books/236926/off-the-sidelines-by-kirsten-gillibrand/9780804179096/excerpt

Gillibrand, Kirsten. "Kirsten Gilibrand: 'We Will Not Allow These Crimes to Be Swept Under the Rug Any Longer.'" *Time*, May 15, 2014. https://time.com/100144/kirsten-gillibrand-campus-sexual-assault/

Kahn, Mattie. "Senator Claire McCaskill and Senator Kirsten Gillibrand Are on a Crusade to End Sexual Assault on Campus." *Elle*, December 15, 2015. https://www.elle.com/culture/career-politics/interviews/a32569/senators-claire-mccaskill-and-kirsten-gillibrand-sexual-assault-on-campus/

Kraushaar, Josh. "Gillibrand, the Fundraising Dynamo." Politico, January 29, 2009. https://www.politico.com/story/2009/01/gillibrand-the-fundraising-dynamo-018121

Merica, Dan. "Kirsten Gillibrand Drops Out of 2020 Presidential Race." CNN, August 28, 2019. https://www.cnn.com/2019/08/28/politics/gillibrand-drops-out-of-race/index.html

Osnos, Evan. "Strong Vanilla: The Relentless Rise of Kirsten Gillibrand." *New Yorker*, December 8, 2013. https://www.newyorker.com/magazine/2013/12/16/strong-vanilla

Peele, Anna. "The Ignoring of Kirsten Gillibrand." *Washington Post* Magazine, July 8, 2019. https://www.washingtonpost.com/news/magazine/wp/2019/07/08/feature/why-america-is-ignoring-kirsten-gillibrand/

Rodrick, Stephen. "The Reintroduction of Kirsten Gillibrand." *New York*, June 5, 2009. http://nymag.com/news/politics/57197/

Terris, Ben. "How Kirsten Gillibrand Shed Her Past on the Way to Liberal Stardom." National Journal, October 25, 2013. https://www.nationaljournal.com/s/636062/how-kirsten-gillibrand-shed-her-past-way-liberal-stardom

Thrush, Glenn. "Full Transcript: Politico's Glenn Thrush Interviews Sen. Kirsten Gillibrand." Politico, April 18, 2016. https://www.politico.com/story/2016/04/off-message-thrush-gillibrand-222071

Van Meter, Jonathan. "In Hillary's Footsteps: Kirsten Gillibrand." *Vogue*, October 19, 2010. https://www.vogue.com/article/in-hillarys-footsteps-kirsten-gillibrand

Wooledge, Scott. "Sen. Gillibrand, the One-Women DSCC, DCCC." Daily Kos, October 3, 2012. https://www.dailykos.com/stories/2012/10/3/1138922/-Sen-Gillibrand-the-one-woman-DSCC-DCCC

Chapter 10: Stav Shaffir

"A Journey with Stav Shaffir — Israeli Elections 2013." Ameinu (blog), January 21, 2013. https://www.ameinu.net/blog/ameinu-video/a-journey-with-stav-shaffir-israeli-elections-2013/

Davidson, Stuart W. "Lessons from Israel's Youngest Lawmaker: Q&A with Stav Shaffir." HuffPost, June 18, 2015. https://www.huffingtonpost.com/stuart-w-davidson/lessons-from-israels-youn_b_7608050.html

Hoare, Liam. "Israel's Year of the Woman" *Slate*, March 15, 2015. http://www.slate.com/articles/news_and_politics/foreigners/2015/03/israel_s_female_politicians_are_becoming_more_prominent_women_are_a_crucial.html

Hoffman, Gil. "The Making of an Activist — How Stav Shaffir Went from Protester to MK." *Jerusalem Post*, November 22, 2018. https://www.jpost.com/Israel-News/Politics-And-Diplomacy/The-making-of-an-activist-how-Stav-Shaffir-went-from-protestor-to-MK-572565

Hoffman, Gil. "Zionist Union MK Stav Shaffir Mulling Run for Tel Aviv Mayor." *Jerusalem Post*, April 23, 2018. https://www.jpost.com/Israel-News/Politics-And-Diplomacy/Zionist-Union-MK-Stav-Shaffir-mulling-run-for-Tel-Aviv-mayor-552533

Kraft, Dina. "On Israel's Left, a Young Firebrand Is Building Her Base." Christian Science Monitor, November 30, 2017. https://www.csmonitor.com/World/Middle-East/2017/1130/On-Israel-s-left-a-young-firebrand-is-building-her-base

Lubell, Maayan. "Social Protest Leaders Hope to Shake Up Israel Ballot." Reuters, January 3, 2013. https://www.reuters.com/article/us-israel-election-protest/social-protest-leaders-hope-to-shake-up-israel-ballot-idUSBRE90207620130103

"MK Stav Shaffir to Join Program of CONNECTIONS 2017." World Union for Progressive Judaism, May 10, 2017. https://wupj.org/news/2017/05/1643/mk-stav-shaffir-to-join-program-of-connections-2017/

Omer-Man, Michael Schaeffer. "The 'Anti-Zionist' Camp Goes Mainstream in Israel Election." *+972 Magazine*, January 23, 2015. https://972mag.com/the-anti-zionist-camp-goes-mainstream-in-israeli-elections/101749/

Sales, Ben. "In Knesset, Former Protest Leader Stav Shaffir Follows the Money." Jewish Telegraphic Agency, October 20, 2014. https://www.jta.org/2014/10/20/politics/in-knesset-former-protest-leader-stav-shaffir-follows-the-money

Sales, Ben. "Israeli Left Resurgent as Campaign Rhetoric Escalates Ahead of March Elections." *Jewish Journal*, January 26, 2015. http://jewishjournal.com/tag/stav-shaffir/

Schulman, Marc. "Stav Shaffir: My Fight Against Corruption in Israel." *Newsweek*, January 14, 2015. https://www.newsweek.com/stav-shaffir-my-fight-against-corruption-israel-298994

Shaffir, Stav, and Cécile Shea. "Deep Dish: Hope and Corruption in Israel with MK Stav Shaffir." The Chicago Council on Global Affairs (blog), March 1, 2018. https://www.thechicagocouncil.org/blog/global-insight/deep-dish-hope-and-corruption-israel-mk-stav-shaffir

Shalev, Chemi. "J Street's Fiery Rock Star Stav Shaffir Has a Suggestion: 'Occupy Zionism.'" *Haaretz* (Israel), March 24, 2015. https://www.haaretz.com/jewish/.premium-mk-stav-shaffir-suggests-occupy-zionism-1.5341786

Shohat, Yehuda. "A Love's Poem." Israel Policy Exchange, December 15, 2017. https://israelpolicyexchange.com/2017/12/a-loves-poem/

Zeveloff, Naomi. "Is Stav Shaffir, Israel's Youngest Lawmaker, Ready for a Bigger Role?" *Forward*, February 17, 2015. https://forward.com/news/israel/214682/is-stav-shaffir-israels-youngest-lawmaker-ready-fo/

Chapter 11: Jaime Herrera Beutler

"40 Under 40 — New Civic Leaders: Jaime Herrera." *Time*, 2009. http://www.content.time.com/time/specials/packages/article/0,28804,2023831_2023829_2025201,00.html

Arter, Melanie. "Congresswoman Tells How She Chose Life for Her Daughter Who Was Given No Chance for Survival." CNSNews, January 19, 2018. https://www.cnsnews.com/news/article/melanie-arter/congresswoman-tells-how-she-chose-life-her-daughter-who-was-given-no

Beutler, Jaime Herrera. "Washington Rep. Jaime Herrera Beutler Speaks on Election Night." Live broadcast, KGW8, November 6, 2018. https://www.kgw.com/video/news/politics/washington-rep-jaime-herrera-beutler-speaks-on-election-night/283-8305689

Brown, Chris. "'Humbled' Jaime Herrera Beutler Prepares for a New Challenge in 5th Term." *Clark County Today,* November 13, 2018. https://www.clarkcountytoday.com/news/humbled-jaime-herrera-beutler-prepares-for-new-challenge-in-5th-term/

Bump, Philip. "Most White Americans Will Be Represented by a Republican in the House Next Year." *Washington Post*, November 27, 2018. https://www.washingtonpost.com/politics/2018/11/27/most-white-americans-will-be-represented-by-republican-house-next-year/?utm_term=.c2f9e8778f38

Camia, Catalina. "GOP Rep Joyous about 'Miracle' Baby's Birth." *USA Today,* July 29, 2013. https://www.usatoday.com/story/onpolitics/2013/07/29/jaime-herrera-beutler-daughter-congress-potters-sequence/2596293/

Durbin, Kathie. "Jaime Herrera: Staying 'True to the Principles.'" *The Columbian* (WA), July 23, 2010. http://www.columbian.com/news/2010/jul/23/3rd-congressional-district-jaime-herrera-staying-t/

Garnick, Coral. "Two Washington State Republicans Voted against Obamacare Repeal." *Puget Sound Business Journal*, May 4, 2017. https://www.bizjournals.com/seattle/news/2017/05/04/washington-state-congress-votes-obamacare-repeal.html

Hair, Calley. "Herrera Beutler Spurns Campaign Finance Reform Bill." *The Columbian* (WA), March 8, 2019. https://www.columbian.com/news/2019/mar/08/herrera-beutler-spurns-campaign-finance-reform-bill/

Hale, Zack. "Obamacare Repeal Talk Dominates Herrera Beutler Town Hall." *Daily News* (southwest WA and northwest OR), June 27, 2017. https://tdn.com/news/local/obamacare-repeal-talk-dominates-herrera-beutler-town-hall/article_acab5787-a46e-5c69-936e-8b9e21b89abc.html

"Herrera Beutler, Peterson, Klobuchar, Sullivan Introduce Bipartisan Legislation to Address the Shortage of Affordable, Quality Child Care." U.S. Congresswoman Jaime Herrera Beutler (website). Press release, March 1, 2019. https://herrerabeutler.house.gov/news/documentsingle.aspx?DocumentID=399419

"Jaime Herrera Beutler." Ballotpedia. Last accessed on October 30, 2019. https://ballotpedia.org/Jaime_Herrera_Beutler

"Jaime Herrera Beutler." Conservapedia. Last updated October 24, 2019. https://www.conservapedia.com/Jaime_Herrera_Beutler

"Jaime Herrera Beutler Successfully Protects Living Organ Donors." U.S. Congresswoman Jaime Herrera Beutler (website). Press release, August 29, 2018. https://herrerabeutler.house.gov/news/documentsingle.aspx?DocumentID=399269

Jayne, Greg. "Jayne: Herrera Beutler Explains It All." *The Columbian* (WA), February 24, 2019. https://www.columbian.com/news/2019/feb/24/jayne-herrera-beutler-explains-it-all/

Jensen, Brad. "Herrera Beutler Is Exactly Who We Need in DC." *The Reflector* (WA), February 4, 2019. http://www.thereflector.com/opinion/article_93f7ace0-28c4-11e9-8478-c37d9e72be75.html

Lystra, Tony. "Candidate Q&A: Jaime Herrera, 3rd District U.S. House." *Daily News* (southwest WA and northwest OR), August 1, 2010. http://tdn.com/news/local/article_20632748-9e01-11df-b947-001cc4c03286.html

Njus, Elliot. "Jobs Take Front Seat in Washington 3rd District Race." *Oregonian* (Oregon Live), October 14, 2010. http://www.oregonlive.com/clark-county/index.ssf/2010/10/jobs_take_front_seat_in_washington_3rd_district_race.html

Peterson, Hayley. "Pregnant Congresswoman Reveals the Tragic News That Her Baby Has a Potentially Fatal Disease." *Daily Mail* (UK), June 4, 2013. https://www.dailymail.co.uk/news/article-2335977/Jaime-Herrera-Beutler-Pregnant-congresswoman-reveals-tragic-news-baby-potentially-fatal-disease.html

Powell, Jared. "10 Questions: Rep. Jaime Herrera Beutler." House Republicans, January 9, 2015. https://www.gop.gov/rep-jaime-herrera-beuter-questions-and-answers/

Schwartz, Karen. "Meet Jaime Herrera Beutler, the Republican Spitfire Who's Rewriting the Rules." *Marie Claire*, April 22, 2015. https://www.marieclaire.com/culture/news/a14174/congresswoman-jaime-herrerra-beutler/

Solomon, Molly. "In Carolyn Long, Jaime Herrera Beutler Faces Her Biggest Challenge Yet." Oregon Public Broadcasting, October 24, 2018. https://www.opb.org/news/article/jaime-herrera-beutler-carolyn-long-washington-race-preview/

Solomon, Molly. "A Darling of Southwest Washington, Jaime Herrera Beutler Faces Her Toughest Race Yet." KUOW, October 24, 2018. https://www.kuow

.org/stories/in-carolyn-long-jaime-herrera-beutler-faces-her-biggest-challenge-yet

Solomon, Molly. "Republican Rep. Jaime Herrera Beutler Wins Tough Re-Election Campaign." KNKX, November 8, 2018. https://www.knkx.org/post/republican-rep-jaime-herrera-beutler-leads-re-election-bid

Song, Kyung M. "Freshman Rep. Herrera Beutler Tries to Set Her Own Course." *Seattle Times*, April 1, 2011. https://www.seattletimes.com/seattle-news/freshman-rep-herrera-beutler-tries-to-set-her-own-course/

Sword, Katy. "Herrera Beutler Pregnant with Third Child." *The Columbian* (WA), January 14, 2019. https://www.columbian.com/news/2019/jan/14/rep-herrera-beutler-pregnant-with-third-child/

Sword, Katy. "Herrera Beutler Running in 2020." *The Columbian* (WA), February 22, 2019. https://www.columbian.com/news/2019/feb/22/herrera-beutler-running-in-2020/

Theen, Andrew. "Father's Day: Meet Dan Beutler, a Congressional Spouse, Stay-at-Home Dad and Organ Donor." *Oregonian* (Oregon Live), June 18, 2017. https://www.oregonlive.com/politics/2017/06/fathers_day_meet_dan_beutler_a.html

"Tracking Congress in the Age of Trump: Jaime Herrera Beutler" (voting record). FiveThirtyEight.com https://projects.fivethirtyeight.com/congress-trump-score/jaime-herrera-beutler/

Chapter 12: Rona Ambrose

"The Canada Institute Names the Honourable Rona Ambrose as Global Fellow." The Wilson Center. Press release, May 16, 2017. https://www.wilsoncenter.org/article/the-canada-institute-names-the-honourable-rona-ambrose-global-fellow

The Canadian Press. "Liberals Tap Rona Ambrose for new NAFTA Advisory Council." *National Post*, August 2, 2017. https://nationalpost.com/news/politics/ambrose-ex-tory-minister-moore-on-council-to-advise-liberal-government-on-nafta

Cryderman, Kelly. "Laureen Harper, Rona Ambrose Throw Support behind She Leads Foundation." *Globe and Mail*, July 23, 2018. https://www.theglobeandmail.com/canada/alberta/article-laureen-harper-rona-ambrose-throw-support-behind-sheleads-foundation/

Ditchburn, Jennifer (The Canadian Press). "The Many Ways Rona Ambrose Differs from Stephen Harper." *Maclean's*, November 6, 2015. https://www.macleans.ca/politics/ottawa/the-many-ways-rona-ambrose-differs-from-stephen-harper/

"Harper Shuffles Cabinet to Create 'Right Team for These Times.'" CBC News, October 30, 2008. https://www.cbc.ca/news/canada/harper-shuffles-cabinet-to-create-right-team-for-these-times-1.706956

Harris, Kathleen. "Rona Ambrose Chosen as Interim Conservative Leader." CBC News, November 5, 2015. https://www.cbc.ca/news/politics/conservative-interim-leader-vote-1.3306152

Kay, Barbara. "Barbara Kay on Rona Ambrose: When the Sisterhood Attacks Its Own." *National Post*, September 28, 2012. https://archive.is/20130208124809/http://fullcomment.nationalpost.com/2012/09/28/barbara-kay-on-rona-ambrose-when-the-sisterhood-attacks-its-own/

Levitz, Stephanie (The Canadian Press). "Interim Conservative Leader Rona Ambrose Announces Retirement from Federal Politics." Global News, May 16, 2017. https://globalnews.ca/news/3454787/rona-ambrose-announces-retirement-federal-politics/?utm_expid=.kz0UD5JkQOCo6yMqxGqECg.0&utm_referrer=https%3A%2F%2Fen.wikipedia.org%2F

Raj, Althia. "Rona Ambrose: Conservatives Must Win Over Young Canadians, Women." HuffPost, December 22, 2015. https://www.huffingtonpost.ca/2015/12/22/rona-ambrose-conservatives-women-young-2015_n_8861902.html

"Rona Ambrose, Interim Tory Leader, and What We Should Know about Her." CBC News, November 6, 2015. https://www.cbc.ca/news/politics/rona-ambrose-5-things-1.3307356?cmp=rss

"Tory Says Child-Care Policy Set by 'Old White Guys.'" CBC News. February 15, 2005. https://www.cbc.ca/news/canada/tory-says-child-care-policy-set-by-old-white-guys-1.567529

Chapter 13: Jenny Durkan

Beekman, Daniel. "Jenny Durkan Draws Big-Time Backers, Overt Opposition in Seattle Mayoral Bid." *Seattle Times*, July 19, 2017. https://www.seattletimes.com/seattle-news/politics/jenny-durkan-showcases-her-experience-in-race-for-seattle-mayor/

Beekman, Daniel. "Seattle Mayor Jenny Durkan Emphasizes Need for Shared Prosperity in First State of the City Address." *Seattle Times*, February 20, 2018. https://www.seattletimes.com/seattle-news/politics/seattle-mayor-jenny-durkan-emphasizes-shared-prosperity-in-first-state-of-the-city-address/

Black, Lester. "Seattle's Police Union Contract Had a Rough Day in Court." Slog (blog). *The Stranger*, November 6, 2018. https://www.thestranger.com/slog/2018/11/06/35085254/seattles-police-union-contract-had-a-rough-day-in-court

Browning, Paige. "Durkan's State of the City Mirrors Her Nickname as the 'Impatient Mayor.'" KUOW, February 21, 2018. https://www.kuow.org/stories/durkans-state-city-mirrors-her-new-nickname-impatient-mayor

Durkan, Jenny. "Hi, I'm Jenny Durkan." Medium, May 11, 2017. https://medium.com/@JennyforSeattle/hi-im-jenny-durkan-f88b5bae8d1f

Geidner, Chris. "The Lesbian Who Could Be the Next U.S. Attorney General." BuzzFeed News, September 25, 2014. https://www.buzzfeednews.com/article/chrisgeidner/the-lesbian-who-could-be-the-next-us-attorney-general#4cniajx

Ghosh, Shreesha. "Who Is Jenny Durkan? Seattle Set to Have First Lesbian Mayor." *International Business Times*, November 8, 2017. https://www.ibtimes.com/who-jenny-durkan-seattle-set-have-first-lesbian-mayor-2611950

Groover, Heidi. "The Prosecutor: Jenny Durkan Embraces Her Place in the Establishment." *The Stranger*, June 21, 2017. https://www.thestranger.com/news/2017/06/21/25227247/the-prosecutor-jenny-durkan-embraes-her-place-in-the-establishment

Howland Jr., George. "Sister's Work Could Raise Conflict Issues for Jenny Durkan If Elected." *Seattle Weekly*, October 13, 2017. http://www.seattleweekly.com/news/sister-could-raise-conflict-issues-for-jenny-durkan-if-elected/

Kroman, David. "Micromanager or Mastermind? Mayor Durkan's First Year Gets Mixed Reviews." Crosscut, November 29, 2018. https://crosscut.com/2018/11/micromanager-or-mastermind-mayor-durkans-first-year-gets-mixed-reviews

"Seattle Council Approves Police Contract with an 8-1 Vote." King 5 News, November 13, 2018. https://www.king5.com/article/news/local/seattle/seattle-council-approves-police-contract-with-8-1-vote/281-614268113

Voelker, Jessica. "Jenny Durkan: 'When Donald Trump Was Elected, the World Started Spinning Differently for Me.'" *Seattle Met*, January 26, 2018. https://www.seattlemet.com/articles/2018/1/26/jenny-durkan-when-donald-trump-was-elected-the-world-started-spinning-differently-for-me

"What Are Consent Decrees?" Criminal Justice Programs. Last accessed on October 30, 2019. https://www.criminaljusticeprograms.com/articles/what-are-consent-decrees/

Chapter 14: Jo Swinson

Adu, Aletha. "Lib Dem Deputy Leader Jo Swinson Recounts Terrifying Moment Man She Thought Was a Friend Tried to Rape Her at University." *The Sun* (UK), February 3, 2018. https://www.thesun.co.uk/news/5494923/

lib-dem-deputy-leader-jo-swinson-terrifying-london-school-economics-attempted-rape/

Bendoris, Matt. "Lib Dem Hopeful Jo Swinson Reveals Her Political Battles as She Takes a Spin around Key General Election Battlegrounds." *Scottish Sun*, May 27, 2017. https://www.thescottishsun.co.uk/news/1068923/lib-dem-jo-swinson-car-share-of-the-vote/

Chakelian, Anoosh. "Jo Swinson: 'Women Need That Extra Nudge.'" Total Politics, September 11, 2013. http://www.totalpolitics.com/articles/interview/jo-swinson-women-need-extra-nudge

Chalmers, Lee. "Women, Your Country Needs You to Stand for Election." HuffPost Blog, March 8, 2018. https://www.huffingtonpost.co.uk/entry/women-your-country-needs-you-stand-for-election_uk_5a9c0558e4b085a5fdd87fe5

"Jo Swinson on the Struggle for Gender Equality and Why Sexism Has to End." *Yorkshire Post*, January 31, 2018. https://www.yorkshirepost.co.uk/news/analysis/jo-swinson-on-the-struggle-for-gender-equality-and-why-sexism-has-to-end-1-8990297

Kane, Patricia. "The Day My 'Nice Young Friend' Tried to Rape Me: Liberal Democrat Deputy Leader Jo Swinson Reveals How She Desperately Fought Off a Fellow Student Who Attacked Her at University." *Daily Mail* (UK), February 3, 2018. http://www.dailymail.co.uk/news/article-5348451/Jo-Swinson-reveals-student-tried-rape-university.html

May, Rob. "Jo Swinson Interview: Part 1 — An Introduction and Life before Politics." Liberal Democrat Voice, May 1, 2017. https://www.libdemvoice.org/jo-swinson-interview-part-1-an-introduction-and-life-before-politics-54122.html

Millar, James. "Can Jo Swinson Win Back East Dunbartonshire for the Lib Dems?" *New Statesman*, June 6, 2017. https://www.newstatesman.com/politics/june2017/2017/06/can-jo-swinson-win-back-east-dunbartonshire-lib-dems

Schofield, Kevin. "Lib Dems Win Council Seats from Tories and Labour in Boost for New Leader Jo Swinson." PoliticsHome, July 26, 2019. https://www.politicshome.com/news/uk/political-parties/liberal-democrats/news/105579/lib-dems-win-council-seats-tories-and-labour

Swinson, Jo. "We Need More Women in Our Public Space — Even Those We Campaign Against." Scottish Liberal Democrats. Jo Swinson, MP (website), March 5, 2018. http://www.joswinson.org.uk/we_need_more_women_in_our_public_space

Swinson, Jo. "Women Now Outnumber Men in Spain's Cabinet. What's Holding Them Back Elsewhere?" *Time*, June 8, 2018. http://time.com/5306197/spain-cabinet-gender-parity-jo-swinson/

Whitelaw, Jonathan. "Who Is Jo Swinson, When Was She Elected as an MP and Could She Be the Next Lib Dem Leader?" *Scottish Sun*, June 15, 2017. https://www.thescottishsun.co.uk/news/1152972/jo-swinson-lib-dems-leader-tim-farron-replacement-westminster/

Wiseman, Eva. "Jo Swinson: New Voice in the Old System." *The Guardian*, May 18, 2013. https://www.theguardian.com/politics/2013/may/18/jo-swinson-airbrushing-maternity-leave

Chapter 15: Beth Fukumoto

"Beth Fukumoto." Ballotpedia. Last accessed on October 30, 2019. https://ballotpedia.org/Beth_Fukumoto

"Beth Fukumoto's Issue Positions (Political Courage Test)." Vote Smart. https://votesmart.org/candidate/political-courage-test/127625/beth-fukumoto/#.W462ly2ZPBI

"Beth Fukumoto's Voting Records." Vote Smart. https://votesmart.org/candidate/key-votes/127625/beth-fukumoto#.W6pnCS2ZPBI

Chappell, Bill. "Hawaii's House Republican Leader Says She Was Ousted Over Women's March." *The Two-Way* (blog). NPR, February 2, 2017. https://www.npr.org/sections/thetwo-way/2017/02/02/513080913/hawaiis-house-republican-leader-says-she-was-ousted-over-womens-march

"Coffee with a Candidate: Democratic Congressional Candidate Beth Fukumoto." Hawaii News Now, July 10, 2018. http://www.hawaiinewsnow.com/story/38615156/coffee-with-a-candidate-democratic-congressional-candidate-beth-fukumoto

Day, Gail. "Beth Fukumoto: Courage (and Style) under Fire." *News Growl*, June 8, 2018. https://newsgrowl.com/beth-fukumoto-courage-fire-hawaii/

Dingeman, Robbie. "Ex-Republican Beth Fukumoto Wants to Be Hawai'i's Next Democratic Congresswoman." *HONOLULU*, March 29, 2018. http://www.honolulumagazine.com/Honolulu-Magazine/March-2018/Hawaii-Lawmaker-Beth-Fukumoto-is-Running-for-Congress/

Harris-Perry, Melissa. "Hawaii State Rep. Beth Fukumoto Explains Why She Might Leave the Republican Party." *Elle*, February 10, 2017. https://www.elle.com/culture/career-politics/a42949 hawaii-beth-fukumoto-leaving-republican-party/

Lee, Traci G., and Charles Lam. "Hawaii Rep. Beth Fukumoto, Republican Turned Democrat, Announces Bid for Congress." NBC News, March 29,

2018. https://www.nbcnews.com/news/asian-america/hawaii-rep-beth-fukumoto-republican-turned-democrat-announces-bid-congress-n860986

Mundahl, Erin. "How Did Beth Fukumoto, Hawaii's GOP Minority Leader, End Up Running in a Democratic Primary?" InsideSources, June 14, 2018. https://www.insidesources.com/how-did-hawaiis-gop-minority-leader-end-up-running-in-a-democratic-primary/

Chapter 16: Shaharzad Akbar

Akbar, Shaharzad. "2009 Ivy Day Speech — Shaharzad Akbar 09." Filmed on May 16, 2009, at Smith College, in Northampton, MA. Video, 8:40. https://www.youtube.com/watch?v=f3WqTvntfMg

Akbar, Shaharzad. "Access for All — The Future for Afghanistan." *Journal of International Affairs* 67, no. 1 (2013): 225–34. Condensed and edited online version, October 25, 2018. https://jia.sipa.columbia.edu/online-articles/archives-access-all-future-afghanistan

Akbar, Shaharzad. "I Don't Want the US to Bargain Away My Son's Future in Afghanistan." CNN, August 22, 2019. https://www.cnn.com/2019/08/22/opinions/united-states-taliban-future-afghanistan-akbar/index.html

Akbar, Shaharzad. "What More Women in Government Would Mean for Afghanistan." Interview with Judy Woodruff. PBS NewsHour. PBS. March 5, 2018. https://www.pbs.org/newshour/show/what-more-women-in-government-would-mean-for-afghanistan

Clark, Meredith. "What Everyone Needs to Stop Getting Wrong about Afghanistan." Refinery29, November 3, 2015. https://www.refinery29.com/en-us/2015/10/95082/shaharzad-akbar-open-society-afghanistan-1400

Qaane, Ehsan. "Beginning of a New Era at the AIHRC: Nine Fresh Commissioners." Afghanistan Analysts Network, July 20, 2019. https://www.afghanistan-analysts.org/beginning-of-a-new-era-at-the-aihrc-nine-fresh-commissioners/

"Shaharzad Akbar." The Forum of Young Global Leaders. https://www.younggloballeaders.org/community?page=2

"Shaharzad Akbar" (alumni profile). Weidenfeld-Hoffman Trust. Last accessed on October 30, 2019. http://whtrust.org/author/shaharzad-akbar/

"Shaharzad Akbar." World Economic Forum. Last accessed on October 30, 2019. https://www.weforum.org/people/shaharzad-akbar

"Shaharzad Akbar Appointed as AIHRC Chairperson." Reporterly, July 18, 2019. http://reporterly.net/live/newsfeed/thursday-july-18/shahrzad-akbar-appointed-as-aihrc-chairperson/

"Shaharzad Akbar Is First Afghan Woman to Study at Oxford University." *The Telegraph*, November 20, 2009. https://www.telegraph.co.uk/education/educationnews/6612574/Shaharzad-Akbar-is-first-Afghan-woman-to-study-at-Oxford-University.html

Chapter 17: Erin Moran

"Erin Moran." The Village of Waunakee. http://www.vil.waunakee.wi.us/457/Erin-Moran

"Erin Morin for Waunakee Village Board" (Facebook page). https://www.facebook.com/erinmoranwaunakee/

LaScala, Kari. "Tribune Profile: Erin Moran: This College Student Is a Village Trustee." *Waunakee Tribune*, November 15, 2018. http://www.hngnews.com/waunakee_tribune/community/arts_and_entertainment/article_64027a8a-eae4-5240-8065-b44aa83be811.html

Wondrash, Kevin. "Giving Back to Her Community." *Catholic Herald* (Diocese of Madison), May 3, 2018. http://www.madisoncatholicherald.org/news/around-diocese/7617-erin-moran.html

Chapter 18: Eva Aariak

"2 Seats Tied, Eva Aariak Loses in Nunavut Election." CBC News, October 27, 2013. http://www.cbc.ca/news/canada/north/nunavutvotes2013/2-seats-tied-eva-aariak-loses-in-nunavut-election-1.2253663

Aariak, Eva. "What It's Like Being a Woman in Office in Nunavut." As told to Kelly Boutsalis. *The Kit*, March 7, 2018. https://thekit.ca/life/eva-aariak/

"Board of Trustees: Eva Aariak — President." Inuit Heritage Trust. http://www.ihti.ca/eng/iht-trus.html

Brown, Beth. "More Than One-Quarter of Nunavut's Next MLAs Are Women." *Nunatsiaq News*, November 2, 2017. http://nunatsiaq.com/stories/article/65674nunavuts_next_legislature_will_be_more_than_one_quarter_women/

Canada Parliament, *Statement of Apology to Former Students of Indian Residential Schools*, 39th Parl, 2nd Sess, Vol 142, No 110 (11 June 2008).

The Canadian Press. "Nunavut Election to Focus on Education, High Cost of Living." HuffPost, October 27, 2013. https://www.huffingtonpost.ca/2013/10/27/nunavut-election_n_4168182.html

The Canadian Press. "Nunavut Premier Eva Aariak Won't Seek Top Job after Election." CTV News, September 5, 2013. https://www.ctvnews.ca/politics/nunavut-premier-eva-aariak-won-t-seek-top-job-after-election-1.1441775

"Five Things to Watch in the Nunavut Election Today." CBC News, October 28, 2013. http://www.cbc.ca/news/canada/north/five-things-to-watch-in-the-nunavut-election-today-1.2251747

Gregoire, Lisa. "Eva Aariak Is Reinventing Politics in the North." *The Walrus*, January 12, 2011. https://thewalrus.ca/madam-premier/

Henderson, Randy, host. "CCLA Questions Nunavut Election Laws." CBC News: Northbeat. CBC News, October 23, 2013. https://www.cbc.ca/player/play/2414130521

"Initial Findings from the Nunavut Government Employee Survey, 2016." Statistics Canada. March 27, 2017. https://www150.statcan.gc.ca/n1/daily-quotidien/170327/dq170327c-eng.htm

Kingsley, Jennifer. "Bringing an Inuit Language into the Digital Age." HuffPost, June 10, 2016. https://www.huffingtonpost.com/entry/inuktitut-digital-age_us_575b1920e4b00f97fba85313

Murphy, David. "Eva Aariak Stresses Early Childhood Education, Addictions Treatment, Mental Health." *Nunatsiaq News*, October 9, 2013. Excerpt reprinted by the Childcare Resource and Research Unit, October 9, 2013. http://www.childcarecanada.org/documents/child-care-news/13/10/eva-aariak-stresses-early-childhood-education-addictions-treatment-m

Murphy, David. "Eva Aariak Won't Seek Second Term as Nunavut Premier." *Nunatsiaq News*, September 5, 2013. http://nunatsiaq.com/stories/article/65674aariak_wont_seek_second_term_as_nunavut_premier/

Nunavut, Legislative Assembly, *Nunavut Leadership Forum (Hansard)*, 3rd Parl, 1st Sess (14 November 20008).

"Nunavut (1999)." Library and Archives Canada. Last modified on May 5, 2016. https://www.bac-lac.gc.ca/eng/discover/politics-government/canadian-confederation/Pages/nunavut-1999.aspx

"Nunavut Will Be Economic Powerhouse, Premier Says." CTV News, July 9, 2012. https://www.ctvnews.ca/nunavut-will-be-economic-powerhouse-premier-says-1.871240

Omand, Geordon (The Canadian Press). "A Tour of Canada's Youngest Legislature in Nunavut." *Toronto Sun*, June 27, 2016. http://torontosun.com/2016/06/27/a-tour-of-canadas-youngest-legislature-in-nunavut/wcm/5d49c939-a13d-4aac-9a68-43e9ef07832c

Snyder, Lorraine. "Eva Aariak." *The Canadian Encyclopedia*, July 26, 2011. Last updated on December 21, 2016. http://www.thecanadianencyclopedia.ca/en/article/eva-aariak/

Strong, Walter. "Calling More Women: Nunavut's 1st Woman Premier Says Equal Representation a Work in Progress." CBC News, October 4, 2017. http://www.cbc.ca/news/canada/north/eva-aariak-female-candidates-needed-1.4321450

Sutton, Tyler. "Female Perspectives in Provincial Politics." *Public Sector Digest*, April 2012. https://www.publicsectordigest.com/article/female-perspectives-in-provincial-politics

"Violence and Abuse Prevention: Residential Schools." Pauktuutit (Inuit Women of Canada). https://www.pauktuutit.ca/abuse-prevention/residential-schools/

Vlessides, Mike. "A Public Government." *Nunavut '99: Changing the Map of Canada.* Iqaluit: Nortext Multimedia Inc., 1999. http://www.nunavut.com/nunavut99/english/public_gov.html

Weber, Bob (The Canadian Press). "Education Common Issue as Nunavut Voters Head to Polls." Global News, October 27, 2013. https://globalnews.ca/news/928485/education-common-issue-as-nunavut-voters-head-to-polls/

Chapter 19: Cori Bush

Buchanan, Larry, Ford Fessenden, K.K. Rebecca Lai, Haeyoun Park, Alicia Parlapiano, Archie Tse, Tim Wallace, Derek Watkins, and Karen Yourish. "Q & A: What Happened in Ferguson." *New York Times*, August 13, 2014. https://www.nytimes.com/interactive/2014/08/13/us/ferguson-missouri-town-under-siege-after-police-shooting.html?auth=login-email

Chavez, Alda. "Insurgent Candidate Cori Bush Wants to End the Dynastic Rule of a Missouri Congressional District." The Intercept, August 7, 2018. https://theintercept.com/2018/08/07/cori-bush-lacy-clay-missouri/

Ellis, Ralph, Brian Todd, and Faith Karimi. "Citing Security Concerns, Darren Wilson Resigns from Ferguson Police Force." CNN, November 30, 2014. https://www.cnn.com/2014/11/29/us/ferguson-protests/index.html

"I'm Bully-Proof." Cori Bush: US Congress | MO-01 (website). https://www.coribush.org/about

Lees, Jaime. "Alexandra Ocasio-Cortez and Cori Bush Are Punk AF." *Riverfront Times* (St. Louis), July 23, 2018. https://www.riverfronttimes.com/newsblog/2018/07/23/alexandria-ocasio-cortez-and-cori-bush-are-punk-af

Lopez, German. "Why Was Michael Brown Shot?" Vox, May 31, 2015. https://www.vox.com/2015/5/31/17937818/michael-brown-police-shooting-darren-wilson

Mindock, Clark. "Ferguson Shooting: Four Years after Michael Brown's Death, How Have Things Changed?" *The Independent*, August 8, 2018. https://www.independent.co.uk/news/world/americas/michael-brown-ferguson-shooting-missouri-death-shot-darren-wilson-trump-obama-police-a8481456.html

Plata, Thalia. "Activist Remembers Ferguson Five Years Later." *Brandeis Hoot*, February 8, 2019. https://brandeishoot.com/2019/02/08/activist-remembers-ferguson-five-years-later/

Ragland, Dr. David. "Protest and Politics, Black Women and Leadership." HuffPost, May 9, 2016. https://www.huffpost.com/entry/protest-and-politics-blac_b_9866598?fbclid=IwAR0NVAlYc-cvzq5nPpZGyMVDQOJuvpSsvlU1aH3jxndBTViVhX08z-gszfA

Reuters. "Michael Brown Shooting: New Footage Raises Questions — video." *The Guardian*, March 14, 2017. https://www.theguardian.com/us-news/video/2017/mar/14/michael-shooting-new-surveillance-footage-video

Salter, Jim (Associated Press). "A Puzzling Number of Men Tied to the Ferguson Protests Have Since Died." *Chicago Tribune*, March 18, 2019. https://www.chicagotribune.com/nation-world/ct-ferguson-activist-deaths-black-lives-matter-20190317-story.html

Solis, Marie. "Meet Cori Bush, the Ferguson Activist Vying to Be Missouri's First Black Congresswoman." Vice, July 31, 2018. https://www.vice.com/en_us/article/gy3dvj/cori-bush-missouri-congress-lacy-clay

Suggs, Ernie. "The Michael Brown Killing: What You Need to Know." *Atlanta Journal-Constitution*. https://www.ajc.com/news/ferguson-brown-faq/

Wicentowski, Danny. "In *Knock Down the House*, Cori Bush Wins Hearts, but Not Enough Votes." *Riverfront Times*, May 2, 2019. https://www.riverfronttimes.com/newsblog/2019/05/02/in-knock-down-the-house-cori-bush-wins-hearts-but-not-enough-votes

PART 2: THE PLAYBOOK

Clark, Nancy F. "Act Now to Shrink the Confidence Gap." *Forbes*, April 28, 2014. https://www.forbes.com/sites/womensmedia/2014/04/28/act-now-to-shrink-the-confidence-gap/#530002075c41

Joy, Tony. "How to Run a Political Campaign." CallHub (blog). https://callhub.io/run-political-campaign/

Mohr, Tara Sophia. "Why Women Don't Apply for Jobs Unless They're 100% Qualified." *Harvard Business Review*, August 25, 2014. https://hbr.org/2014/08/why-women-dont-apply-for-jobs-unless-theyre-100-qualified

Nir, David. "Just How Many Elected Officials Are There in the United States? The Answer Is Mind-Blowing." *Daily Kos*, March 29, 2015. https://www.dailykos.com/stories/2015/3/29/1372225/-Just-how-many-elected-officials-are-there-in-the-United-States-The-answer-is-mind-blowing

O'Connell, Shannon, Samantha Smoot and Sally Abi Khalil. "Campaign Skills Handbook Module 6: Message Development — Creating Powerful and Persuasive Messages." National Democratic Institute, May 8, 2013. https://www.ndi.org/sites/default/files/Module%206_Message%20Development_EN.pdf

O'Day, J. Brian. "Political Campaign Planning Manual: A Step by Step Guide to Winning Elections." National Democratic Institute, March 12, 2007. www.ndi.org/sites/default/files/1541_ru_election_5.pdf

Rose, Chris. "12 Basic Guidelines for Campaign Strategy." campaignstrategy.org, October 12, 2006. http://www.campaignstrategy.org/articles/12basicguidelines.pdf

Sweeney, Camille and Josh Gosfield. "8 Master Strategies for Public Speaking." *Fast Company*, August 5, 2015. https://www.fastcompany.com/3049322/8-master-strategies-for-public-speaking

Zeoli, Richard. "Seven Principles of Effective Public Speaking." American Management Association (blog), January 24, 2019. https://www.amanet.org/articles/seven-principles-of-effective-public-speaking/

ACKNOWLEDGMENTS

There are many people who supported and encouraged me in writing this book: Thank you, Lisa Lyons Johnston, for suggesting we have lunch and talk about a book idea, and for your enthusiastic support throughout! Thank you to the whole Loft/Kids Can team, especially Kate Egan, whose guidance and steady hand were invaluable. A very special thank you my editor, Susan Knopf of Scout Books and Media, who was with me every step of the way, who patiently answered endless rookie author questions, put me back on track when I veered off, and with whom conversations about politics, life and writing were as enjoyable as they were enlightening.

Thank you to: my friend Penny Collenette, whose sound judgment and keen perception have made her such an invaluable sounding board. I am also grateful for her generosity of spirit in helping me make many of the connections that were vital to the writing of this book; Lili Campbell for her long and loyal friendship, for listening to endless "what ifs …" and for her scathingly brilliant ideas; Gretchen Van Riesen for her encouragement and for asking such good questions. A special shoutout also to Diane Morris, who, in this project and many others, has been a stalwart support, sounding board and source of wise advice. And, of course, my dear friend Mary Morris.

Thank you to Haifa Al Kaylani, the inspiring leader and chair of the Arab International Women's Forum, for graciously connecting me to Hala Lattouf. Several others also provided suggestions on interview subjects and/or connections to enable me to reach out: thank you Sally Armstrong, Pamela Caudill, Tara Kimbrell Cole, Pauline Couture, Lisa Mezzetti, Shelley Murphy, Jane Rounthwaite, Bruce Rowlands, Dr. Sima Samar, Kevin Shea and Peg Weir.

To my many other friends at TIAW who are too numerous to list, your collective support was a big part of this.

Katarina Rowlands — thank you for an early review and providing excellent advice from a young woman's perspective. Lawrence Surtees, thank you for your expert advice on writing and research.

To my advisory group at Verity, extraordinary women all, your support and friendship mean so much: Janet Cloud, Sue Folinsbee, Anne Lamont, Angela Mitchell and Lisa Taylor.

To my husband, Gordon, who always said, "You can do it," whenever things seemed impossible. And finally, to my mother, Joan MacKendrick, who never set limits on what I could aspire to.

STEPHANIE MACKENDRICK is a former journalist dedicated to women's career advancement and non-profit leadership. She served as board vice chair for The Samara Centre for Democracy, engaging Canadians in politics, and played a key role in establishing the Canadian chapter of the 30% Club, which aims to increase the representation of women on corporate boards. Stephanie was president of the board of The International Alliance for Women (TIAW) and co-founded the TIAW World of Difference 100 Awards. She has twice been recognized by the Women's Executive Network as one of Canada's Most Powerful Women: Top 100, and in 2010 she was admitted to the Freedom of the City of London (UK).